# What Are Children For?

# What Are Children For?

## On Ambivalence and Choice

Anastasia Berg
& Rachel Wiseman

ST. MARTIN'S PRESS
NEW YORK

*To Lila*

# CONTENTS

# What Are
# Children For?

# Under Pressure

## *—Rachel*

I thought the day would come when I would just know. The most likely sign would be an urge, *the* urge. The desire to nurture would emerge unbidden from some nether region of my being, and babies would gain an irresistible power over me, exerting a magnetic pull whenever I saw one in the wild. Or, as the trial period of adulthood came to its end, maybe having kids would come to seem like the "natural next step," sometime after moving in with my boyfriend, consolidating our furniture and streaming accounts, buying a used station wagon. Or, cliché of clichés, a panic might set in, as if to preempt the regret of not having them. Who would I have to keep me company on the holidays when I got old? What if the only things I'd have to look forward to in my waning years were Amazon package deliveries and my online book club?

Even if I never had a biological awakening or pragmatic epiphany, perhaps the weight of social pressure would one day force the issue. By most accounts, the world is not a very hospitable place for women who don't want children. Was I bound to meet disapproval? Would I be judged by those who think that a woman prioritizing her career is selfish? Become undesirable to men for not wanting to start a family? Would I lose my friends, one by one, as they settled down? A terrifying prospect: a chasm would open between us, and I'd watch impotently as our day-to-day concerns became inaccessible to one another. Perhaps then I would feel pressed to answer the question once and for all: yes or no.

I was almost thirty, but my appointment with fate hadn't come up. In truth, I felt strangely indifferent. If there was any pressure, it was not some deep-seated urge, abstract maternal longing, or fear of loneliness that was nagging at me, but the familiar anxiety of not knowing what shape I wanted my life to take and how children might or might not fit in.

There was, on rare occasions, the stray awkward remark from my parents to contend with. Shortly after my twenty-ninth birthday, my parents were visiting from out of town. Over French toast and diluted diner coffee, my mom turned and looked at me intently. She lowered her voice—a tell we were about to enter a delicate discursive zone. She had something she wanted to discuss with me, she said: she and my father could help me out if I wanted to start a family.

"We know it can be very expensive to have kids," she explained. She didn't want financial anxiety to be holding me back. My dad, nodding beside her, looked embarrassed at the intrusion, as much into my finances as into my sex life. "That won't be necessary"—I cut her off before she could complete her pitch. It wasn't that I was too proud to take their money (I was still freeloading on their Verizon family plan). And I knew that I was very fortunate to have supportive parents with resources to help me—many are not so lucky. But the truth was that I had hardly gotten far enough with any deliberations to consider the practical implications of having children, let alone the actual costs. My parents were grasping for an explanation about why I wasn't having kids—why I seemed to be barely even thinking about it—and settled on the one they felt equipped to address. But I didn't even know what the explanation was myself. All I knew for certain was that I wasn't yet "there," wherever *there* was.

BECOMING A PARENT, for those of us on the outside, can seem less like a transition and more like throwing yourself off a cliff. When my friends and I talked about the prospect of having children, we spoke about it with casual detachment, as if conducting a thought experiment populated by people who were not us but total strangers. Well into our early thirties, when the conversation veered closer to our lives as we were actually living them, we retreated to a familiar place of uncertainty: *I dunno, maybe one day, I guess, it depends, we'll see.* No matter how demanding, all our attachments—to our one-bedroom apartments, our midlevel jobs, our romantic partners—felt tenuous and temporary. Adding a child into the mix was practically unthinkable. Something about parenthood seemed inimical to my existence; I suspected it would change me so much that I'd become unrecognizable to myself. I worried that everything I enjoyed or that made me a halfway interesting person would recede beyond my reach, that I'd never be able to finish a book again. We all said that if we had kids we would "somehow make it work," but no one really believed the halfhearted propaganda. How do you figure out how to throw yourself off a cliff?

Perhaps this is why more and more American millennials are experiencing vertigo as we look over the ledge. Many in our generation are waiting to have kids until later in life, or are forgoing it altogether.[1] Even before COVID-19 hit, millennials were having fewer children than any cohort in recent history before them.[2] After declining steadily for thirty years, the national fertility rate reached an all-time low in 2020.[3] Though the pandemic was a volatile time for fertility rates (falling sharply during the lockdown before making a slight recovery),[4] they have dropped below pre-pandemic levels once more, and demographic analysts aren't optimistic that they will recover over the long term.[5] People are not just waiting longer to have kids or having fewer of them; there is mounting evidence that more are choosing to have none at all. Rates of childlessness have fluctuated over the past fifty years, but they are generally trending up.[6] More than one in seven women between the ages of forty and forty-four had no biological children in 2018, up from one in ten in 1976.[7] And according to a 2021 Pew Research Report, 44 percent of nonparents between the ages of eighteen and forty-nine say they do not expect to have children eventually—an increase of seven percentage points from 2018—suggesting that rates of childlessness are unlikely to decrease in the future.[8]

Bringing up declining birth rates at best comes off as gauche and, at worst, can smack of demographic panic and the most dangerous kind of racist ideology. In recent years, the topic has been so thoroughly co-opted by the far right that one could be forgiven for thinking it belongs strictly in alt-right forums dedicated to the Great Replacement theory, not in serious conversations about our personal and collective futures. What, after all, is there to worry about? All those statistics might make for good clickbait, but don't they express the outcome of inexorable historical progress? Birth rates decrease in inverse proportion to access to contraceptives and abortion; women's rising education levels and income; the modernization of the economy, with its diminished reliance on children to keep up the farm or family store; secularization. (Not to mention that, with the requisite political will, any lasting declines could be offset by immigration.[9]) Some point out that falling birth rates might not just be inevitable but themselves a sign of positive social change—evidence that women have finally begun to break free from the confines of the biological and social positions they had been relegated to by patriarchy. For the first time in human history, women can freely exercise choice over their life trajectories and realize their full potential. If women are having fewer children, might it not just be a reflection of the extent to which they are taking their personal destinies into their own hands? And who could blame them for hesitating, at a time when the right to end an unwanted pregnancy is once again severely restricted or banned outright in much of the country, maternal and infant care are prohibitively expensive, and giving birth continues to be a physically dangerous and painful trial, especially for women of color and those of lower incomes?[10] On the margins, others are reaching an even starker conclusion: in our ecologically and politically degrading world, the choice to remain childless is the only morally responsible one.

I tried to see how I fit into these grand narratives. But while I could recognize that my experience might constitute one tiny data point in a sweeping generational scatterplot, knowing that I was part of a trend didn't make things any easier. When it came to my own so-called family planning, I didn't feel like an agent of the march of history, or its victim—I felt confused. When I tried to look ahead ten years, to imagine the life I wanted for myself, I saw either more of the same—my daily existence no different from what it had been for years, just transposed a decade into the future—or I saw a blank screen, nothing at all.

I took comfort in ambivalence. The rejection of easy certainties seemed like the intelligent attitude to take toward a responsibility so big. It felt prudent and sensible to approach motherhood just like this—carefully, introspectively, sidelong, keeping in mind all the risks and trade-offs. The ambivalence was its own mode of sophistication, the poise of a thinking person. But not knowing was starting to make me unhappy, and privately I wondered if it would ever end. Tired of wavering, one day I caved and called my mom. I asked how she came around to deciding that she wanted a family. "I always knew," she told me. "It was never even a question."

Now, having children *is* a question, more open-ended and fraught than ever before. My mom's easy-won certainty has become harder for women like me to adopt, and harder still to sustain. What changed? I wanted to understand why this desire had been so available to her and yet felt so alien to me. Why didn't she pass it on to me, like her curly hair, coffee addiction, and eagerness to please? Why are so many of us hovering in indecision, or not thinking about this at all?

The longer I waited, the less I believed I might one day just happen upon the answer.

How to resolve a seemingly intractable personal dilemma of life-altering significance? Like anyone with a shortage of practical wisdom and a strong broadband connection, I turned to the internet. Scanning news stories and blogs about "motherhood ambivalence," I came across a website titled "Motherhood—Is It for Me?" *Can't decide? Want clarity?* the website banner read. *Tired of not being able to figure this out?* Ann Davidman, a licensed marriage and family counselor, has been running "parenting clarity" seminars since the early nineties—that is, for most of my life—and now regularly offers online courses directed at those struggling with the decision whether or not to have children.

The homepage featured a muted photograph of a boardwalk extending out onto a sandy shore; the logo, a heart composed of two sinuous question marks. The site advertised a three-month correspondence course consisting of guided meditation exercises, a series of writing prompts, an online forum, and biweekly check-in calls with the other women registered in the class. There are countless support groups for moms, but Davidman's course is still one of the only groups meant for women and men who are actively deciding whether or not to become parents. Those who completed the program, the website promised, would come to better understand the "subliminal messages" that had contributed to their state of uncertainty: *End the cycle of "I don't know" so you can get on with your life and feel at peace.* It was the end of summer, and I was about to turn thirty-one. I signed up.

I ordered the textbook and downloaded the first "guided visualization." I was instructed to lie down in a quiet place and breathe deeply. The voice on the recording instructed me, in a soothing, assured monotone, to close my eyes and concentrate on my breathing. There was no wrong way to experience the exercise, it said; all I had to do was to trust and pay attention to where my mind wanted to lead me—a special place I could always return to when I needed to feel safe and secure. I was invited to envision the space, to roam freely in it, to furnish it to my liking down to the most delicate detail. I pictured a boardwalk opening out onto a rocky shore. *Great*, I thought, I had just reproduced the website cover photo. Starting over, I conjured the image of an armchair, a green banker's lamp, and a whiff of dust on old bookshelves. I had just swapped out one tired trope for another, but I decided to stick with it—let's face it, being hypercritical and overly self-aware hadn't gotten me very far up to this point. And I did feel a bit calmer, more attuned; the anxious hum in the background of my thought process seemed to get quieter. I was ready to begin.

The class opens with a mantra:

> *I don't know.*
> *I don't know why I don't know.*
> *It's not my fault that I don't know.*
> *It's okay that I don't know.*
> *I have had clarity before about many things.*
> *My true desire matters and no one can know it better*
>     *than I.*
> *I am the definer of me.*
> *The answers will come because they never left.*
> *Only I can know what's true for me. . . . It's all within me.*[11]

Participants are asked to abide by this mantra for the duration of the program. We pledged to fully embrace "not knowing," postponing trying to reach any kind of certitude until after the course concluded.

"Motherhood—Is It for Me?" is premised on the idea that there are no "right answers,"[12] only your answer, and it lies within. In order to unearth this deeply buried truth, participants must excavate their family histories and reexamine their preconceptions about parenthood. At one point, we were instructed to draw a family map and scan it for patterns that could have shaped our attitudes toward having children: separations, infertility, mental-health issues, abuse. I color-coded my family's emotional damage: divorce, illness, addiction, death. I searched the map for meaningful connections. We were told to notice any feelings that came up—anything could be a clue. What was I afraid of? Was there some kind of trauma in my family's history I was trying to avoid repeating? I was the baby in my family—did

I not want to give up that privileged status? Did my grandparents' painful divorce shake my confidence in lasting love?

At another point, my classmates and I were prompted to imagine running into our inner child during a walk on the beach. Are there messages she needed to hear but didn't receive growing up? We were told to deliver those messages to her now (e.g., "you're beautiful," "you're smart," "you're loved"). Later, we composed a letter to one of our parents in order to finally express, if only on paper, the needs they failed to address when we were growing up. By vocalizing these needs and recognizing these lacks, the theory went, we could begin to see more clearly which of our feelings were merely the residue of old traumas. Only then could we move past them, onward to our deeper and more authentic desires.

Though most of the course is conducted privately, via journal entries and meditative exercises, there is an important social component to "Motherhood—Is It for Me?" that takes the form of biweekly phone calls and an optional online forum. There were nineteen of us in my class, and once a week we would get on the phone to share how we were feeling about motherhood or living without children, or what having a family meant to us that week. Some of the women were my age or a little younger, just beginning to consider whether they wished to have children. Many were in their late thirties and early forties, anxious to make a choice they wouldn't regret before it was too late. Some came to the course because they were truly baffled about their feelings; others had partners who were "hard yeses" or "hard noes," and they had no idea how to navigate the decision without destroying their marriages. One was in her fifties and no longer considering biological motherhood but surrogacy or adoption. Some called in from Europe or as far away as Australia. Many spoke about how alone they had felt in their ambivalence. Before finding the class, they felt as though they were the only ones who didn't "just know." Despite their different backgrounds and life trajectories, they had expected that one day they would no longer have to wonder whether they wanted to be mothers—the answer would become clear, and they could get on with the rest of their lives. But, for one reason or another, the answer never arrived, and they kept wondering and doubting, running through the possible scenarios in their minds, again and again.

One week we were instructed to pay close attention to our professional and personal interactions by tracking all the mundane requests we received and taking note of our responses. Many of the participants—myself included—reported finding it difficult to say no. They described themselves as caretakers and pleasers, women who were reluctant to disappoint others and were always eager to help. In turn, they expressed misgivings about how the potentially infinite demands of motherhood might cause them to lose track of themselves.

I recognized myself in their accounts. I tend to avoid conflict at all costs. I struggle to deliver bad news. Only on one occasion have I successfully ended a relationship; usually I'd just wait for the other person to do it, which could take years. I'd often get roped into drawn-out, one-sided conversations with total strangers about their side projects, quixotic business ventures, and love lives. Once, on a farm in Patagonia, I drank a shot of fresh sheep's blood because I was worried about offending my hosts (I'm a vegetarian). It was no shock, then, to learn that I reflexively accepted others' requests or contorted myself to make them happy. But the exercise didn't just alert me to my inability to set boundaries; I realized I was so beleaguered by the specter of others' needs that I experienced simple instructions at work or even my friends' venting as entreaties requiring my personal intercession. Managing others' feelings was paramount, and always fraught. And though it was often stressful, being made to feel needed gave me purpose. If only I could somehow fill in the outline of my existence with what others needed me to be, I wouldn't have to face the task of figuring it out on my own.

Perhaps this is why having a child seemed like such an unnerving risk: When confronted with the many potential demands of caring for a small infant—their constant, urgent needs—would my sense of self completely dissolve? For many of the participants, this was not just an abstract worry; they had seen it happen to the women in their lives—to their friends and sisters, and, up close, to their mothers. Listening in on the group call that day, I thought about how sometimes our fear of children can have its roots not in dramatic patterns of inherited trauma but in some of the most quotidian aspects of our family lives.

WHEN I WAS a child, the word "family" was invoked as a talisman against the uprootedness of an insular life that had revolved almost entirely around my parents' careers. It was the kind of comfortable existence that was shared with minor variations by many children of the enterprising late-twentieth-century American professional class. We moved up the eastern seaboard as my parents completed their medical training and sought out better jobs. My dad, the youngest son of a trinket salesman and a typist in Montreal, went into private practice as a cardiologist to give us the privileged childhood he hadn't had. My mom had grown up in a middle-class suburb on Long Island, the bookish peacemaker in a loud, turbulent family of shoe salesmen; she was the first in her immediate family to get an advanced degree. Together, my parents landed a pair of placements in a quiet corner of New England known for its long grassy commons and colonial homes tastefully updated with Sub-Zero refrigerators. While working full time as a geriatrician, my mother assumed most of the responsibility for taking care of us. She invested a large share of her salary and emotional energy into managing a rotating cast of nannies and babysitters—a task she undertook, like everything she does, with administrative precision and zeal. Though motherhood came naturally to her, though I never heard her complain, being a mother seemed to me, even then, like a massive headache.

"We're family," my mom would remind me and my sister. "We always have each other. You can tell me anything—I'm here for you always." Yet despite my mother's assurances, I knew there were no guarantees that this would really *always* be the case. On my dad's side, my aging Canadian grandparents lacked the wherewithal to cross the border to visit more than once a year. We saw my mom's side more frequently. But when we did, I observed how carefully she had to navigate family events and weddings, fine-tuning the seating arrangements to prevent flare-ups of old squabbles, or walkouts in the middle of the function. She tried to make our home a haven amid this strained web of family relations, but it was obvious to me, even as a kid, that no amount of planning could completely insure against breakdown. My maternal grandparents, who split up while my mom was in college, were so embittered by the divorce they couldn't stand to be in the same building together. It felt like everything was precarious—old-world tempers without the geographic or emotional closeness that would have incentivized humility or restitution for past wrongs. When my parents tried to instill in us the message that family is the most important thing in life, it felt at times more asserted than believed, as if it had to be asserted, again and again, for it to be made real.

Gestures of love in our home were over the top and effortful.

"Free time" together was hard to come by. Now and then we'd have a leisurely meal out, or go apple picking or hiking in the woods. But it only happened according to some laborious plan, concocted ex nihilo, rarely by chance or habit. And these activities required so much fussing and compromise to keep everyone happy that it was hard to remember that all this work was in the service of having fun.

With extended family far away, and our nuclear family spread thin, there was little in the way of shared traditions or mutual experience for us to fall back on. Dinner was not a collective activity, more of a necessity to be squeezed in between scheduling conflicts. Because we are Jewish, my parents would usually cover for their colleagues in the hospital on Christmas and Easter. We'd cook big meals for Thanksgiving and Passover, and my dad would gather us in the kitchen for an annual latke fry for Hanukkah, which consisted of peeling, pureeing, and frying twenty-five-pound bags of potatoes. But this ritual sometimes felt less celebratory than like a performance, half *MasterChef* family showdown, half gulag reenactment. Why were we doing this?

In starting their own family, my parents hoped that they could get things right where their parents had faltered. For my dad, this meant protecting us from the financial insecurity that he'd suffered in his childhood. So he worked as hard as he could—coming home after our bedtimes, working weekends, forgoing vacation days, taking on extra consulting gigs. My mom always took pride in being supportive of us, unlike her overbearing mother, who judged her taste and choices and took credit for her accomplishments. She'd pour her energy into fostering any nascent interest or talent we exhibited. But her reluctance to impose her will on us, grounded as much in a lack of confidence about her own judgments as it was in her love for us, often meant that my sister and I were the ones she turned to for advice. Moving away from their hometown and university friends to start over in suburbia had left them without much of a support network. This was especially hard on my mom. When our new house was being built, my mom looked to me for my considered opinions on floor plans and roofing tiles. Marital spats, conflicts with coworkers, even healthcare decisions were laid out for me in detail. At the time, I didn't know what I was supposed to do; I was twelve, and she was the one who had gone to med school. When I was a small child, I enjoyed feeling that I could be her helper and the closeness this afforded. But as I grew older, the responsibility began to weigh on me. Would everything fall apart if I stopped playing my role well?

When I was in eighth grade, we moved from Massachusetts to Maine after my dad got a new job; my older sister stayed behind to finish up high school. Not long after, my mother fell ill. With no friends or family close by and my mom sick with cancer, it felt like the responsibility of holding the family together fell to me: fixing dinner, watching TV with my mom after her chemo appointments, talking to my dad when he came home exhausted from the hospital. Right at the moment when most teenagers would be in the throes of rebellion, sneaking out of the house, trying on new identities, doing whippets under the bleachers, I mostly stayed home. Maybe this was when I stopped being able to register my desires as important, or fully real.

About halfway through the "Motherhood—Is It for Me?" course, we were instructed to imagine a dialogue with a parent with whom we had "unresolved issues."[13] We were to picture them sitting before us with an open heart, granting us their full attention. Long-simmering resentments, undervalued accomplishments, anger, or grief—it was all fair game. Things could be different, in the fantasy, at least. Perhaps this time we would have our needs met. What could I say to them? I wasn't sure. I considered the standard generational complaints about boomer parents—that they were shallow, narcissistic capitalist consumers, that they've left us with little more than a burning husk of a planet to live on. But they rang hollow.

Most of the women in the course chose to address their mothers. I did too. In the imagined dialogue, I told her that I felt she could be too quick to look for solutions to my problems. I tried to say what I couldn't that day in the diner: that it wasn't money that was stopping me from having kids or growing up but something much harder to pin down. I thought about how lonely it felt at home, especially in those dark cancer years. I thought about how hard she worked to make sure everyone was okay, and how much I hated seeing her stressed out. I thought about how although she was, by any objective standard, a great mom, the truth was that none of it looked fun, none of it felt easy. Driven by service, she was always looking for something, searching for it in us or other people, doubting herself. Though it pained me to admit it, when I took stock of my life and asked myself whether I wanted the things she had, whether they would be worth the sacrifices, the answer was not obviously "yes."

For my parents, it was clear what it meant to do things better, to give us the kind of upbringing they wished they'd had. But when I envisioned my own hypothetical family, there was nothing specific, nothing major, that I could point to that I would have tried to change. Sure, I'd want to have more family dinners. I'd try to really listen to my children and not hold on to any fixed notions of who they were. But would this be enough? Could I make them feel any less adrift? All my life, my parents have wanted my sister and me to be happy. I was offered every individual freedom possible—freedom to choose my career, to find love, to attain creative satisfaction. But what pleasures and pursuits to seek out and which to avoid, what aspirations and projects merit sacrifice, what challenges are worth the trouble—all of these judgments were to be worked out on our own, more or less played by ear.

One day I asked my mom if there was anything I could have done that would have fundamentally changed the way she felt about me, anything that would have really disappointed her. What if I, who got shipped off to peace camp every summer of middle school, had decided to enlist in the military? What if I, the scion of science nerds, opted not to go to college? My mom gamely paused to think about it, but refused to take the bait: "College isn't for everyone. If that was what you wanted . . ." Okay, what if I, who made them both proud by blowing the shofar at High Holiday services throughout high school, accepted Christ as my savior and became an evangelical convert? "Well, I wouldn't want you to try to convert me." Is that all? Surely she would have had some misgivings if I repudiated everything she and my father held dear. Her purported indifference was sweet, but also baffling.

Like many parents today, my mother did not wish to impose a vision of happiness on us; we were meant to discover it for ourselves. Of course, in aiming at their children's happiness, parents "have always justified themselves with reference to the future," as the philosopher Agnes Callard has written. But there is something different about how parents think of their role today: "What's radically new is not, at heart, how concerned or permissive we've become, but how fully we have given over to our children the job of defining 'happiness.'" Callard calls this new paradigm "acceptance parenting." "Traditional" parents, she explains, drew "on culture and tradition to set standards relative to which children are to be assessed." (Think of Tevye in *Fiddler on the Roof,* who disowns his daughter when she announces her plan to wed a non-Jew.) "Those standards now come from the people they are to be applied to—more specifically, from *future, which is to say, not yet existent,* versions of those people."[14] Instead of moral guides, parents become talent scouts and trend forecasters in their own homes, doing their best to expose their children to as many activities and opportunities as possible in the hope that something will take root.

Naturally, parents still wish to see their kids "succeed," in some ways perhaps more than ever before, but the onus is on children to figure out what that actually means. This is why acceptance parenting and intensive parenting are not only compatible but complimentary. Parents fret about preschool admissions, extracurricular activities, SAT scores, and college rankings. But beyond that it's up to their children to make sense of the world, more or less on their own—with little meaningful direction aside from the injunction to be kind and not bully the other kids on the playground. As parents watch apprehensively from the sidelines, praying nothing goes terribly wrong, kids are left to deduce the deeper, unarticulated expectations of the adults through shrouded patterns and signs. Without a model to reproduce or rebel against, growing up with acceptance parents can feel tractionless, like a wheel spinning in a void.

For most of us today, there's simply no going back to traditional parenting, even if we wanted to—and not many of us would want to, even if we could. Once lost, traditional ways of life cannot easily be recovered. For the generations reared through acceptance parenting, this change has and will continue to have immense consequences: shaping not just how we think about ourselves but how we understand what family is and what it can be.

What would a happy family look like? When I blinked, I

couldn't picture it. And, even if I could conjure some image of the kind of familial mutuality I thought I was after, I had no reason to think I'd be any better at executing it than my parents. Why would I be able to succeed where so many others had failed? I'd spent so long straining to meet the nebulous expectations of others, following their cues, and yet I knew that, when you had kids, this was neither a wise nor a sustainable strategy—you can't just chase your kids around and hope they'll tell you how they want to be raised; you have to make a life *for* them. There was still so much, it seemed, I had left to figure out.

At one point in the "Motherhood—Is It for Me?" course, we were asked to spend a week imagining that our answer to the central question of the course was *yes*. When I applied myself to fantasizing about motherhood, I could summon up pleasant scenes—reading to my children, cooking with them, going sledding, collecting sea glass on the beach. Yet none of these seemed adequate to the monumental task of cultivating another human being. And though it felt like a betrayal to admit it, when I looked back on my childhood, I couldn't quite say what I'd want to re-create, were I to have children of my own. Raising a happy family presented itself as an impossible challenge, like trying to build a house on sand.

I'D BEGUN TO entertain the possibility that I might end up not having kids—not by grand design or willed intention but almost unwittingly, by putting the decision off, over and over again. The time for deliberation was not infinite. In *The Bell Jar*, Sylvia Plath analogizes the process of choosing between possible futures—motherhood, writing, traveling, a career—to an Edenic dilemma of picking fruit from a tree: "I wanted each and every one of them, but choosing one meant losing all the rest, and, as I sat there, unable to decide, the figs began to wrinkle and go black, and, one by one, they plopped to the ground at my feet."[15] A decision delayed long enough makes itself.

I had spent my twenties admiring the figs of possibility dangling overhead. I went to college to read books with those who liked them as much as I did, eager to leave behind the bored kids who copied my homework and the grade-grubbing nerds I competed with in high school—finally, I could be among my own people. On campus I could feel myself expanding in many thrilling directions. After graduation, most of my friends moved out of Chicago, and I was left behind. I didn't have a real career, or a plan. I gravitated toward people who seemed smarter or more self-assured than me. It was only through exposure to others' strong opinions that I felt capable of fumbling, however tentatively, toward my own. My ideas, which felt embryonic and only ever partial, needed to be coaxed into the light; they needed friction to take form. Aimless and striving, a year and a half out of college, I quit my full-time publishing job and gave up my health insurance to become the first employee at a small literary magazine run by three idealistic, hyper-earnest grad students. When I was hired, it was a one-year gig with no promise of renewal, and the whole enterprise felt like an experiment: Could we, could I, make this magazine work? I was in charge of managing the production schedule and keeping the magazine administratively afloat, but of course what I really wanted was to write. If only I could land on a subject I could speak about with any authority. (For two years I had a draft of an essay on the Museum of Broken Relationships languishing in my drafts folder, only to be scooped by Leslie Jamison.)

It was there that, in 2015, I met Anastasia. She was writing a dissertation in philosophy and had just joined the magazine's staff as a part-time editor. The first memory I have of meeting her was at one of our release parties, where she showed up straight after canvassing for Bernie in Iowa. Her big parka was covered in campaign stickers. "I just convinced all these nice Iowan grandmas to vote for Bernie," she beamed. "I'm not even American!" From the first time she came to visit our small, closet-like office in downtown Chicago, I knew I wanted to be her friend. She was tall and put together, all hard angles and strong feelings, full of fresh thought. I was indecisive; she took unapologetic stances. I was tentative and overaccommodating, slow to come around to my own convictions; she was very impatient. Once or twice a week, she'd join me in the office to edit and work on projects for the magazine. Sometimes she'd arrive and declare—to the interns or no one in particular—that she was kidnapping me, which meant dragging me to a "Russian-French bistro" for a lunch that consisted of crepes and vodka martinis and lasted until 4:00 P.M.

After finding purpose for so long in being merely useful, here was someone who treated me as a peer and coconspirator. I wanted to live up to her expectations. With Anastasia around, I no longer saw myself as being relegated to shuffling around commas and turning double hyphens into em dashes. Now, every assignment, down to the most modest tweet, was important, imbued with excitement and urgency. She didn't just nod along or commiserate with me; she pushed me—to share my offhand remarks in office-wide emails, to shed my veneer of cautious professionalism and betray my sense of humor, to write.

It was the ethos of the magazine that there was nothing more serious than everyday life. And it became the ethos of our friendship, too. Our work together spilled out of the margins, and soon we were talking, and talking, about everything in our lives. Before long, we were interpreting each other's dreams. Amid the ardent discussions of the magazine drama and grad school gossip, a deeper current of thought emerged, one that led, searchingly, into the future. Anastasia was more confident in her desire to start a family, but even then there were obstacles: a very long-distance relationship, the bleak academic job market. It was during these conversations that we began asking each other: *What would it be like to have kids? What would a life without them look like? How would we reconcile family with our intellectual and social lives? Why did it all evoke so much fear? What are children for?*

Where before, my conversations with friends about these subjects felt weightless and conjectural, now I saw my thoughts become sharper and more concrete. We knew the stakes of these questions were high—it was, after all, the rest of our lives we were talking about. We kept trying to zero in on the source of our dissatisfaction with the narratives that we saw circulating, with increasing frequency, about the choice to have children. Those discussions were the seeds of this book. We knew the answers we were looking for couldn't be found through amateur self-analysis or by scanning the endless streams of millennial trend pieces and memoirs on offer. Maybe, though, we could find them together, in conversation. In her poem "Dreams Before Waking," Adrienne Rich asks, what would it be like to live "in a city whose people were changing / each other's despair into hope?"[16] We didn't have a city, but maybe the two of us would do.

And yet we realized that this was not really a task we could undertake all on our own; we had to invite others in. Our experiences gave us a starting point, but to penetrate to the core of the contemporary mood of ambivalence, we had to look outside ourselves: to history and sociology, to literature and film, to philosophy. Above all, we had to talk to other people. Through in-depth interviews and surveys, we asked hundreds of our contemporaries about their attitudes toward children and family.

We felt the conversation about millennial ambivalence about children was shallow. But how could we loosen the grip of hackneyed generational narratives while still doing justice to people's real, legitimate concerns? We shared the conviction that defending women's right to decide their reproductive fates did not mean that each of us had to deliberate alone. But how could we begin to publicly discuss the ultimate private decision, and especially at a time when reproductive freedom is coming under fatal attack once again?

The repeal of *Roe v. Wade* and the wave of antiabortion laws that followed it have made any conversation about the potential value of having children fraught, to say the least. In a representative essay published a year after the *Dobbs v. Jackson Women's Health Organization* decision, the journalist Andrea González-Ramírez described how she began thinking more seriously about becoming a mother when she was about to turn thirty, but then *Dobbs* put an end to all that: "I have never been sure that I desire to be a mom, let alone that I desire it enough to assume the risks. These days, however, that door is shut. I choose myself."[17] This sentiment testifies to the ways that right-wing attacks on women's reproductive freedom not only threaten women's access to birth control and safe abortion but also affect how they approach the very question of whether they want children for themselves. The conversation has become highly politicized, seeding real, and understandable, aversion. But to permit the antiabortion movement to alienate women and men from the very question of whether they want children in the first place, to let it prejudice their capacity to deliberate about their own future, only allows conservatives to set the reproductive agenda for the rest of us in yet another way. Simply put, the question of whether or not to have a family is too important to allow it to be a casualty of the culture war.

Any invitation to reevaluate how we are living will touch on live nerves, and we felt we couldn't ask our readers to grapple with such a personal topic without sharing and risking something of ourselves in turn. This is why we decided that I would write the introduction and Anastasia would write the conclusion, not only to establish the personal stakes of these questions for us but to show how the social and cultural forces that we will go on to probe can shape individual lives. As of this writing, I still do not have children. But this is no longer because I am undecided. I started IVF in the spring of 2023. I'm still nervous about motherhood, but I have different worries—not so much abstract fears about an unimaginable future but more concrete concerns about fertility, pregnancy, and parenthood. Anastasia gave birth to Lila, my goddaughter, while we were researching and writing this book. The chapters in between these personal essays follow the arc of our conversation as we tried to peel back the layers of resistance: What do material concerns—about money, career, and the desire for autonomy and flexibility—reveal about our priorities and what "happiness" has come to mean to us? What do people look for in love today, and how do these pursuits align or conflict with the possibility of one day starting a family? Is the choice to become a mother the fulfillment of a feminist ethos or a betrayal of it? Where do *men* fit in? Isn't it perverse that the question of parenthood is so frequently treated as only a women's issue? How do we acknowledge ambivalence without letting it make the choice for us? And, above all, for all its cruelty, for all the suffering it entails, is human life still worth the trouble?

If you're reading this book, it is unlikely you're asking these questions in the abstract. You are asking them because you are thinking about children: whether to have them, whether to have more of them, how to justify having had the ones you have. Perhaps you are wondering how to talk to your partner about your desire for them, or lack thereof, or worrying about how to ask your children whether they've ever given thought to having their own. Maybe you were not able to have them, or never wanted them in the first place. If you are facing the decision yourself, we cannot make it for you, just as you cannot make it for others. We can, however, reassure you that if you're finding the choice paralyzing, you are not alone, and you are not simply indecisive, or cowardly, or selfish. It's anxiety-provoking even for those to whom the decision comes with relative ease. It requires a precise and elusive alignment of circumstances—material, biological, and personal. And it requires risking the unknown not only because you cannot predict how parenting would go for you—whether it would be physically possible, whether you would enjoy it, what costs it would exact—but also because in having a child, you tie the uncertain fate of your own life to that of another human being, vulnerable in body and heart just like you. It is possible, however, to approach the decision with a better understanding of the sources of our ambivalence and fear, as well as the deep philosophical stakes of the question; it is possible not to face it alone.

# CHAPTER 1

# The Externals

In 1991, Ann Davidman, a marriage counselor by training, teamed up with Denise L. Carlini, another therapist, to found a support group for women who were unsure about whether or not they wanted to have children. Davidman and Carlini were looking to expand their practice and decided that the life transition around motherhood would be a good topic for group work. Setting up weekend workshops in the San Francisco Bay Area, they invited women to come together to reflect on their unresolved feelings about starting a family. Davidman eventually branched out on her own and began to offer the program remotely, allowing English-speaking women from all over the world to participate by phone. The "Motherhood—Is It for Me?" founders were among the first to recognize the growing demand for opportunities to explore the question of whether or not to have children in a therapeutic setting. Thirty years on, Davidman's course remains one of the only programs of its kind, and certainly the best established.

Over the span of ten to twelve weeks, participants try to penetrate their ambivalence and discover whether or not they really want to become parents. This insight will not necessarily translate into a decision—perhaps they will realize they don't have an innate desire to have children but choose to have them anyway because it is important to their partner; maybe they will discover that in fact they want them very much, but circumstances render having them out of the question. Whatever happens, they will, at least, know *what* they want—a necessary precondition for making any well-considered choice.

One of the key tenets of Davidman's course dictates that participants distance themselves from what she calls the "externals" to the decision: age, fertility, health, finances, their relationship status and partner's preferences, familial expectations, the fate of the environment. These factors, she counsels, can interfere with the ability to truly get to know oneself, and only by putting them aside, at least temporarily, can one reach inner clarity. "What needs to be known first," according to the course book, "is what you want for yourself *regardless of the circumstances of your life.*"[1] The "externals" are literally cast away: participants are instructed to write out their circumstantial concerns on scraps of paper and place them inside a "tightly lidded jar."[2] If they'd like, they can make a craft project out of decorating the container—perhaps this will help them see its contents in a new, lighter way!—before placing it squarely out of sight.

After the course Rachel took part in concluded in fall 2020, we spoke to some of Davidman's former students about their experiences. The call to mute external influences, even temporarily, could be liberating, they said. All too often, women are asked to prioritize others' desires before their own. For such women, the invitation to focus on their own wishes and needs was a welcome change. For others, it was an immense relief to shrug off, if only for a moment, the material anxieties that had hijacked their decision-making process. Whatever might have been holding them back, the promise was the same: Cut through the static, and you will finally be able to hear your inner truth. An authentic desire lies dormant within you ready to light your way forward, if only you can uncover it.

Still, sidelining their externals wasn't always easy. Some participants in the program struggled with the demand to silence their worries: they might run out of time, disappoint their parents, damage their careers, or lose their partners. When we asked them what they might have changed or added to the program, they expressed surprise that they did not get to return in a meaningful way to the externals they'd initially been instructed to put away. The course book includes a short final exercise prompting readers to revisit these factors, in order to see which "no longer apply and which have shifted in importance."[3] But there's no serious attempt to investigate what those externals mean to the women and men taking the course, let alone guidance on how to confront them in view of the new insights they'd gained. Of course, there's only so much one can cover in an hour-long biweekly call, especially in a group setting. But, like it or not, when the twelve weeks are up, participants must return to their lives—to their partners, parents, and bank accounts. In the end, the externals can't stay in the jar.

The decision whether or not to have children is too important to be made according to someone else's preferences or the vagaries of circumstance alone. But no one lives in a vacuum; taking personal responsibility for the choice can't possibly mean bracketing off everything else that goes into making it. After all, becoming a parent is not a self-contained activity, and this is not just because having a child comes with many personal and social repercussions. To have a child is to reconstitute the shape of your life. If you are doing it with a partner, it will mean binding yourself not just to your mutual offspring but to them, in one constellation or another, in perpetuity. It will also likely mean radically reconfiguring your existing material and professional priorities and your relationship to leisure, to your existing family members, to time itself. The "externals" aren't just distractions from what matters; they make up the substance of our lives.

According to the narrative of the course, one's internal desire, precious and pure, needs to be rescued from outside interference. But these so-called external factors—chief among them concerns about money and relationships—are inescapable. It is hopeless to try to rid ourselves of their influence over our deliberations by fiat. We have to examine these forces, and not just because of their immediate consequences for our lives; in facing them, we find ourselves confronting some of our deepest and most entrenched attitudes toward family formation. Behind the façade of straightforward concerns about financial security or the difficulty of finding a partner lies an intricate web of convictions and doubts: What ought to matter to us? What goals should we pursue and how should we adjudicate conflicts between them? To determine the proper place for such considerations in our deliberations about having children, we will have to do nothing less than probe the very frameworks of meaning and value that constitute our lives.

THERE ARE MANY reasons people give for hesitating about or choosing not to have children: climate change; mental illness; health problems; traumatic family histories; intellectual, artistic, religious, or other higher callings; simply not having the desire for it. But which factors are most decisive for those facing the dilemma?

To find out, we interviewed dozens of Zoomers, millennials, and Gen Xers and conducted in-depth qualitative surveys that received responses from three hundred more. We distributed the surveys through our social media platforms, friends, and acquaintances. Our goal was to get beyond the media headlines and hear, firsthand, from as many people, with as many diverse perspectives on the question of children, as possible. The vast majority of the replies came from people we do not personally know. The median age of respondents was thirty-six; 75 percent identified as female, 24 percent as male, and 1 percent as nonbinary. They were mostly highly educated: 95 percent of respondents had a college degree, and 68 percent had an MA or above. Their education levels and careers suggest most, though not all, were middle to upper-middle class. Most were either married or in a serious relationship, and roughly 40 percent had kids. Some of the people we spoke to came from religious backgrounds, though most did not. The majority identified as straight or mostly straight, but we heard from queer, lesbian, gay, bisexual, asexual, and pansexual people as well. We did not ask them to identify their race or ethnicity; based on volunteered information, we know it was a diverse group, but we estimate that most were white. (All names of interview and survey subjects have been changed.)

When we asked our survey respondents and interview subjects what might have made it easier for them to make the decision, they cited some variation on financial security more frequently than any other factor. Of course, given the demographic composition of our surveys and interviews, we cannot assume that any particular response or trend is representative of the American, let alone global, population. But in foregrounding financial anxiety, these respondents were expressing a widespread mood. Responding to a news story about the "crisis" of declining birth rates, the millennial political phenom Alexandria Ocasio-Cortez took to Twitter in March 2021 to express her

annoyance: "The actual crisis," she said, "is how entire generations are sunk with inhumane levels of student debt, low incomes,
high rent, no guarantee of healthcare and little action on climate
change which creates a situation where feeling stable enough to
have a kid can feel more like a luxury than a norm."[4] Ocasio-
Cortez's cry sounded a familiar refrain. The high cost of raising
a child is one of the most tangible external obstacles to starting a
family today, certainly in the United States. Concerns about the
affordability of housing, feeding, dressing, educating, and enter-
taining children are exacerbated by anxieties about the lack of
affordable health- and childcare, student debt, and the state of
the economy. As the feminist *Guardian* columnist Moira Donegan has argued, these pressures are felt especially acutely by
women, who suffer from career and pay stagnation, pregnancy
discrimination, and the unequal distribution of housework and
childcare duties, and who, in the United States, are not entitled
to paid parental leave by law: "Women are not given enough material support by the state to be able to raise children while still
leading prosperous, economically productive lives."[5]

Among our respondents, financial anxiety took many forms.
For some, the risks were straightforward. Camila, a thirty-four-
year-old graduate student in anthropology who said she would
eventually like to have children, told us that "precarious labor
conditions and increasingly expensive healthcare and education
systems make the decision seem more momentous—more of a
'gamble,' even." Similarly, Anthony, a gay thirty-two-year-old at-
torney, said that the challenges of his own upbringing had affected
his attitude toward parenting. He fondly recalled his experience
babysitting in France after college: "I really enjoyed spending time
with the children and teaching them about Black American history and culture. I taught them how to sing Aretha and Whitney,
and memorize poems by Langston Hughes. I got excited about the

idea of having children and passing on culture and tradition." But though he was happily married and gainfully employed, financial concerns made children a distant hope. "Seeing how my mom and everyone else struggled makes me not want to be unprepared financially for kids." He was "just waiting to crawl out of a mountain of debt and make sure that my mother is secure." He added that the situation was "very stressful." Amal, a literary agent who, at forty-three, did not have kids, put it most succinctly when we asked what might have swayed her: "A shit ton of money."

Other middle- and upper-middle-class millennials worried not so much that children would be unaffordable but that they would not be able to give their children the same standard of living that they had growing up. "I think about student debt a lot," said Meera, a twenty-eight-year-old magazine writer who grew up in India and now lives in New York, "because I don't have any." She was afraid that she would not be able to guarantee the same for her own children: "I would consider it a failure (both to the child and to my parents) if my child had to have debt, or if it were not able to benefit from or maintain the security I grew up with and that my parents worked so hard to give us." Danielle, a thirty-six-year-old diplomat, shared this concern: "I would not want to raise kids if I didn't feel I could provide them with the same standard of living I enjoyed growing up, which included things like summer camp, sports lessons, vacations, and private college tuition." For these respondents, bringing up children responsibly meant not only shielding them from financial precarity but providing them with the same opportunities they had access to in their childhood, or more. Trouble was, they hardly felt confident in their capacity to secure either.

ACCORDING TO A widespread generational narrative, millennials and Zoomers have experienced substantial precarity, especially as compared to their predecessors. This impression is hardly base-less: by many gross economic metrics, millennials have gotten off to a very shaky start. They graduated into the worst recession since the Great Depression and have been saddled with historic levels of student debt.[6] Despite being the highest-educated American generation to date and having worked in the most productive economy in history, millennials have suffered from job insecurity, rising costs of living (especially in large cities), record levels of personal debt, stagnant wages, and a tattered social safety net.[7] Meanwhile, millennials have earned the unfortunate distinction of being the "first American generation to experience as much downward mobility as upward mobility," with 49 percent in lower-status positions than their parents.[8] Though they are currently the largest cohort in the American workforce, and with the oldest millennials now entering their forties, millennials have amassed just 5.6 percent of the national wealth.[9] They struggled to gain professional footing well into the peak of their productive years and then had to contend with the effects of a global pandemic. "After accounting for the present crisis," the *Washington Post* reported in May 2020, "the average millennial has experienced slower economic growth since entering the workforce than any other generation in U.S. history."[10]

The Great Recession hit at a formative moment in many millennials' lives, shaping their self-understanding and life choices. It's no wonder that, amid such continuous disruption, they have grown disillusioned with the promises of progress. In a 2023 YouGov poll, nearly one in four people under the age of forty-four responded to the question "How attainable is the American Dream for you personally?" with "the American Dream does not exist."[11] Promised that education and hard work were the only sure pathways to success, by now many millennials have lost the blind confidence in the system but have kept its obsession with productivity. And while millennials are well aware that they may have to work even harder to offer their children a standard of living comparable to the one they have enjoyed themselves, they must also contend with an even more basic dilemma. In our hyper-competitive economy, where the gap between rich and poor only continues to grow, will having children cause them to lose their edge and forfeit whatever gains they have managed to claw away for themselves?

The mood of precarity, distress, and resentment is undeniable. But exactly how much worse off millennials are compared to previous generations is not as obvious. In recent years, millennials have started to reach some of the benchmarks of prosperity set by previous generations. While in absolute terms millennials are still poorer than their predecessors—owning seventy-two cents in 2023 for every dollar boomers had when they were the same age, back in 1989—according to economist Jeremy Horpedahl, when adjusting for the significant differences in generation sizes, as of 2022, millennials were roughly equal in wealth per capita to boomers and Gen Xers at the same age.[12] In addition, after some years of stagnation, millennials earn more—with a median adjusted income per household of $71,566 in 2022—than nearly all earlier generations on record.[13] (In large part this is due to more millennial women participating in the workforce than ever before, and being paid significantly higher salaries.) Their rates of homeownership, though still trailing behind earlier generations, are rising, too; now, more than half of American millennials own their own homes.[14]

When economists with the Federal Reserve examined the impacts of the Great Recession in 2018, they warned that millennials were at risk of becoming a "lost generation."[15] But when they revisited the data in 2021, they found that millennials had "staged a remarkable comeback," increasing their median wealth by 29 percent between 2016 and 2019, with more "time to gain lost ground." While older millennials (those born in the 1980s) were 40 percent behind wealth targets for their age in 2016, by 2019 the gap was only 11 percent. And though millennials' debt-to-income ratio remains the highest of any age group, the researchers added that, given the high levels of education among younger cohorts, "it is possible that younger generations will simply have a steeper wealth life cycle than older generations . . . and will eventually make up the difference."[16] Among other achievements, during the pandemic, millennials' net worth more than doubled, from an average of $62,758 in early 2020 to $127,793 in early 2022 (largely because they were able to buy homes and build equity when interest rates were low).[17] And while they may have gotten off to a slow start, many millennials will soon get a lot richer. In what economic analysts are projecting will be one of the "greatest wealth transfers" in history, millennials are projected to inherit as much as $68 trillion from their parents by the end of this decade, coming to hold five times more wealth than they do today.[18] Reflecting on similar findings suggesting millennials have caught up with or even surpassed previous generations, in an April 2023 essay in *The Atlantic* titled "The Myth of the Broke Millennial," Jean Twenge wrote that, "all in all, this is a generation on the cusp of middle age that looks successful, not lost."[19]

These gains are far from evenly distributed and vary sharply by education level, socioeconomic status, and race.[20] But the millennial turn of fortune, unequal as it is, is not lost on those lucky enough to benefit from it. Indeed, many Americans report being fairly optimistic about their long-term material prospects. While on average American millennials, like their global counterparts, report lower financial well-being at present than other generational cohorts, a 2019 T. Rowe Price survey on attitudes toward future finances among over three thousand working

American adults found that millennials were the most sanguine age group, with 74 percent reporting being "somewhat or very comfortable" that they're on track to reach their financial goals.[21] In a similar vein, in a nationally representative survey in late 2020 of more than four thousand young Americans (aged thirteen to thirty-nine), 81 percent of respondents reported believing that if they work hard, they will succeed in life. Seven in ten said that their hard work will enable them to rise up the economic ladder. And nearly eight in ten maintained the belief that their lives will be better than or roughly on par with their parents'. More recently, in Schwab's 2023 "Modern Wealth" survey of one thousand Americans of various ages, millennials were the most likely generation to report that they "feel wealthy" today, with a majority of millennials and Gen Zers surveyed saying that what makes them feel wealthy was "being able to afford a similar lifestyle as my friends."[22]

One should not be too credulous about the conclusions of polling and isolated survey results, not least when the populations whose attitudes they purport to represent are as large and diverse as generational cohorts. And none of this is to deny that, whatever millennials' long-term economic prospects may actually be, and however confident they feel about them, there remain many in the cohort who are struggling materially, and for whom optimism is well out of reach.[23] The mounting evidence of millennials' improving material conditions and financial confidence does no more and no less than complicate the caricature of millennials as uniformly financially insecure and terminally anxious. In turn, it raises doubts about the claim, so often taken for granted, that the reason people aren't having kids today boils down to money. As attractive as economics may be as a solution to the riddle of the growing ambivalence about having children, it is partial at best. Many millennials are not as financially stressed as they are often assumed to be. As for those who are, birth rates by and large correlate negatively with income and still remain highest among women below the poverty line.[24]

International comparisons put even more pressure on the hypothesis that financial deprivation and precarity are the main cause of millennial hesitancy about having children. Stepping out of the American frame of reference, it becomes evident that there is little assurance that removing financial hurdles to childbearing will reverse the trend of birth-rate decline.[25]

Even in countries with robust pro-family policies—including those that have attempted to encourage child-rearing by guaranteeing free or subsidized prenatal support and childcare as well as paid parental leave—millennials are often no more likely to start families than their American counterparts. In many cases, they're even less keen on it. For example, while the fertility rate in the United States in 2021 was 1.66 children per woman, in Germany it was 1.58, in Canada 1.43, in Portugal 1.38, in Japan 1.3, in Italy 1.25, and in South Korea just 0.81.[26] While the introduction of free universal childcare and generous family leave programs in Nordic countries at first increased marginal fertility rates, even then the long-term effects have been modest.[27] Until relatively recently, the Nordic welfare states were viewed as fertility success stories by remaining at or above population replacement while enjoying high levels of gender parity and female workforce participation. Over the past decade, however, Nordic birth rates have declined dramatically across the board, despite public campaigns directed at slowing the trend.[28] "The Nordic countries are in general . . . good welfare states," noted Nora Sánchez Gassen, a political scientist and demographer at the Nordic research institute Nordregio. "They have good social support, they are stable countries with high levels of social trust. In general, these should be considered good conditions to raise children, but nonetheless we see that fertility is declining." One reason for these fertility declines, Sánchez Gassen suggested, is that there are more couples remaining childless, whether voluntarily or involuntarily.[29] In 2022 Sweden's fertility rate was 1.52, Denmark's 1.55, Iceland's 1.59, and Finland's 1.32.[30] In Norway, which has universal healthcare, free college tuition, a monthly child benefit, public daycare, and one of the most generous family leave policies in the world—granting mothers forty-nine weeks at full pay or fifty-nine weeks at 80 percent pay, in addition to up to fifteen weeks of paternity leave—the fertility rate reached a record low of 1.41 in 2022.[31] The fact that Nordic birth rates continue to fall, despite such extensive social support, suggests that additional economic benefits and incentives would likely do little to turn the tide. As a UN report from 2019 put it, "Policies supporting children and families are clearly important, but often other factors and policies not pertaining directly to families"—like changing work, parenting, and gender norms—"might have a stronger impact on reproductive decisions."[32]

The prevalent American tendency to suppose that it is economics, and, in particular, the lack of social-welfare infrastructure, that is keeping those who want kids from having them persists in the face of such evidence to the contrary. A representative example: in a popular *New York Times* essay from 2019 titled "The End of Babies," journalist Anna Sussman attributed the steep declines in birth rates across the globe to the "barely perceptible contraceptive" of the market economy and its direct economic, as well as social and environmental, repercussions. Sussman's starting point is the reported gap between how many children people say they want—their so-called ideal family size—and how many they end up having. "It seems clear," she writes, "that what we have come to think of as 'late capitalism'—that is, not just the economic system, but all its attendant inequalities, indignities, opportunities and absurdities—has become hostile to reproduction."[33] Sussman is keen to reveal how our current economic system makes it "inconceivable" for people to have as many children as they would have liked, not just in the United States but around the world.[34] But why is it, then, that the removal of financial barriers to child-rearing in places like northern Europe and South Korea has so little effect on people's individual choices? Addressing the global failure of existing pro-family policies to raise birth rates, Sussman argues that while it is true that many European states offer generous material support for prospective parents, their citizens nevertheless "find themselves contending with the spiritual maladies that accompany late capitalism even in wealthy, egalitarian countries."

> With their basic needs met and an abundance of opportunities at their fingertips, Danes instead must grapple with the promise and pressure of seemingly limitless freedom, which can combine to make children an afterthought, or an unwelcome intrusion on a life that offers rewards and satisfactions of a different kind—an engaging career, esoteric hobbies, exotic holidays.[35]

If late capitalism is responsible for declining birth rates both in the United States and in northern Europe, critics like Sussman must show why the ostensible removal of the "inequalities, indignities, opportunities and absurdities" that characterize life in the United States has done so little to alter the outlook on children in Scandinavian social democracies. But by her own analysis, in countries like Denmark, what people are facing is not an insurmountable series of obstacles to having children but rather "limitless freedom." For them, children are not a longed-for object of fantasy, regretfully out of reach, but "an afterthought." In other words, their "spiritual maladies" do not render children impossible to afford so much as they make them increasingly undesirable to have.

Many of the social policies considered in such contexts— child tax credits, debt forgiveness, guaranteed livable wages, subsidized rent, healthcare, childcare, and paid parental leave— would no doubt make it easier for American families to raise children with far greater confidence and dignity than they can under current conditions. But the question we are exploring here is not whether such social policies are just, whether they would benefit both children and parents, or whether they should be enacted, but whether such measures would touch upon people's deepest sources of ambivalence about children and family. If the global evidence is to be trusted, there is little reason to think that they would. Ultimately, it seems that no amount of money or social support can help you answer the question of whether or not you want to be a parent. To begin to answer *that* question, we must look more deeply into what our contemporary financial insecurities and preferences reveal about what we take to be important in life, and what we no longer do.

ACCORDING TO A 2019 global survey of 13,416 millennials across forty-two countries and territories, just 39 percent of millennials worldwide listed having kids as one of their life ambitions—in last place in the rankings, behind goals such as traveling the world, earning high salaries, buying a home, and making a "positive impact."[36] In a 2018 national *New York Times* survey of over 1,800 American millennials, the most common explanation given by those who did not want kids or were uncertain about having them was wanting "leisure time."[37]

Many of the millennials and Gen Xers we've spoken to who

were ambivalent about having children or who had decided against it also named different concrete priorities—career, travel, romantic relationships—as the things pulling them away from starting their own families. Work, in particular, featured prominently. For young professionals today, work is no longer just something they do for a paycheck; it has become one of the primary spheres of meaning in their lives. For those who take themselves to pursue a vocation, work is a way of leading a purposeful life and making a mark on the world. For those still going to the office, work is where people find others to talk to and, if they're lucky, people who care about the same things that they do. Often, it's where people fall in love. Above all, it's how many people in the middle and upper-middle classes define their value and sense of purpose: it is against the standards of their professions that people measure their level of success and personal growth. And it is in large measure on the social status of their professions that they base their self-worth.

Because work has become so central to people's identities, self-esteem, and social lives, it is easy to lose sight of its many dry demands. For full-time employees, work takes most of our waking hours. And for whole swaths of highly skilled white-collar workers, the willingness and ability to give more and more time to their careers has become a professional virtue in itself. In principle, under conditions of gender parity in the workplace and the home, these pressures ought to have jeopardized equally the capacity of men and women to function as parents. But the reality is that external and internalized expectations about who should care for children often place a higher burden on women than on men, with the disparity exacerbated by the failure of contemporary workplaces to accommodate dual-earner households.[38] As a result, among parents, women are disproportionately the ones who end up having to compromise their careers.

In a landmark 2012 essay for *The Atlantic*, "Why Women Still Can't Have It All," Anne-Marie Slaughter argued that employers' insatiable hunger for workers' time made it near impossible for professional women, in particular, to pursue ambitious, demanding careers at the highest levels. But it wasn't just ordinary sexism that was keeping women from reaching the very top of their professions. In many corners of the professional world, a "culture of 'time macho'" reigns, Slaughter wrote, "a relentless competition to work harder, stay later, pull more all-nighters, travel around the world and bill the extra hours that the international date line affords you."[39] In this environment, those who choose to opt out of the rapid and steep career climb in order to care for their children are often met with bewilderment, condescension, and pity. This is true of both men and women but, in practice, men are still more comfortable prioritizing career over family, which means it is still mostly women who try to juggle both. While mothers can and do, of course, work—and work hard—and often attain significant measures of success, even now they rarely reach the pinnacles of their professions.[40] Contrary to the popular line, Slaughter concluded, women simply "can't have it all"—nor should they be expected to.

We heard the same from many of the women we interviewed. When we asked Allison, a thirty-four-year-old civil servant and mother of one who was undecided about having more children, what would make her decision easier, she said, "A society that is more supportive of work-life balance so it isn't always an exhausting tug-of-war between work demands and family needs." The inability to pursue both family life and the highest measure of success, Slaughter insisted, is not due to lack of skill or effort or commitment; there simply are not enough hours in the week. The few women who have made it to the very top of their professions while raising children are the exceptions that prove the rule. Focusing attention on the accomplishments of women like Susan Rice, Samantha Power, and Sheryl Sandberg—"genuine superwomen"—and suggesting their paths are replicable will leave most women, even high-achieving ones, with little more than "a sense of failure."[41]

Slaughter observed that while it was hard for women of her generation to give up on the dream of having it all, almost none of the younger working women she'd spoken to seemed to still believe that it was possible to manage both work and family without fatally compromising one or the other. Something has got to give—and as time goes on, no longer just for women. Slaughter herself noted that men have also begun to struggle to satisfy the demands of both work and family.[42] Whereas men of previous generations had few qualms about the unequal division of domestic labor, today they are finding it far less acceptable, and less desirable, to neglect their responsibilities at home in favor of professional advancement. Indeed, among the men we surveyed, several reported feeling that the foreseen conflict between childcare and work was keeping them from having kids, too. Michael, a thirty-six-year-old university lecturer, told us, "I don't want kids now, if I ever have them, because it's just not compatible with my career. Later it might be. I know everyone is supposed to say that, and it's naïve. But I feel like my career is just picking up right now, and I wouldn't want to give that up."

The idea that starting a family is a trade-off that very ambitious people can no longer afford has become increasingly commonplace. One can excel at one's career or one can be a good parent, but not both at once. Some people we spoke to said they manage the conflict by just giving up on the dream of doing either particularly well. Lauren, a thirty-seven-year-old writer, told us this was a lesson she learned from her own mother, who made it clear to her that her children had "cost her a career":

> Prior to giving birth, I had a huge amount of anxiety (still do have quite a bit) about having both children and a career. That has dissipated a bit and made way for the somewhat crushing awareness that I can have both, but I might always feel as if I'm not really hitting the marks at either.

But others reported finding it hard to resign themselves to such compromises. "Having children would destroy my career and the fulfilling life that I've built for myself," said Kelly, a thirty-four-year-old diplomat. In our surveys, such an attitude was especially prominent among intellectually and creatively ambitious women. "At the end of the day," Leah, a thirty-five-year-old academic philosopher, told us, "I think I'd grow to resent a child if it hindered my ability to work and pursue my career." Naomi, a twenty-nine-year-old book critic, said, "I want to have as much time as possible for writing, thinking, and traveling. Children seem both time-consuming and expensive, and I think I am too single-minded or selfish in my ambitions to be a good parent." She added, however, that "maybe if I had tons and tons of money—enough to know for certain I could afford to hire a caretaker for the child forever—I would be more ambivalent and more open to the possibility."

In this, Naomi echoed several other women and men who claimed that they would be more receptive to the idea of children if only they could guarantee that having kids would not jeopardize the things that really mattered to them. "If money were truly no object," said Caroline, a thirty-year-old government worker, "I'd probably be at least neutral about the subject."

If she knew she would be "able to afford childcare at any/all levels, schools of choice, household help, etc.," she might consider it. "But that's not real life, and I don't want to give up the life I've built for myself by directing resources that make my life comfortable and enjoyable as is to raising a child." When she contemplated the prospect of having children, all Caroline could envision was the prohibitive cost:

> If I imagine having kids now, my first several thoughts are about what I would lose from that choice rather than what I would gain. Every time I have a lazy day or have a hard day at work or spend way too much money on something trivial or go on a great vacation, I think, "Thank god we don't have kids."

Having kids posed a similar threat to freedom for Matt, a thirty-five-year-old video producer in the Bay Area who took Davidman's private fatherhood ambivalence course. "I've done fairly well in my career—I've had good jobs, I'm kind of on 'the path,' if you will, relative to what I do," he told us in an interview. Though he was satisfied with his professional status, he said, "at the same time, there's been times when I just don't want to do it and I just want to walk away. And actually, the only way I could do that is if I had enough of a cushion financially to say 'fuck it,' just take off, without having a security blanket of finances or another job or something like that. I see having a kid as this extra layer of confining in terms of my choices." When we have kids, he said, "we lose that ability to say 'fuck it.'"

Wanting to achieve professional distinction, to travel, to pursue fulfilling creative projects, to make new friends, to promote worthy political causes, to enjoy leisure time, to maintain one's independence—none of these desires are frivolous. For women in particular, the freedom to foreground such ambitions has been hard-won. So it isn't surprising that individuals—and young women, especially—are reluctant to give them up. What is surprising is just how salient these considerations have become when measured against the possibility of having children.

The resistance to compromising on professional, personal, romantic, and social fronts may seem to suggest a straightforward shift in priorities: that children have become less important, a possible life choice that has lost its erstwhile appeal, an aspiration that no longer has the same value and no longer confers the advantages it once did. But contemporary ways of thinking about children indicate something more than a reshuffling of preferences. The thought that children have just become a less appealing or advantageous choice than they once were obscures a more fundamental transformation: that they have become, for the first time, a matter of choice.

Until not too long ago, for most people around the globe, child-rearing was a basic part of becoming an adult. It was not, as it is steadily becoming today, one possible path to take among several equally legitimate ones. This was not just because children used to perform various political, religious, and economic functions in the lives of their families that they no longer do. Children worked on the family farm, provided and cared for parents in old age, secured alliances. But the role of family in people's lives was not exhausted by concrete dependencies like these. Such practices—which included inheriting property, or praying for the ancestral dead—were often as much an expression of the central role family played in people's lives as they were its cause. Children were not just a biological or economic or political necessity; rather, human life was understood as essentially intergenerational, not just on the level of the species but also that of the individual.

Certainly, childlessness is hardly a contemporary phenomenon.[43] But to be childless was often understood to be a misfortune, or a sacrifice—at any rate, a state of exception that usually involved a form of radical compromise or renunciation. That at some point in life one would start a family of one's own was, for the most part, as inevitable as growing older. That one would bring forth life, or at least try to, was just about as certain as death. Like moving out of your parents' house and getting a job today, having children was just what people did, not something one had to weigh against a sea of other options. Like sleep, children were something one had to work around while pursuing other goals. Under those conditions, it made little difference that one might die in childbirth, that one might not be able to provide for one's family, that one's children might suffer, that they might die young. And it certainly made very little difference that one had other hopes, such as traveling or advancing in one's career.

Today, by contrast, for many people, having and raising children is no longer understood as a necessary part of a full human life. Having children is but another possible project, with its own attendant emotional experiences, social obligations, and financial responsibilities. According to a September 2023 Pew Research report, only 26 percent of Americans today say having children is important for living a fulfilling life, whereas 71 percent consider "having a job or career they enjoy" to be essential, and 61 percent say the same for "having close friends."[44] As the demographers Samuel H. Preston and Caroline Sten Hartnett found in an overview of the forces affecting fertility patterns today, "Increasingly, people justified childbearing in terms of its impact on their personal well-being, satisfaction, and happiness."[45] When children are seen in this light, it's understandable that many people, certainly those whose lives feel uncertain and precarious, dread giving up their time, energy, resources, highest ambitions, and—perhaps above all—freedom to the task of raising another human being. When you compare having children—a resource-guzzling enterprise that comes with no guarantee of mental or material satisfaction—to all those other possible attractive ends, how could it ever measure up?

Scratch the surface of the ostensible concern with the financial viability of having children, or their compatibility with career ambitions, or travel plans, or spontaneity, and you will quickly discover a profound revolution in meaning and value: having children is steadily becoming an unintelligible practice of questionable worth. Now when it comes to justifying the necessary risks and sacrifices required to start a family, we find ourselves at a loss. Why should we have kids at all? Is it worth the trouble? We lack the resources to answer such questions. The old frameworks, whatever they were, no longer seem to apply. And the new ones provide us with hardly any answers at all.

This shift in the attitudes toward children is not an isolated phenomenon but a part of a reconfiguration of value that touches on every part of our lives. As the French feminist Élisabeth Badinter observed in her 2010 book *The Conflict,* "In a civilization that puts the self first, motherhood presents a challenge, even a contradiction."[46] When parenthood gets pitted against individual freedom, the choice to have children becomes a matter of personal preference: "The individualism and hedonism that are hallmarks of our culture have become the primary motivations for having children, but also sometimes the reason not to. For a majority of women it remains difficult to reconcile increasingly burdensome maternal responsibilities with personal fulfillment."[47] Of course, as we've discussed above, reconciling parental

responsibilities with personal fulfillment should be equally difficult for men, if only they prioritized their domestic duties as highly
as women do. If and when they do, the impossibility of "having it
all" will weigh as heavily on their shoulders as it does for women.
But the conflict Badinter is pointing to goes deeper than work-life
balance or the impossibility of having it all; it's about what having
it all has come to mean. The dominance of what Badinter calls
"individualistic hedonism" means that, for those under its sway,
all choices are primarily beholden to the same standard: Does it
make me happy? The point is not that every choice is shallow or
self-serving. The point is that the individual assesses possibilities
from the standpoint of how they will affect her, what concrete
benefits they will confer, and what costs they will exact.

It is often assumed that such prioritizing of personal satisfaction is the reserve of the privileged few—the upwardly mo-
bile professionals with the time and resources to invest in their
own happiness. But working-class Americans are displaying
similar concerns about whether having a family is compatible
with personal fulfillment. In her ethnography *Coming Up Short:
Working-Class Adulthood in an Age of Uncertainty*, the sociologist Jennifer M. Silva demonstrates how the goals that previously
supplied working-class Americans with a sense of purpose and
meaning—marrying and starting a family, along with a steady
blue-collar job—have now largely been supplanted by the idioms
of "therapeutic self-expression," "emotional self-management,"
and an intent fixation on "self-sufficiency." In what Silva terms
the "mood economy," young Americans feel a heightened responsibility to control their own emotional well-being; under
this system, happiness gets "privatized," a matter of psychology
rather than character or social standing. As a result, "in today's
increasingly individualized and competitive world," she writes,

"family-centered and career-centered markers of adulthood confront working-class young people as mutually exclusive."[48]

Happiness can mean different things to different people—for some, professional distinction; for others, intellectual, creative, or personal fulfillment. And hedonism is not hegemonic: it is still possible for people to choose their life paths out of a sense of higher purpose, or willingly sacrifice their personal well-being for a greater good. But the expectation of physical and psychological satisfaction—combined with expanding opportunities, particularly for women—trains our gaze on our immediate, present concerns. This, in turn, can push the possibility of children further out of our frame of sight. It is not that people refuse to think about the future; in fact, the future looms large. (Millennials started saving for retirement nine years earlier than their boomer parents.[49]) Rather, people are becoming increasingly reluctant to embrace the possibility that their future will look radically different from their present.

In 2021 we spoke to Isabelle, a thirty-one-year-old therapist from California who described herself as a "very social person" who valued her freedom to "go somewhere with a friend at the drop of a hat, or take a trip with my husband on a whim." She was delaying having kids, she said, anxious that her life would lose its familiar shape: "What's terrifying to me about losing my independence is essentially a fear of the unknown. And this gut feeling that the person I've been up until the point that I have that kid will change or disappear completely." Isabelle worried that children would destabilize her very identity, and therefore hoped to come well into her own, personally and professionally, before settling down. This is why, in an effort to resolve the conflict between competing life goals, people like Isabelle frequently attempt an ordered stacking of their pursuits, with children as the final big step. (Since speaking with us, Isabelle and her husband have welcomed their first child.)

In a common aspirational script, having kids is understood as a "cherry on top" of an already fulfilled life, a bonus. This form of sequencing—holding off on having kids until you've reached major educational and professional benchmarks—is likewise no longer just the prerogative of the well-to-do. "For decades, delaying parenthood was the domain of upper-middle-class Americans, especially in big, coastal cities," the *New York Times* reported in June 2021. "Highly educated women put off having a baby until their careers were on track, often until their early 30s." But, the report continued, the same trend is now visible across all sectors of society: "Over the past decade, as more women of all social classes have prioritized education and career, delaying childbearing has become a broad pattern among American women almost everywhere." One of the women they interviewed, a twenty-seven-year-old married Arizonan, said, "I still don't think I have everything I want to set myself up for success." She was poised to graduate as an aesthetician that summer but wanted to build up a client base before becoming a mom: "I want to have a house and career first."[50]

In this way, even for those who think they might want to have kids, the exhortation to "find" or "fulfill" themselves before deciding how family will fit into their life can encourage indefinite waiting. The thought of starting a family remains suspended, something you're meant to get to eventually, once you've checked off enough of your personal and professional to-dos: a degree, a satisfying and well-paid job, a few key accomplishments, a vital social life, sorting out your issues in therapy. But at the same time, the indeterminacy of the standard of readiness can make it difficult to know when you've reached it, contributing to an ongoing, and often paralyzing, cycle of introspection and self-doubt.

Not to mention that there is one more thing most will feel they have to accomplish before they have kids: enter into a stable relationship. And, unlike the other tasks on the list, it's not one that anybody can complete all on their own.

AMBIVALENCE, ANXIETY, AND calculation may characterize much of contemporary life, but love has not yet lost its luster. Eighty-six percent of respondents to a 2022 CBS News poll—both men and women—said they believe that true love exists. Among those who had not found it yet, 69 percent said it was real, they just hadn't met the right person.[51] But the search for love and the winding path toward family do not necessarily align. In the 2018 *New York Times* survey of American millennials, the second most common reason for not having any children—after not wanting them—was "haven't found [a] partner."[52] The situation in the UK is remarkably similar: in a 2012 survey of 1,821 forty-two-year-old childless Brits, the second most common reason given for not having kids, after not wanting them, was that they had "never met the right person."[53] While the American survey did not provide a breakdown of the responses by gender, the UK survey indicated that its gender distribution was relatively uniform. Among respondents, 23 percent of men and 19 percent of women attributed their childlessness to not having found the right partner. (Though of course childless men at forty-two have a higher chance of still becoming parents than forty-two-year-old women.) What these results indicate is that, at least as far as individuals' subjective assessments are concerned, the struggle to find suitable partners can present itself as a more significant obstacle to parenthood than even more familiar sociological explanations like women's increased participation in higher education and the workforce, the instability of the labor market, or the rising costs of living, childbearing, and child-rearing.[54]

Many of the women we've spoken to who had kids late, or none at all, have raised the same issue: "It was more important to have a solid partner than to have kids, just for the sake of having kids," said Aparna, a project manager for a software company, who, at forty, was engaged to get married and hoping to start trying for kids soon. Mia, a thirty-one-year-old who worked as a right-of-way agent, acknowledged that "a willing and stable partner would make the decision a lot easier" for her, but she hadn't yet found herself in the "position in a relationship to have the conversation, let alone the children themselves." Colleen, a fifty-year-old woman who works in international development, realized she wanted children in her thirties but could never find the right person to have them with: "The guys ended up not being serious . . . they weren't able to demonstrate commitment." "I never felt like I made an active choice not to have kids; it was just the way life worked out," said Hannah, a forty-five-year-old government employee. "For me, having children was tied to the prerequisite of having a partner."

Although both men and women struggle to find partners to start families with, the difficulty of finding a suitable partner is frequently presented as strictly a women's issue, especially in the popular press. In *The Guardian*, for example, the columnist Martha Gill has attributed a "shortage of Mr. Rights" to the gains of "female empowerment." While our mothers and grandmothers might have been forced to settle down with less desirable or worthy men, she suggests, nowadays women have the luxury to be more discriminating. In a similar vein, the Norwegian population economist Vegard Skirbekk has argued that women's lower rates of childbearing are due to women having "become increasingly selective," with the pool of eligible partners shrinking in proportion to the rising standard of suitability.[55] According to Gill, "Women may not in theory want to be single and child-less, but they can afford to be if the right person doesn't come along. That is how increased choice might paradoxically result in women who want children not having them."[56] According to this hypothesis, men and women today are failing to find part-ners with whom to start families because women no longer have to compromise and accept substandard matches. Gill concludes that the predicament calls for policymakers to "better support single mothers," while Skirbekk enumerates the benefits of de-clining birth rates for both individuals and societies and argues that childlessness, whatever its causes, is nothing to be too con-cerned about.

But pinning the difficulty of finding a suitable partner on "choosy" women risks overlooking a phenomenon of equal, if not greater, significance: women today are not just more selec-tive than they once were; rather, the scripts of romance have been radically rewritten in ways that make it harder for poten-tial family partners, men and women alike, to find one another.

Consider the traditional—though, really, nineteenth-century—romantic ideal: keen and swift, true love leaves no room for doubt; once it is declared, lifelong commitment (barring intervention by ill fortune or meddlesome relatives) will surely follow on its heels. "They were gradually acquainted, and when acquainted, rapidly and deeply in love," writes Jane Austen in her final completed novel, *Persuasion*. "It would be difficult to say which had seen the highest perfection in the other, or which had been the happiest; she, in receiving his declarations and proposals, or he in having them accepted."[57]

Many today would recognize the appeal of such a picture, however skeptical they might be about the likelihood of this fantasy coming to life. But, for the most part, the way we actually date could hardly be more different. Today, love takes *time*. When looking for a soulmate, people no longer rely on blind dates or chance encounters. They cast wider nets than ever before and date across great geographical divides. They test the waters for long periods over text before meeting in person. They vet partners for financial stability and shared interests. Every stage of the relationship is drawn out: they wait longer to become "official" or exclusive, to move in with each other, to introduce their partners to their families, to marry and have children. In a 2016 reissue of her book *Anatomy of Love*, Helen Fisher, a biological anthropologist at the Kinsey Institute who has served as an adviser for Match.com for nearly twenty years, gave these new, extended courtship practices a pithy name: "slow love."[58]

If the results of Match.com's *Singles in America* report are any indication, this trend only intensified during the COVID-19 pandemic.[59] Hesitant about meeting in person, people were spending more time texting and video chatting, holding off on physical contact for longer than they did before. Relationship goals have shifted, too: according to the 2022 survey, only 10 percent of singles expressed interest in just dating casually. The new, more "intentional" approach to dating, some experts claimed, is likely to lead to happier, deeper, and more lasting relationships over time.[60]

Two years into the pandemic, Fisher told us cheerily that despite our social isolation, uncertainty, and challenges of making new connections, "Cupid beat COVID by a country mile." It's "a historic change!" she exclaimed, evidence of "post-traumatic growth" in the wake of the pandemic. "You were always an extremely serious generation," Fisher, a wisecracking and proud boomer, told us—"much more serious than mine." According to her, millennials like us were "leading the way in wanting a serious partnership. And I think you're going to take your time to do it."[61]

Her argument has intuitive appeal and echoes the sort of romantic advice often given to young people today: "There's no need to rush," "Enjoy your twenties," "Figure out who you are." Such imperatives have become axiomatic in an age defined by self-realization on the one hand and instability on the other. Today, even hardcore romantics bear no illusions about the permanence of lust, limerence, or wedlock. It is common knowledge that roughly one in two marriages fails, and most young Americans have seen divorce up close, in their own or their friends' immediate families.[62] In a 2015 report on Gen X and millennial attitudes toward marriage, nearly two in five said that "marriage has not worked out for most people I know," and nearly half of all singles who had lived with a partner expressed "pessimism" about the institution.[63] When deciding to marry, few of us truly feel it's unquestionably forever. We say "I do," *for now*. (In this way, Noah Baumbach's choice of title for his 2019 film *Marriage Story*, which chronicles an excruciating, drawn-out divorce, was not all irony.) And what's a better way to insure against heartbreak than to hold off on committing until you're absolutely certain? "For the past 10,000 years," Fisher has observed, "marriage was the beginning of a partnership; today it's the finale."[64]

When it comes to love, however, it's not clear that patience is always a virtue. For all its apparent shrewdness—and however preferable it might be to so-called hookup culture—slow love leaves many on the dating market dissatisfied. The new norms encourage ambivalent daters to play it safe while forcing more serious ones to downgrade their expectations. Today, far from securing better connections, app users will often find themselves engaging in empty chitchat for days, or weeks, only to get unmatched or ghosted. Rebekah, a single thirty-six-year-old psychiatrist from Philadelphia, told us that she dislikes dating online. She hates the drawn-out texting period: "I find that if there is too much of a lead-up, then there's too much of a well-formed idea in their minds of who you are. And then, inevitably, you refute that when you meet them in person." That's assuming that one ever makes it to an in-person date at all. Amanda, a thirty-nine-year-old senior marketing manager from San Francisco, explained: "A few years ago, I would go on so many bad first dates. And it's such a waste of your time and their time." During the pandemic she started vetting her dates over video chat, which had the advantage of being "more efficient." That way she doesn't have to worry about taking Ubers to and from a bar just to meet someone it'll turn out she's not interested in. Better for the bad first encounter to happen from the convenience of one's own home. But when we asked Rebekah about how newly popularized dating formats like video chat might improve her dating experience, she dismissed the idea out of hand: "It would take a lot for me to actually meet someone in person."

For those who make it past the gauntlet of texting and video dates, the pace of the relationship often remains glacial. Slow love is not just a strategy for finding a partner; it permeates every stage of the relationship. Commitment is postponed, and the relationship gets stretched out until it can become thin and brittle. Crystal, a thirty-five-year-old physician from Orange County, California, met her boyfriend online during the pandemic. When we spoke to her in December 2021, she had just completed a round of egg freezing. She told us she would like to try to start a family as soon as possible, and she would prefer not to do this on her own. She had been dating her boyfriend for six months, but when she told him she'd like to have kids within a year, or at most two, he just "kind of laughed." He said he wanted to travel and have a couple years of "just us," though in reality he was spending most of his time at work. They had planned to move in together in December, but he kept delaying their move-in date. Though they barely saw each other, "he doesn't think anything is wrong," she told us. "He thinks our relationship is perfect. And I'm like, 'What are we doing here?'" She was getting fed up and said she intended to end things soon. All the trips and dates in the world couldn't fix the fundamental issue: "Is the relationship the priority, or is it work, and how long is this going to be?" "There's romance," she said, but "there's no intimacy."

ONLY FOOLS RUSH in, or so the saying goes. But slow love can turn out to be a losing strategy. It doesn't just threaten the possibility of finding love, which always involves the sacrifice of opportunities and exposure to chance. It might actually stand at cross purposes with what many people still hope their relationships will eventually enable: serious commitment—particularly of the sort that might one day lead to starting a family together. Ask the average secular, educated person in their late twenties what they're looking for in a potential partner and you're not likely to hear anything related to a willingness or suitability to parent children in the near (or even far) future. Common deal-breakers for ending relationships include being "at different places in life," having trouble "committing," and having different approaches to conflict and emotional expression, but rarely the lack of interest or desire to make a family together. Even when a young person knows they would like to start a family, raising the subject with a potential partner is often difficult. Slow love isn't just about taking one's time: dating in search of a co-parent threatens to interfere with the primary question a young person is supposed to be focused on while looking for a partner—namely, that of personal, romantic compatibility.

From this perspective, love and family should be kept apart. A 2018 study by the sociologists Eliza Brown and Mary Patrick bears this out starkly.[65] Brown and Patrick interviewed fifty-two American women from diverse racial and ethnic backgrounds who had at one point frozen or considered freezing their eggs. To their surprise, Brown and Patrick found that most women were resorting to egg freezing not, say, in the hope of advancing their professional ambitions but in order to "disentangle the trajectory of finding a partner from the trajectory of having children."[66] Despite the popularity of the hypothesis that women are freezing their eggs primarily "because of demanding corporate careers," Brown told us in an interview, "we just did not find that to be the case." To the extent that their careers "propelled" women into egg freezing, it was only "indirectly . . . through the pathway in which it was sort of difficult for them to find a partner because of their career." And as for the nature of those careers, they were hardly all corporate overachievers: "Many of the people who are part of our study," Brown said, "are teachers, social workers, acupuncturists. This is the most expensive thing they've ever purchased in their life. They don't own an apartment. They don't own a car, they did this instead." Contrary to the "media image" of egg freezing, Brown said, "this wasn't an easy purchase for them. They really thought about whether or not this is something they could afford to do."[67]

For the women in the study, the desire for disentanglement was twofold. First, they wanted to preserve the purity of romance: "Women were fearful that rushing to find a partner with whom to have children was rationalizing their search for a romantic partner, making the process calculative and contrived."[68] And, secondly, Brown and Patrick found that "romance" was understood to consist less in passionate desire than in secure attachment:

Narratives of fast, immediately intense romance, or love at
first sight, permeate popular culture. . . . Nevertheless, our
participants idealized a slow build in their romantic lives
that they hoped would lead to stable partnerships; a romantic temporality they hoped egg freezing could help them
access.[69]

In other words, the sociologists discovered that women's fear of
the biological time crunch wasn't just rooted in their refusal to
start a family with a hastily found partner, or their longing for
the intrinsic pleasures of courtship. Rather, women identified a
"slow build" as the necessary condition for long-term stability
in their relationships. In this way, egg freezing has become a key
instrument employed in the service of the slow love program.
Egg freezing dangles the possibility of transcending biological
necessity, allowing women's dating lives to stay on their proper
course—one that aims at a stable romantic bond and is allowed
to go on for however long that takes.

Among the various reproductive technologies and treatments
available today—hormone therapy, intrauterine insemination
(IUI), in vitro fertilization (IVF), and surrogacy—egg freezing
addresses most directly the desire to start a biological family on
one's own terms. The supply of viable eggs, and with it a woman's
ability to naturally conceive and carry a pregnancy to term, begins to decline as early as one's twenties—a steady drop that ac-
celerates after thirty-five and continues until the possibility of
natural pregnancy bottoms out around the age of forty-five.[70]
Egg freezing, a process by which egg production is stimulated
and eggs are collected and frozen for later use, promises freedom from such limitations by offering women, in the words of
Brown and Patrick, the chance to "manipulate time in the life
course."[71]

The women they interviewed often expressed the worry that dating with a view to finding a partner with whom to start a family would put them at risk of "compromising" or lowering their standards for love and personal fulfillment. (In this, they seemed to confirm the claims of demographic analysts like Skirbekk, who attribute declining birth rates to women's increased selectivity in their choice of partners.) Hadiya, a thirty-seven-year-old nurse, told Brown and Patrick that she didn't "want to have a child with [just] anyone. . . . I want to be with the person that I want to be with and out of that have a child, and I think egg freezing will allow me to do that instead of doing it the other way."[72]

Others who shared Hadiya's concern put it in terms of wanting to distinguish themselves from those in their social circles who they thought had settled in order to meet an arbitrary deadline. Chloe, a thirty-three-year-old woman working in product management who was considering freezing her eggs, contrasted her goals with those of her friends, who'd attained only "70 percent compatibility" with their partners. "I want 90, 95 percent compatibility," she told the researchers. Dating with the prospect of a future family in mind would endanger the possibility of attaining what she called this desired "super compatibility":

> My number one priority is to find a play-partner to have a blast with who stretches me, grow, and we can learn, and I'm not willing to give that up to have a family at the right time. So [egg freezing] is my way of putting the family thing over here, so that I can focus on the super compatibility, and not feel like, *Oh, sometimes you have to give things up in life, and people aren't perfect.*[73]

This way of conceiving of interpersonal compatibility in mathematical terms attests to the steady creep of the logic of the dating app algorithms into our private lives. Bridget, a young history PhD student we spoke to, likewise described watching her friends try to calculate the marginal benefit of throwing a "93rd percentile match" back into the pool so that they could wait "just a little bit longer" and find someone "that's even just a little bit better."

But the problem the women in the study described goes even deeper. It isn't only that by resigning yourself to your natural fertility timeline you might run out of time before finding the perfect partner and be forced to settle for less. Wanting to start a family and conveying this to prospective partners is itself perceived as a liability on the dating market. In this way, fertility pressures can make dating *anyone* fraught, no matter how good a fit they might be. Catherine, a thirty-nine-year-old acupuncturist Brown and Patrick interviewed, explained:

> Just the fact that, you know, you didn't have to date people thinking, *Oh God, I have like a year. Are you right for me? Are you right?* It makes you sort of anxious to try to find a partner because you feel like you have to do it fast, which can lead to you making wrong decisions because you have this goal of a baby as opposed to this goal of a partnership, which I think could be dangerous.[74]

One of Brown and Patrick's subjects went so far as to call egg freezing a "desperation avoidance strategy." Wanting—really wanting—to make one's desire for a family known can seem an overwhelming ask in the early stages of courtship, especially in a world that places a high premium on independence and autonomy. "I don't know if I was just putting out a vibe," another woman in the study wondered, "like I need to find someone quick and make it work so we can do the normal, date for a year and then maybe get engaged, okay, and then like a year from then get married and maybe a year from then have kids." Olivia, a forty-one-year-old woman who works for a healthcare company, froze her eggs after separating from her husband. "What I think I accomplish with freezing my eggs," she explained, "is to give myself time to let things organically happen and not run around like a crazy person trying to make something happen. That doesn't make sense."[75]

The desire to let things run their "organic," "normal" course was echoed by Ana, a forty-year-old real-estate broker who froze her eggs at age thirty-seven and complained that her friends had their children "with people who they probably wouldn't have had children with if they had taken the time to form a real relationship with someone and do it traditionally." And for Kayla, a thirty-seven-year-old social worker who was single for most of her adulthood, not even egg freezing succeeded in alleviating the distorting effects of the desire to start a family on her dating life: "There wasn't any space for like, naturally getting to know someone."[76] These comments point to a striking inversion. Getting to know a potential romantic partner while sidelining one's desire to start a family is now perceived as the "natural," "organic," and even "traditional" course of action. By implication, dating with a view to starting a family would be artificial or forced.

To date authentically—naturally, organically, traditionally— one must suppress the desire to have kids. This is a peculiar idea, and not merely because in the past people used to seek out partners, as a general rule, in order to have a family. The risks of a bad partnership are significant, no doubt, and it is no surprise that a technology that allows us to take our time to execute such an important search would be embraced with open arms. But it is strange that the willingness to start a family and suitability as a co-parent (presumably necessary attributes of a life partner with whom one eventually would like to have children) are often absent from the descriptions of what these women are looking for in a potential mate. Francine, a thirty-nine-year-old tech worker, for instance, froze her eggs and then decided to become a single parent. All the while she "actively struggled," as Brown and Patrick describe it, to harmonize what she perceived as the distinct projects of romance and family: "There is one path where I am moving forward with my plans to have a family. There's another path where I am moving forward with dating, which could affect the plans to have a family, but I'm not relying on one to make the other one happen."[77]

Using egg freezing to enable this sort of indefinite postponement can backfire. Despite the rosy promises of the assisted-reproduction industry, egg freezing can be exacting, and it is by no means a sure bet.[78] The hormonal drugs used to stimulate egg production can have substantial physical and emotional side effects; during the treatment cycle, one's evenings are dominated by a strict injection schedule, and one must abstain from having sex due to the potential complications of artificially induced extreme fertility.[79] The data on success rates is scarce, because the technology is still new and, as of today, relatively few women have attempted to unfreeze their eggs. But according to a large-scale study published in *Fertility and Sterility* in 2022, the likelihood of a live birth resulting from frozen eggs was, on average, only 39 percent. The study's authors argue this is due, in large part, to women waiting too long to start fertility preservation (the median age of the women when they froze their eggs was 38.3).[80] Freezing eggs young and banking large numbers of eggs can improve one's chances of having a child, but even then it's a coin toss: the women in the study who froze eggs before turning thirty-eight ended up with a 51 percent live birth rate.

But the problem is even more basic: finding the right partner with whom to start a family is not simply a function of time. Of course, it is possible to stumble upon a willing and suitable co-parent by accident, and having more time increases the likelihood that such an accident will take place. But the trouble is not just that the clock might run out on our best-laid plans for love. We're more intentional and selective than ever before in our choice of partners, but when it comes to commitment and the prospect of family, our approach has become remarkably passive—as if we believe that starting a family is something that's supposed to just *happen*, if only we wait long enough. Small wonder that consciously refusing to direct one's dating efforts toward finding a potential co-parent can result in the failure to find one.

Elizabeth, a forty-year-old writer we interviewed in late 2021, assumed that she would one day have children with her husband, whom she married at thirty. A few years later, her marriage fell apart. Seeing that children were no longer a given, she froze her eggs when she was thirty-six. But the realization had little effect on her choice of partners. Describing her dating life, she said, "I don't know that I necessarily was thinking of it so much through the child lens." Though she did go on dates with men who "clearly would have been very happy to settle down and were perfectly nice," she "just wasn't that into" them. "And the people I was into," she went on, "were, by and large, pretty unsuitable—just kind of messes, kind of assholes." When asked whether she ever ended a relationship on account of a date's lack of seriousness, Elizabeth said she didn't: "I would just let things run their course." After years of online dating, an email correspondence with a fellow writer turned into an unexpected epistolary romance. Within six months she moved across the country to live with him in Montana. They started trying for kids almost immediately. Not wanting to waste time, they tried using the eggs Elizabeth had frozen years before. When all attempts failed, they did three cycles of IUI. None of it worked. When we followed up with Elizabeth two years later, she said that though it took her a long time to come to terms with not having a biological child of her own, she and her partner had decided to pursue egg donation.

Elizabeth's story illustrates the pitfalls of slow love, especially for those who wish to start families. A bad breakup can understandably leave one wary of commitment, no one can summon attraction by force of will, and toxic men can be intoxicating, no matter what dating paradigm you uphold. But slow love encourages romantic procrastination: it derogates any sense of urgency and instead counsels patience and nonchalance. In doing so, it can severely underserve its disciples. It is possible to hit a target without trying, but even with time, what are the odds?

WHILE MANY FIND the desire to have children difficult to embrace and express without reservation, the yearning for adult, romantic love remains constant and strong. "Love," sociologist Eva Illouz writes in her 1997 study *Consuming the Romantic Utopia,* is "one of the most important mythologies of our time."[81] Like religious devotion, love—true love—is supposed to be unconditional, given and received as its own reward, without questioning or qualifications. With so few other means of accessing transcendence and connection in modern life, we have become attached to the idea of love as a redoubt from the market and market-like demands that dictate so many of our other choices. Illouz concludes that love has deep affinities with the experience of "the sacred": it is an exceptional state—a force strong enough to break us out of old habits and release us from the ruthlessness of the external world. Love, however, tends to be defined

narrowly: as the erotic and social bond between romantic partners that is independent of and often takes precedence over
familial love, which by contrast is spiritually stultifying, encum-
bered by dead traditions, and literally mundane. The idea that
passionate love and filial obligation can come apart is not new.[82]
What is unprecedented is the particular notion that while romantic life is the proper precursor to family, conducting one's
dating life with a view to that goal might be, paradoxically, contrived.

In today's popular imagination, romantic love is still understood to be the preferred gateway to family, but now the inchoate desire for children is meant to materialize into intention, as
if alchemically, when *and only when* you find the right person.
Like the bloom on the cheek of youth, the child will arrive as the
concrete proof of the depth and intensity of the romantic relationship. Choosing to have a child will turn out, once again, to be
no choice at all. But now not because having children is understood as a given, as it once was, but by virtue of the overwhelming power of the romantic bond. One's relationship would be so
loving, stable, and nurturing that children would come to seem
not just like a "logical next step" but fate. This is why declaring
that one is dating not merely for the sake of ideal companion-
ship but also with a view to having children would debase the
relationship in its precious early stages—it would instrumental-
ize love itself. From this perspective, childbearing and -rearing
cannot be calculated and summoned at will (let alone rushed);
they are meant to emerge spontaneously, like Venus from the
seafoam. To channel one's dating efforts directly toward this goal
would be self-defeating.

When the romantic unit is prioritized in this way, having a
child, insofar as it is still desired, is seen as a kind of capstone
or reward for having succeeded in the long journey to find ro-

mantic fulfillment. Raising children is conceived as yet one more unique "experience" that the couple will undertake together, sure to strengthen their bond. Family life becomes a way of seeing and experiencing your partner anew. Early parenthood—beginning with the miracle-trauma of birth to the boot camp of sleep training and the endlessly documentable developmental milestones—is idealized as a two-person adventure to be shared with one's true love and, most importantly, best friend.

Perhaps the most dramatic example of this vision is found in the fantasy series Twilight, which was wildly popular among millennials in their teenage years. Although the newly married couple—he a vampire, she a human—have intentionally saved themselves for marriage, it is a complete surprise when Bella gets pregnant after they have sex. They certainly weren't *planning* to start a family! How to face the challenge posed by this new life—Bella will have to become a vampire for the hybrid fetus not to destroy her from the inside—becomes the ultimate test of their otherworldly love.[83]

Another kind of magical transformation preoccupies the popular imagination, whereby babies again emerge without planning or effort, but this time not as the result of the perfect romantic union—but rather, by accident. Although it's uncommon for women to explicitly express the desire to accidentally conceive a child, unplanned pregnancies form the narrative backbone of two of the most popular shows millennials watched growing up (albeit at different periods in their lives). First in *Friends* and then in *Girls*—both generation-defining series in their own way—the character arc of one of their central protagonists, Rachel and Hannah, respectively, ends in an unexpected pregnancy. Both shows are dedicated to the self-exploration of their main characters—more or less independent New York City creatives whose daily dramas are consumed with their own lives and their immediate social group. For the majority of their story arcs, the characters are hardly preoccupied with the prospect of starting a family, and both shows end not long after one of their female protagonists gets pregnant by accident. The stories they tell are thus ones of stunted growth, rocky friendships, and romantic travails, which reach their conclusion only when the characters have a baby they did not plan to have. At last, they are forced to grow up. The unexpected baby serves as the deus ex machina that can conclude the meandering plot of becoming a "real adult." But equally significant is the fact that the audience's interest is presumed to dissipate once they do. *Friends* lagged on for two more seasons after the baby arrived; Hannah gave birth in the last episode of the final season of *Girls*. After she learns to nurse her child, the action ends and the screen fades to black. Parenthood remains metonymic with adulthood, but cannot be aimed at directly. If one is fortunate, it just happens.

The conceit of languorous self-realization and aimless romantic entanglement resolving itself in parenthood also serves as the basic template for Sally Rooney's much-hyped and best-selling 2021 novel *Beautiful World, Where Are You*. The novel charts the circuitous relationship developments of four Irish millennials and owes its critical acclaim in large part to Rooney's ability to reflect back to readers how they experience their own love lives: listless and without direction, wistful but also poisoned with irony and detachment. In Rooney's world, romance is an aimless slog because everything is an aimless slog: work, socializing, making art. There are no grand gestures or feelings, just undefinable attraction, overthinking, and doubt. The novel ends when one of the two central characters, Eileen, moves in with her boyfriend and gets pregnant. This comes as somewhat of a shock to her, and she must deliberate about how to proceed. Though she and her love interest, Simon, have known each other since adolescence and have been in an on-again, off-again relationship that they have been reluctant to pin down for over a decade, Eileen worries they have not waited long enough: she writes to her best friend that they "have only been together for eighteen months (!)." She decides to go through with it anyway, ending her final letter, and the book, by sharing how amused she is to imagine herself, now in her early thirties, for the first time ever, as "a mother, a married woman, owning a little terraced house somewhere in the Liberties."[84] A textbook practitioner of slow love, Eileen is forced to grow up, and the book ends.

In the real world, things rarely turn out quite like this. Long cohabitation practices, the stresses of modern life, and the mismatch between women's biological clocks and men's emotional timelines all conspire to frustrate the hopes of enacting the ideal of independent soul-seeking and patient testing of the romantic waters, capped off by more or less spontaneous pregnancy. Women who want kids often come to realize this at some point in their early thirties—sometimes only as a hurried afterthought. If they are lucky, their partners (if they have any) will fall in line. If they are not, they will have to face the choice of returning to the dating pool, freezing their eggs (if they haven't done so already), single parenting, or giving up their dreams of having kids of their own.[85] No matter the outcome, the trials of slow love can make starting a family—already a fraught prospect—feel even more doubtful and uncertain. The one marker of "seriousness" that Match.com's singles score lower on than ever before is the desire for kids.[86]

IF, AS THE story goes, romance and women's happiness have been sacrificed on the altar of family for too long, now the dynamic is being reversed. When we spoke to her in 2021, Abby, a forty-two-year-old music teacher living in Brooklyn, told us she had been torn for years between her desire to be a mother and her love for a man who decidedly did not want children. She and her partner had finally moved in together in the middle of the pandemic after five years of dating. At the same time, she was preparing to start IVF, a process in which he was not involved. After years of trying and failing to move on—from the dream of parenthood as much as from her partner—she felt no less conflicted than before. "What's so heartbreaking for me," she told us, "is, like, this is the person I want to have kids with, and I've been looking for him my whole life, and he's just anti-kids."

Abby is an ebullient, self-declared "oversharer," who grew up on the Upper West Side in an upper-middle-class Jewish household. She always wanted to be a mother, she told us, and hoped to re-create the experience of her "perfect" childhood. Her family life was far removed from what she referred to as the "cookie-cutter" standard American upbringing. Her parents, two quirky New Yorkers, delighted in her precocity and encouraged the expression of her whimsical imagination. "It feels like I'd be missing out on the biggest ride or adventure if I don't do this," she said. But her desire has been frustrated by her circumstances: "Everything in my life is cosmically pointing toward not having kids."

A lifelong romantic and "maximalist," Abby had spent years in search of a person with whom to realize "the perfect vision" of a partnership, which she hoped would eventually yield children. But her desire for children never came to inform the romantic ideal she held before her. The model partner, she said, was "really similar to the guy I'm with now—you know, funny, like, keeps me laughing, keeps me interested." A relationship with such a man, Abby imagined, would improve the experience of having children, and parenthood would develop and deepen their connection to each other:

I always envisioned my love for my partner growing through having a connected human between us. I just think that's so magical, that you can make another person with a person, and then you really do become, you know, through the love like modus tollens or the distributive property, or whatever it is—like, a equals b equals c. You're just, you know, all connected in this web, and just looking at how they parent is just another lens on your partner.

She longed for "an easy relationship with a great person, who was going to be so value-added to the experience of having kids, and then we can really share and fall even deeper in love by doing this amazing project together, of raising a child." The trouble was that her current partner, while being so close to her idea of "perfect," had no desire for children himself and was not open to persuasion.

Abby's boyfriend was explicit with her from the beginning that he had no interest in becoming a father, that he would prefer to maintain the freedom to travel and was disinclined to sacrifice his financial stability and spontaneity to have children. Before Abby met him he had even gone through a breakup over the same issue. "I think he's more of a 'Why would you have kids?' kind of person" than genuinely ambivalent, she told us. Shortly after they met, on Abby's thirty-sixth birthday, the two discussed this mismatch in their desire to have children and how to deal with it. When recalling this conversation, Abby struggled to describe what happened next: "We just couldn't or, let me not say couldn't—we just didn't really do the thing we needed to do in order to stop seeing each other. And, you know, in order to grow apart." After years of couples therapy, countless conversations, and an extended break during which Abby attempted three rounds of IUI, they were still at an impasse as of our last full interview in February 2021.

Abby had difficulty envisioning how they could move forward. She described her partner as "the hardest no ever": "He's just anti-kids. And you know, he likes kids, but I don't think— he's not great with kids. He doesn't really know what to do with them." And yet, she would not give up the hope that he would one day change his mind. She felt he would, most likely, "love his own kid" and would make a great dad, though she also readily admitted that any time she expresses this hope to him it "makes him mad."

Abby's situation is unique, but the basic mismatch in desires between her and her partner is not. Sooner or later, many couples find themselves having to negotiate the differences in their conceptions of a fulfilling life. How important is education and intellectual stimulation to one's happiness? How much time should one devote to work, and how central is it to one's sense of self? What role should religion occupy in one's life, if any? How necessary are physical attraction and sex to satisfaction in a relationship? People often end up with partners who disagree with them on such questions, and it is not surprising that at a time of growing ambivalence about having children, more and more people find themselves diverging from their partners on the question of whether or not they want any. What is remarkable about Abby's situation is that the way she and her partner diverge on the question "What role should family play in our lives?" did not really affect her estimation of their compatibility. Their disagreement about having children weighed heavily on her and was causing them both great unhappiness, but in her telling, this conflict did not make her partner any less of a match for her. It was an obstacle they faced, but it did not really detract from the quality of their bond. Although she was going forward with fertility treatments that, if successful, would end the possibility of their life together, Abby expressed confidence in their relationship: "Of course we have our 'things,' but they're easily worked on—like, everybody's rowing the boat."

When we checked back with Abby two and a half years later, in September 2023, she was planning to go to Europe to start a cycle of IVF using a donated embryo. "My partner and I are still together," she told us. "But this is very difficult to navigate together." Before signing off, she added, "I think we're doing a pretty amazing job."

A careless observer might be tempted to dismiss Abby's narrative as a case of tragic self-deception. But her story touches on a widely shared experience. Her conundrum is just an extreme manifestation of the widespread separation and compartmentalization of romance and family. Just like the participants in Brown and Patrick's egg-freezing study, Abby was struggling to disentangle the romantic and family trajectories. And she was never entirely unaware of how her quixotic efforts could end up. She told us that in her dark moments she has a "sort of a conspiracy theory" about herself: "The conspiracy is that I don't actually want kids. I just want to think I want kids."

THE IDEAL OF "slow love" that underlies contemporary dating practices seems, at first blush, to be at a far remove from the calculative demands that dominate so many other areas of our lives, chief among them the financial and professional anxieties with which we opened this chapter. Dating in search of love is supposed to offer reprieve from the daily grind, while the years of vetting and practice are meant to secure the kind of stable, lifelong connection that would serve as a refuge from the threat of economic, political, and ecological precarity. But our romantic lives are hardly insulated from the oppressive dynamics of the market. After all, as we have seen, the standards of "romantic fit" are often themselves suffused with the logic of maximization (recall the egg-freezing study participant's appeal to "super compatibility"). And while being on the same page as one's partner about having kids is no longer seen as a prerequisite for a committed relationship, in the 2022 *Singles in America* survey, 96 percent reported feeling that "having similar attitudes about debt and spending is an important partner trait."[87] Once in relationships, millennials are keen to protect their personal interests—a change reflected in their embrace of prenuptial agreements, the unprecedentedly high rates at which they maintain separate bank accounts, and even in the way they negotiate domestic affairs and disputes.[88]

In a vivid example of the encroachment of the norms of corporate efficiency into couples' private lives, many now turn to professional management tools—Excel spreadsheets, project management apps, shared calendars, and HR-derived communication protocols—to divide up their chores as well as manage their relationship's emotional challenges.[89] The modern stressors of intensive parenting are familiar to the point of cliché. Overworked parents operate nonstop to orchestrate multiple schedules, coordinating meal prep, school drop-offs, doctors' appointments, gymnastics, sports practice, music lessons, teacher-parent conferences, date nights, self-care. These challenges are exacerbated by stubborn gender disparities in domestic and familial duties, wherein women still end up doing the lion's share of the work. Everything has to fit in, or else be triaged. All the while the "work-from-home revolution," far from easing the parental time crunch, has meant that many white-collar workers are expected to be responsive at all times.

Perennially logged on, parents search for systems to tame the chaos at home and end up replicating the models and practices of the modern office. Having a family and kids is "the same thing" as "running your business," CEO and mom-to-be Meghan Asha told the *New York Times* in 2020. "What's our mission as a family? How do we organize ourselves? How do we create trust, transparency and communication when the going gets tough?" Asha and her husband have created a system they call "My Relationship Is a Start Up," with organized task lists and prescheduled sessions for discussing emotionally demanding topics such as how to deal with their parents or when to have children.[90]

More than a twenty-first-century update to the old family chore wheel, the turn toward domestic project management points to a fundamental change in contemporary conceptions of family. No doubt, as sociologist Allison Daminger told the *Times*, "more formal systems" can help overcome domestic disparities in the division of labor.[91] But implicit in the assumption that having a family and kids is the same as running your business—that they function according to the same dynamics and can benefit from similar management strategies—is the blurring of any real distinction between home life and the corporate world. If for a previous generation of working women the goal was to achieve "work-life balance"—where that balance meant not just being able to do both well but entailed that they constitute different, heterogeneous spheres of value—now, as professional standards and practices remake intimate relations in their image, the distinction between the spheres is gradually being erased.

Private life today looks more and more like work—and not just because we are very busy, or because of hybrid office arrangements, or because we digitally manage our itineraries and track our performance with "life-hacking" tools. Nothing wholly escapes the reach of the productivity mindset; even our desire for recognition, support, and intimacy morphs into just so many items in a flowchart. This is most nakedly apparent in the insinuation of HR language into interpersonal communication: excusing unavailability as a "lack of bandwidth," protecting one's "mental capacity," making demands for "consent" for the performance of "emotional labor."[92] A copy of one of Asha's to-do lists ("the Weekly Sprint") showed the couple had scheduled to "talk through our fight"—broken down by key questions to be addressed. One wonders when they found the time to argue in the first place.

THE SO-CALLED EXTERNAL concerns we've addressed in this chapter—concerns about money, career, and our love lives—no longer seem so unrelated, or even all that distinct. It is no coincidence that the integration of family into both one's professional and romantic trajectories so often unfolds as a kind of rigid sequencing. From both perspectives we take for granted that having children is only possible when we have achieved some indeterminate standard of sufficient readiness: well before one can even contemplate introducing children into the equation, professional stability and success, on the one hand, and a stable romantic partnership, on the other, must be secured.

The case for doing things this way appears unassailable. In an essay reflecting on what is keeping people from having children young nowadays, journalist Elizabeth Bruenig described the dilemma that many find themselves in: How can you think of "making somebody else" before establishing yourself, before knowing who you really are? "The standard-issue airline safety warning comes to mind," she wrote: "*In the event of an air pressure change inside the cabin, secure your oxygen mask in place before you attempt to assist other passengers you may be traveling with.* They don't say *or you'll both be screwed.* But you know that's what they mean."[93] From this perspective, pursuing family while your own identity is still in flux can seem downright irresponsible. Surely a professionally secure parent is better than an anxious one (for both the parent and child), and no one wants to subject kids to growing up in the shadow of a loveless and unstable marriage. But what might seem in theory to be a mature and thoughtful approach to life could itself be a symptom of anxiety or a mere coping mechanism: an overwhelming commitment to maintaining agency over one's own life, a reluctance to foreclose one's options, a need to stay in control and never end up the victim of circumstance.

Dating and finances are stressful, and at a time when so much in the world feels perilous and uncertain, proceeding with caution is sensible. The logic of patient sequencing, at work and in love, is so compelling, its norms so pervasive, that it can sometimes seem like there is no viable alternative. Throwing caution to the wind and running off with the next stranger you meet on Hinge sounds hardly more promising. But the opposite of caution is not necessarily naïveté or blindness. We should remain open to questioning the prudence of delay. Professionally, the more established you are in your career, the more of a hit it might take when you finally decide to have kids; romantically, slow love might push the question of family off until it's no longer an option. One thing seems right no matter what your actual goals are or come to be: it is good to start asking the important questions early—early enough to ensure that the future is not decided for you. That's what it really means to be in control.

No one can tell you whether having children is the right decision for you, and if it is, when to have them. But when it comes to children, asking those important questions is not the same as searching for some secret inner desire while abstracting from everything else you care about. The "externals" must be contended with. It might be liberating for a moment to bracket your financial concerns and professional insecurities, but that won't dislodge the fear of losing your independence or dull the force of your ambition. Insulating your deliberations about having kids from your romantic entanglements might offer a semblance of self-sufficiency, but if you don't attempt a synthesis, in the end you could lose out on both.

The idea of "finding yourself" and discovering "what you really want" presupposes the presence of some stable fact waiting to be discovered by conscious effort, like an item in a scavenger hunt. But there is rarely such a static truth to be found. If having your life all figured out is the bar for being "ready" to have kids, no one will ever reach it. It is the choices you make—what to study, where to work, whom to love, and how—that will form you and shape your life, setting and delimiting the horizons of possibility, one day at a time. Raising the question of children, as personal as it inevitably is, requires more than soul searching. It takes a certain kind of courage, an open-minded willingness to probe into the meaning and value of having children, with the sober recognition that there is no past conception we can easily recover or resuscitate.

There are many places to start such a journey. For us, it had to begin with the feminist tradition. Examining the feminist record is not just a matter of paying dutiful homage to our intellectual foremothers; it is an intellectual necessity. It was feminists, after all, who first systematically explored the value of parenthood to a human life by questioning the value of reproduction to a woman's life. Their attempts to think through the ethical, political, and personal significance of the decision to become a parent remain unsurpassed. And the theoretical contradictions that they sought to resolve continue to animate our very real ambivalence today.

CHAPTER 2

# The Dialectic of Motherhood

When Adrienne Rich asserted in 1976 in *Of Woman Born* that women are as valuable as men and that their worth does not depend on whether or not they become mothers, her claim was hardly self-evident. Whether or not they had children, women were "seen primarily as mothers." At the same time, "all mothers," she wrote in the *New York Times*, "are expected to experience motherhood unambivalently and in accordance with patriarchal values; and the 'non-mothering woman' is seen as deviant."[1] The trouble, the feminist writer Nancy Friday wrote a year later, was not only that women were thought of as mothers from the outside, but that they often understood themselves in just the same way. Reflecting on the specter of "the mother" in women's lives, Friday wrote:

> We try for autonomy, try for sexuality, but the unconscious, deepest feelings we have picked up from her will not rest: we will only feel at peace, sure of ourselves, when we have fulfilled the glorified "instinct" we have been trained, through the image of her life, to repeat: you are not a full woman until you are a mother.[2]

In the mid-seventies, pronatalist, pro-motherhood norms seemed so deeply internalized that some feminists doubted women would ever willingly give up the prospect of having children. Motherhood was so central to modern female conceptions of self, Nancy Felipe Russo wrote in 1976, that "even if the perfect contraceptive were developed and used . . . social and cultural forces that enforce the motherhood mandate would continue."[3]

One often hears that the situation has not changed much. In many quarters it is taken for granted that women experience significant social pressure to become mothers and suffer censure when they hesitate or refuse to do so.[4] "We, unfortunately, live in a pronatalist world," motherhood-ambivalence coach Ann David-man wrote in an article for *Vox*, "where the unspoken message is that everyone should want children and should have them, the end."[5] These pressures, she has written elsewhere, are directed with special force at women: Our pronatalist society is one "that through numerous spoken and unspoken signals, continues to assume that women will 'naturally' want to become mothers." As a result, "those women who do not want to pursue motherhood feel inadequate, as if something is wrong with them. And if they're not sure what they want, they often feel more broken."[6] The sociologist Amy Blackstone, author of *Childfree by Choice* (2019), has observed similarly: "Girls are taught from a very early age that motherhood is their destiny, and that it is the singular most important and fulfilling role they will have. One need only take a stroll down the 'girls' aisle of any children's toy store to see this."[7] In an essay about his experience as a childless man, the cartoonist Tim Kreider took note of the differential treatment childless men and women receive: "Men who don't want kids get a dismissive eye roll, but the reaction to women who don't want them is more like: *What's wrong with you?*" "Women who don't want to have children," he explained, "are regarded as unnatural, traitors to their sex, if not the species."[8] This assessment is frequently echoed by popular women's media. "If ever there was proof that gender inequality is still alive and well," announced Ella Alexander in a 2019 piece for *Harper's Bazaar*, "it's the pressure on women in their 30s to have children." Progress is imperceptible: "*Bridget Jones*, a story about the struggles of a single journalist, came out 20 years ago—and yet still the attitudes towards childless women beyond the age of 30 remain largely unchanged."[9]

The actual situation on the ground, however, is more complicated. When we asked women about the external pressures they have experienced with respect to having children, their responses rarely conformed to this totalizing narrative. Across our surveys and interviews, it became evident that for many educated, working women—the kind of women who might have ended up in a course like Davidman's or picked up a copy of *Harper's Bazaar*—motherhood is no longer the ineluctable mandate it once was.

Among the women we spoke to, a little over half said that they felt little to no external pressure to have children. Among the rest, one form the pressure took was social: "Society assumed I wanted kids," said Aria, a fifty-one-year-old government worker, "no pressure from family." More concretely, women reported having to put up with casual, unsolicited inquiries and remarks. Vicky, a thirty-six-year-old organizational strategist, said she felt "no external social pressure from women (or men) within my immediate social circle" but that she and her husband would hear "passing questions, comments and judgments" from male coworkers who "simply assume in passing that 'kids must be next!'" Deirdre, a thirty-seven-year-old digital marketer who took Davidman's class, put it in terms of an "expectation that this is what everyone does" and "strangers who ask, 'when are you having kids?'" A few others mentioned the pressures implicit in being told that time would eventually run out or that they would make good parents.

Frequently, though, when responding to our question about external pressure, women spoke not of social expectations but of their partner's wishes or, more often still, the pestering of parents or in-laws who vocalized a desire for grandchildren. Correspondingly, when elaborating on the absence of pressure, both women and men would sometimes mention that their own parents, and especially their own mothers, were okay with them not having kids. (We also learned that it was more likely for parents not to ask for grandchildren if they had already procured some by means of their other children.) Often, when answering the question about "external pressure," our respondents pointed to what would perhaps more intuitively be considered internal pressures and anxieties: their own private wish to give their parents grandkids, the fear of missing out (exacerbated by watching friends' children grow up on social media), or worries about their ticking "biological clocks."

Rarely did the women we spoke to report receiving the message that they would be "less" as women, let alone as human beings, were they not to have children. One of the few who did, Priya, was a twenty-seven-year-old daughter of Bengali immigrants who trained as a classical musician before attending Yale and then getting a job in tech. In her culture, she said, "there is pressure to have kids," but, she added, "it's frowned upon to actually *talk* about the decision to have kids, as it's not seen as a 'decision'; rather it's the 'fate' of one's daughters to produce children." At the same time, the experience of several other women who grew up in conservative or religious communities where having kids young was still par for the course was markedly different. "My parents were adamant that I could be anything I wanted to be (within some Christian religious confines)," said Erin, a thirty-year-old who was raised Christian and knew from a young age that she never wanted children. "I played sports and overall did masculine things, and they didn't steer me away from that." After marrying her wife, she received some hectoring from family, but, Erin said, it was "honestly only verbal questions, and the follow-up, 'Really? You're sure?' And when the answers are direct and unwavering, people tend to get the hint." Haniya, a twenty-six-year-old studying to be an occupational therapist who grew up in a Pakistani Muslim family, reported that she felt "no overt pressure. Implicit expectation from cultural and religious sources. Post-marriage, some slight pressure (i.e., comments) from my mother-in-law that she would like grandchildren, but not at all excessive."

But many women simply denied feeling overt pressure outright. Meera, twenty-eight, who was born in India and now works for a magazine in New York, said, "No one has ever even tried to sell me on the idea, and if I were to ask my parents/husband they would say it's my choice entirely, and they would mean it." Some women even reported experiencing the opposite kind of pressure. "I was very much pressured to succeed in school and prepare for a future career, not an MRS degree," said Michelle, a thirty-seven-year-old diplomat who does not wish to have kids. In academia, media, and the arts, in particular— all fields that historically have been crucibles for progressive thought and activism as well as conduits of ideas from the avant-garde to the mainstream—women described receiving messages from their friends and colleagues cautioning them against having kids. "I experienced active pressure from my family not to have children!" said Leah, a thirty-five-year-old academic who was raised by lesbian parents:

My parents were very focused on achievement, and my biological mother especially really worked to give me the idea that it would be a failure on my part to place family over career. When I was ten or eleven she'd often remind me that if I ever got pregnant as a teenager, the only option would be abortion, because having a baby would prevent me from going to college and grad school. Apart from that, I don't think I ever received other pressure one way or another from anyone about having children.

Similarly, Sasha, a thirty-four-year-old artist, grad student, and mother of one, told us, "I feel there was some judgment from people in the arts, as a previous generation of women artists has chosen not to have kids in order to focus on their art." Gabrielle, a twenty-eight-year-old writer who grew up in an interracial family, said, "I think my parents and in-laws would like to be grandparents but they're pretty cool about not pressuring us. I feel no pressure from peers/friends—if anything I feel pressure *not* to have kids yet." A Catholic philosophy professor and mother of six replied bluntly, "I'm an academic, so if anything, there's the pressure not to have kids, and that pressure is extreme."

Recent polls and research into attitudes toward parenthood likewise attest to the weakening of the motherhood mandate. In a 2022 YouGov poll of 15,975 American adults, only four out of ten women and three out of ten men said that women in the United States today come under pressure from society to have children.[10] Analyzing changing attitudes toward childbearing in the twentieth century, the sociologists Arland Thornton and Linda Young-DeMarco have argued that the insistence on the importance of parenthood declined dramatically between the 1960s and the 1980s. While 85 percent of American mothers in 1962 said that "all married couples who can ought to have children," by 1980 the figure was only about 40 percent. Writing in 2001, they concluded that "the 'oughtness' that used to be associated with parenthood has been removed for a substantial fraction of people in the United States today." Marrying and having children are "now much more voluntary and less obligatory than they were in previous decades."[11]

At this point, two qualifications are in order. First, recognizing that social norms about the legitimacy of childlessness are shifting should not be mistaken for minimizing the effects of rearguard campaigns to roll back women's reproductive rights. Both things are happening at one and the same time. In the United States, reproductive rights have been under some form of attack ever since they were secured in 1973 with *Roe v. Wade.*[12] The ongoing assault on women's reproductive freedoms culminated in the Supreme Court's *Dobbs v. Jackson Women's Health Organization* ruling in 2022, a decision that set off a wave of new conservative laws aimed at restricting or eliminating access to contraceptives and safe abortion. As of this writing, fifteen states have made abortion illegal, and two more states have issued bans on abortions after six weeks of pregnancy.[13] In many parts of the United States today, women who want to prevent or terminate a pregnancy are finding it hard, or impossible, to do so, as they are forced to navigate a byzantine, overbooked system in order to schedule the appointments and travel long distances to receive care, at great personal cost.[14] This new legal landscape means that access to abortion is becoming stratified: those with the resources to travel, take time off work, and/or secure childcare will likely be able to get an abortion; those less fortunate will not. The effects are already being felt. According to the Society of Family Planning, in the nine months after *Dobbs,* an estimated 65,920 fewer women were able to obtain abortions in the states where bans were in place.[15]

The second, more complicated, point concerns the question of the extent to which the social and legal campaigns against reproductive freedoms contribute to pressures on women to become mothers, not only in cases of unplanned pregnancy but as a matter of deliberate choice. On the one hand, it is clear that the American conservative movement combines the traditional "New Right" pro-family agenda with grassroots "pro-life" anti-abortion activism and legislation. Accordingly, in many of the conservative religious communities in which abortion is now under threat or wholly denied, traditional family structures are still embraced and promoted, and these produce external pressures to start a family as a condition of mature womanhood or adulthood. But these two elements of contemporary right-wing politics do not necessarily constitute a single unified ideological system and have historically sometimes come into conflict with each other. Conceptually, contemporary antiabortion arguments, especially among evangelical (as opposed to Catholic) adherents, are for the most part based in claims about the moral status of embryos and fetuses, not in the spiritual, ethical, or existential benefits that motherhood may confer upon women.[16] And, practically speaking, from the standpoint of many antiabortion activists, it is not even essential that a woman chooses to assume parental responsibilities for the fetus she carries; adoption and no-questions-asked drop-off boxes are touted as viable options for dealing with unwanted pregnancies.[17]

But as necessary as it is to acknowledge the curtailing of reproductive rights and the persistence of exclusionary pro-motherhood sentiments among conservatives, we must be able to do so while also recognizing that natalist pressures on women in progressive and liberal secular society are lifting. Once we do, we are confronted with a question: How are we to reconcile the popular assessments of our society as a pronatalist monolith in which women find themselves under unrelenting pressure to have children with the contravening evidence—the sociological findings as well as women's own far more qualified testimonies? The onslaught of regressive antiabortion policies, which will result in birth and motherhood being in effect forced upon unwilling women, certainly goes a long way toward explaining the discrepancy. (It is worth mentioning that in the YouGov poll, Democrats were far more likely to attest to the pressure on women to have children than either Republicans or independents.) But paying attention to the contemporary social, political, and legal state of affairs reveals only part of the story.

To better understand these contrasting assessments of the motherhood mandate it will be necessary to trace the evolution in attitudes toward motherhood, both theoretical and practical, that preceded them. For underlying this controversy is a long-standing contest of perspectives that transcends our current political moment: Is motherhood a profound calling, or is it so far from being a necessary part of a fulfilled and fulfilling life that it is actually incompatible with it? The history of the feminist movement in the twentieth century bears witness to the depth and intractability of this question, as well as the conflicting assumptions about the meaning and significance of motherhood at work. This is why to clarify our own situation we will first have to tell the story of the women who have attempted to answer this question before us.

MOTHERHOOD HAS ALWAYS been at the very heart of attempts to examine and address the condition of women. Going back to Medea's lament that she'd "rather stand three times with a shield in battle than give birth once," motherhood has been deemed a site of struggle, intimately connected to women's hopes and fears, highest aspirations, and thwarted dreams.[18] The fact of "motherhood" and the fundamental difference that it introduces to human existence—that only some but not other human beings are naturally endowed with the ability to support the development of an embryo in pregnancy, to give birth, and to nourish children with their bodies—has historically been understood to underlie many, probably most, of the disparities that characterize the lives of women and men. In almost every historical configuration known to us, motherhood has been recognized at one and the same time as a hallowed duty and a stamp of inadequacy, and has placed disproportionate and often devastating burdens on women. Confined to the role of caretakers and homemakers, women were treated as intellectual, moral, social, and political inferiors.

By the middle of the twentieth century, the wish to overcome this predicament has given rise to two seemingly contradictory theoretical and practical impulses: women were to be delivered from motherhood and its trappings, or motherhood would have to be reconceived so it could be once more embraced as a noble calling, but this time on women's own terms. The stakes of this project were first articulated by the French philosopher Simone de Beauvoir. The publication in 1949 of Beauvoir's opus, *The Second Sex,* was a landmark event in the development of feminist thought. It was the first serious philosophical investigation dedicated in its entirety to women—not just "the idea of womanhood" but their actual lives, from the earliest awakening of their consciousness to old age and death. Beauvoir started by noting that, aside from the coincidence of a few brute biological facts, what it was "to be a woman" was essentially unclear. A woman was defined by what she was not—a man—remaining hazy even to herself. Beyond that, to be a woman meant taking on qualities imposed on her by others, according to their wants and preferences, never her own. It followed that while men could be many things—they were able to pursue original projects, shape the arc of their own existence, create great art, and leave lasting legacies—women rarely displayed such self-determination. Why, Beauvoir demanded to understand, have women never been able to achieve genuine human freedom?[19]

For Beauvoir, to be truly free meant achieving "transcendence"—that is, rising above the biological, familial, social, and political conditions into which you were born and paving a path for yourself of your own accord. Free human beings are not simply defined by their past or present circumstances but are capable of determining themselves and their lives with a view to an open-ended future and its untold possibilities. This is hard for any human being to achieve, but for a woman especially so. The reason? Motherhood: the fact that women are the involuntary seats of biological and social reproduction. "From puberty to menopause she is the principal site of a story that takes place in her and does not concern her personally."[20] The capacity to mother is women's greatest obstacle to attaining an authentic form of life.

The binds of motherhood are not, however, just imposed on women from the outside. Denied access to men's traditional forms of transcendence, Beauvoir argued, women came to attach themselves to motherhood as its simulacrum. In this way, motherhood becomes a siren song: it diverts women from loftier callings with the promise that being a mother is the highest form of activity available to them. Once enthralled, women are imprisoned in their own bodies and confined to the home. Pregnancy is "an enrichment and a mutilation": the fetus gestating inside a woman is both "part of her body" and "a parasite exploiting her."[21] So destabilizing is maternity to a woman that her body often rebels against it with morning sickness, which Beauvoir interprets fantastically as a form of existential nausea caused by the subjection to such violent forces outside her control.[22]

Within the strictures of her limiting circumstances, Beauvoir wrote, motherhood is the closest a woman may come to achieving transcendence. For the expectant mother, the child "encapsulates the whole future and, in carrying it, she feels as vast as the world; but this very richness annihilates her, she has the impression of not being anything else."[23] This form of transcendence will always be partial and distorted, for childbearing is not something a woman does *for herself.* A woman's aspirations and efforts are circumscribed in the service of others; she finds meaning primarily by living vicariously through those in her care—her sense of purpose emerges only in the negative image of *their* happiness and success, not her own. She is relegated to a submissive, contingent existence: "Even in cases where the child is a treasure within a happy or at least balanced life," Beauvoir writes, "he cannot be the full extent of his mother's horizons."[24]

A few years later, a version of the same line of thought could be found in Betty Friedan's 1963 cultural sensation, *The Feminine Mystique.* Though far more concrete and pragmatic in its ambitions and style than its French counterpart, the American bestseller described a similar postwar malaise: the boredom and unhappiness of housewives confined to the home, the yearning and unfulfilled desires of women who dreamed of an active life and career defined by more than the narrow band of "feminine" activities. In articulating the "problem that has no name," Friedan's book was enthusiastically embraced by millions of women across America who were relieved to see their dissatisfactions recorded and legitimized.[25]

Beauvoir's main ambition, shared by Friedan, was to point the way for women out of the constraints imposed on them by "physiological destiny" and their social circumstances and encourage them to seize on newfound opportunities for women outside the home.[26] She was at great pains to express the human deprivations that resulted from deceiving and forcing women to see motherhood as their deepest calling, the source of their personal value, and so the altar upon which all other opportunities were to be surrendered. At the same time, Beauvoir grasped the pull of motherhood—the joys and seductive mysteries of pregnancy, birth, and child-raising. "There is," she wrote, "a wondrous curiosity in every young mother. It is a strange miracle to see, to hold a living being formed in and coming out of one's self." Even though mothering under the current conditions was necessarily oppressive, she acknowledged that "if the circumstances are not positively unfavorable, the mother will find herself enriched by a child." And in the face of all critique, caring for children remained for her an "undertaking one can validly aspire to," though it must be "desired for itself, not for hypothetical benefits." The shaping of the character and intellect of a human being, she wrote, was "the most delicate and the most serious of all undertakings."[27]

For all that, Beauvoir remained mostly tight-lipped about the role that motherhood *ought* to play in women's lives. While she never went so far as to recommend against motherhood, she also never quite found room for it in the vision of the kind of complete human life that she would have wished upon the women who would follow her.

This subtle ambiguity—a sober examination and unsentimental repudiation of motherhood, on the one hand, and a recognition of the tremendous responsibility vested in those who assume the task of creating and nurturing new human life, on the other—is a tension that underlies *The Second Sex*. And in turn, the split attitude embedded in Beauvoir's work came to constitute the central axis of disagreement in the many feminist debates that ensued about the status of motherhood. Was motherhood to be transcended in the name of progress? Or was a more thorough revolution of values needed, one that would be centered on the reevaluation of the meaning of motherhood and a recognition of its unique significance?

Beauvoir's thinking laid the groundwork for a string of subsequent feminist critiques of motherhood, which gradually went beyond questioning the notion of motherhood as the natural destiny of women or rebuking the institution of motherhood in its contemporary forms. The most radical critiques suggested that we would have to do away with "motherhood" and perhaps even "the family" altogether.

Twenty-one years after the publication of *The Second Sex*, Shulamith Firestone was inspired by Beauvoir's attempts to loosen the ties between the conceptions of womanhood and biological sex. In her polemic *The Dialectic of Sex*, Firestone argued that the role of biological sex must not simply be rethought but *overcome*—totally and unconditionally. Dedicating *The Dialectic of Sex* "to Simone de Beauvoir, who endured,"[28] Firestone found one serious failing in her intellectual forebear: while Beauvoir vividly captured the myriad restrictions and indignities meted out on women, in her analysis of the grounds for the inequality of the sexes she relied far too heavily on abstract philosophical categories like "transcendence" (or "immanence," or "the Other"). Firestone thought there was a far simpler explanation for inequality: it "sprang from the sexual division itself." For Firestone, the very fact that we divide humanity into "men" and "women" based on their differing roles in reproduction necessarily produced inequality. It was a matter of "biological reality" that the traditional family was based on "an inherently unequal power distribution," and, as a consequence, it would remain inegalitarian and unjust as long as it existed.[29]

The hard truth, Firestone contended, is that the mutual dependence of mother and child—and, in turn, their dependence on men—is inescapable. Children are always helpless and require monitoring and care, and it is women who must bring them into the world. Women, Firestone observed, are necessarily "at the continual mercy of their biology" for the better portion of their lives.[30] Stuck in a cycle of pregnancy, labor, breastfeeding, and childcare, women remain reliant on men for sustenance and protection. These fundamental realities result in a division of labor within the home, *any* home, that is the root of inequality in all societies around the world. The problem, Firestone insisted, was not that men were not doing their share or that patriarchy, heterosexuality, and monogamy have restricted the horizons of women; as long as humankind seeks to reproduce itself "naturally"—that is, through the bodies and labor of women— inequality will persist. To remedy the situation would require nothing short of eliminating the sex distinction as such. If sex differences could not be leveled, feminist liberation required that they be exploded:

> To assure the elimination of sexual classes requires the revolt of the underclass (women) and the seizure of control of *reproduction*: not only the full restoration to women of ownership of their own bodies, but also their (temporary) seizure of control of human fertility—the new population biology as well as all the social institutions of child-bearing and childrearing.[31]

Gender equality demanded the reinvention and reengineering of the whole of human reproduction.

*The Dialectic of Sex* sought to raise the consciousness of newly politicized women: "A revolutionary in every bedroom cannot fail to shake up the status quo," Firestone quipped memorably.[32] But this, as Firestone saw it, was only the beginning. Writing in 1970, with the winds of midcentury technological progress at her back, Firestone reminded her readers just how quickly what seemed impossible only a few years earlier was now being realized: the discovery of the structure of DNA (1953), which promised to unlock the mysteries of human genetics; the availability of hormonal birth control (1960), which transformed women's lives in and outside the bedroom; and the moon landing (1969), which made moving beyond our earthbound existence look less and less like a pipe dream. Test-tube babies and in vitro fertilization were "just around the corner," and Firestone saw no reason to limit the application of such technologies to shoring up the family in its present configurations. Technology's "ultimate cultural goal" for Firestone was "the building of the ideal in the real world." With continuing scientific advances, she argued, we could divorce reproduction from women's bodies altogether. In her speculative vision of the future, machines gestate fetuses and nurture babies until they're no longer completely defenseless, women and children are endowed with full personal autonomy, the gender divide falls apart, and full "cybernetic communism" reigns.[33] These proposals, she acknowledged, could seem far-fetched, but progress always requires us to look beyond the visible horizons of possibility and into distant, now only dimly imaginable futures.

Firestone's ambitions might sound like retro science fiction. But the underlying diagnosis—that the biological facts of reproduction and the social institution of the nuclear family render true gender equality intrinsically and necessarily impossible—is one that feminist thinkers have been returning to ever since the publication of *The Dialectic of Sex*.[34] Calls for "family abolition," in particular, which can be traced back to Marx and Engels's critique of the family in the mid-nineteenth century, are being heard with increasing frequency among progressives today. While such provocations have typically remained confined to specialized environs—the academy, radical feminist activist circles—one recent restatement of Firestone's utopian demands has received a considerable amount of popular attention: Sophie Lewis's 2019 book *Full Surrogacy Now*. Updating Firestone's arguments for the twenty-first century, Lewis abandons the fantasy of artificial wombs alleviating the hardships of pregnancy in favor of another speculative solution: the fully equal distribution of reproductive labor through universal surrogacy. Priming her readers, Lewis opens her book by graphically recounting the physical ravages of pregnancy and childbirth (a "biological bloodbath").[35] If we cannot rid ourselves of the physical necessity of playing human hosts to gestating fetuses that must tear their way into the world through our bodies, she argues, at the very least we can eliminate the uneven distribution of the costs exacted by the reproduction of our species. In doing away with biological parentage, full surrogacy would also loosen the ties that at present irrationally bind adults to their own children, ties that are responsible for the entrenchment of unjust disparities in the distribution of economic, social, and intellectual goods. Equality calls for a global "gestational commune":

> Let's bring about the conditions of possibility for open-source, fully collaborative gestation. Let's prefigure a way of manufacturing one another noncompetitively. Let's hold one another hospitably, explode notions of hereditary parentage, and multiply real, loving solidarities. Let us build a care commune based on comradeship, a world sustained by kith and kind more than by kin. Where pregnancy is concerned, let every pregnancy be for everyone. Let us overthrow, in short, the "family."[36]

It is Lewis's hope that if we just acknowledge how interconnected we all are, wanting a child of one's own will become an "unthinkable" proposition. In her "gestational commune," children will belong to no one but themselves, and the work of birthing and raising them will be a collective project, not a familial one. What this might look like in practice, however, is hard to pinpoint. Lewis gestures to the history of alternatives to the normative nuclear family—lesbian-separatist communes, the queer kinship networks that provide support to those rejected by or alienated from their families of origin, and practices of collective mothering in Black communities—as examples of less degrading forms of relationship. But she never offers a clear vision of how the actual business of reproduction is meant to take place.

The provocative title of her book, *Full Surrogacy Now*, suggests the wholesale redistribution of gestational responsibility among all those who are capable of bearing children, with or without technological intervention. "The whole world," Lewis says, "deserves to reap the benefits of already available techniques currently monopolized by capitalism's elites." But in Lewis's telling, pregnancy is a living nightmare. "It is a wonder we let fetuses inside us," she says, before giving an inventory of the many physical and psychological atrocities involved in carrying a fetus to term and laboring to birth it. "It seems impossible that a society would let such grisly things happen on a regular basis to entities endowed with legal standing," she adds. Later, she wonders "whether motherhood and pregnancy are viable cornerstones of a livable world" at all.[37]

Lewis decries pregnancy and labor in vivid terms, arguing against "romanticizing childbirth" as a justification for the pain and trauma that go along with it.[38] But she has little to say about why we should ever expect individuals to opt into such an arrangement voluntarily, under any conditions. Or why we should want them to.[39] Lewis, who aims to attack the maternity mandate in all its forms, would never go so far as to say that individuals who do not wish to carry or care for children, their own or those of strangers, should be required—or even encouraged—to do so. What would it take, then, for pregnancy to truly be "for everyone"? Lewis's arguments against the horrors and injustices of pregnancy, childbirth, and child-rearing leave us in the dark. We never learn why it might be desirable or good for anyone to choose to become pregnant, in her ideal gestational commune no less than in our actual world. In her follow-up volume, *Abolish the Family,* Lewis calls the family "a normative aspiration and a last resort: a blackmail passing itself off as fate, a shitty contract pretending to be biological necessity."[40] But to those who would ask her, "What would you put in place of the family?" Lewis endorses the retort given over thirty years ago by the feminist theorists Michèle Barrett and Mary McIntosh: "Nothing."[41]

Of course, the vagueness of the proposed alternative is almost beside the point: the force of Lewis's critique—as with many of the unqualified critiques of "the family" today—leaves us so despairing about human reproduction that we can hardly muster interest in alternative systems anyway. In this light, Lewis's rallying cry—full surrogacy now—seems less like a practical program and more like a *reductio.* "The work of social reproduction brings forth new hope for revolutionary struggle," Lewis writes at the end of *Full Surrogacy Now,* "but also produces more lives for oppressors to suck and crush."[42] This self-undermining logic is not unique to Lewis. For all their audacity and ingenious futuristic speculation, family abolitionists from Firestone to

Lewis tend to be so scathing about human life that they give us little reason to continue bringing about the people their radical future depends on.

NOT ALL FEMINIST thinkers have located the solution to the afflictions and indignities of motherhood in its elimination. Within the ongoing conversation about motherhood, feminists have explored how "motherhood" might be rehabilitated: either by revolutionizing the practices of parenting and redefining the role of mothers in society or by trying to "universalize" mothering— recognizing that the forms of thinking, feeling, and acting associated with motherhood ought to be embraced far more broadly.

Six years after Firestone issued her call to arms for "the freeing of women from the tyranny of reproduction by every means possible," the poet and critic Adrienne Rich published her landmark text, *Of Woman Born*.[43] "We know more about the air we breathe, the seas we travel, than about the nature and meaning of motherhood," Rich observed in its opening pages.[44] Before we can decide motherhood's fate, Rich said, we must first work to understand it better.[45] Like Beauvoir, Rich thought that a careful examination of cultural history, mythology, and contemporary female experience was crucial to grasping the causes of women's oppression. And like Firestone, Rich believed that the key to overcoming reproductive oppression was a recognition of the intrinsic role "motherhood" played in constituting the experience of "womanhood," not just biologically but also insofar as the mother-child relationship was at the root of psychosexual identity formation. But while Firestone suggested that technology might yet enable us to do away with the basic biological facts altogether, Rich thought such measures were neither likely nor desirable. Instead, she called for rethinking wholesale what forms pregnancy, birthing, and mothering might take under different, as-yet-unthought-of, political and cultural conditions.

The epigraph to *Of Woman Born* is taken from the first canto of Dante's *Inferno*: "but to treat of the good that I found there, I will tell of other things I discerned."[46] Like Dante returning from hell, Rich recounted her descent into and return from darkness—in her case, the darkness that marked her early experiences as a mother—in order to claim, or reclaim, another way for women and their children to coexist. The hell of motherhood consisted for Rich in loneliness and anger, but also in the severe contrast between her resentment and the wonder and love that she felt when she was with her young children. "My children cause me the most exquisite suffering of which I have any experience," Rich quoted from her diary. "It is the suffering of ambivalence: the murderous alternation between bitter resentment and raw-edged nerves, and blissful gratification and tenderness." She had to return to the suffering of ambivalence, shameful as it is painful, in order to draw the crucial distinction between what motherhood *is* and what it *could be*: between "the *potential relationship* of any woman to her powers of reproduction and to children; and the *institution,* which aims at ensuring that that potential—and all women—shall remain under male control."[47]

Rich refused to romanticize motherhood in any of its previous iterations. In her telling, there is no mythical matriarchal past for us to retrieve or state of nature to return to. She was sympathetic to Firestone's criticism of the then-ascendant (and still enduring) movement of "natural" childbirth, which Rich readily acknowledged was reactionary to a worrying degree. But in the same breath, she found Firestone's aversion to childbearing superficial (as she might have found Lewis's) and detected in it a male-derived loathing of women's bodies:

> Firestone sees childbearing, however, as purely and sim-
> ply the victimizing experience it has often been under pa-
> triarchy. "Pregnancy is barbaric," she declares; "Childbirth
> *hurts.*" She discards biological motherhood from this shal-
> low and unexamined point of view, without taking full ac-
> count of what the experience of biological pregnancy and
> birth might be in a wholly different political and emotional
> context.[48]

Firestone's quick dismissals of pregnancy, Rich warned, are as facile as her blind faith in technology's benign potential. She had ample reason to doubt this techno-utopianism. Made to deliver her three sons under heavy sedation, Rich went on to examine in detail how the hijacking of traditional female-centered birthing practices by modern medicalized obstetrics had done women harm. Modern obstetrics had inflicted upon women not just physical injury, resulting from unnecessary interventions that often led to preventable complications, but also the emotional suffering entailed by alienating them from their own bodies and turning pregnancy and childbirth into terrifying unknowns. And while Rich agreed with Firestone that the mother-child re-lationship is *the* essential human bond, the root of sexual iden-tity, and the template for all other forms of intimacy, she urged her readers to remain suspicious of simple vilifications of the singular capacity to nurture life.

The central, most stirring chapter in *Of Woman Born*—Rich referred to it as the book's very "core"—is dedicated to the subject of "Motherhood and Daughterhood."[49] Here Rich considered the potential inherent in close relationships between women. The

THE DIALECTIC OF MOTHERHOOD

most elemental human relation there is, for Rich, is the one that mothers and daughters share.

> This cathexis between mother and daughter—essential, dis-
> torted, misused—is the great unwritten story. Probably there
> is nothing in human nature more resonant with charges than
> the flow of energy between two biologically alike bodies, one
> of which has lain in amniotic bliss inside the other, one of
> which has labored to give birth to the other. The materials
> are here for the deepest mutuality and the most painful es-
> trangement.[50]

Both men and women, Rich explained, taste "warmth, nour-
ishment, tenderness, security, sensuality, mutuality" first in
the arms of their mothers. But unlike the mother-son bond,
which continues to serve as a model for men's relationships with
women throughout their lives, the elemental mother-daughter
bond is gradually erased as daughters reach adulthood. The relationship between mother and daughter is obfuscated by the institutions of heterosexuality and motherhood under patriarchy
that demand that the maturing, "normal" girl direct her capacities for affection, eroticism, and mutual dependency away from
her mother—and by implication away from women altogether—
and toward men, instead.

The first feminist priority, according to Rich, is therefore
to help women recover and restore their identities as daughters and mothers, literally and figuratively. Building a meaningful women's movement would require women to face their
longing for their mothers and apply themselves to the task
of mothering one another in their absence. For many centuries this relationship was the site of violent, forced intersub-
jective strife and self-alienation among women. "The small

female who grew up in a male-controlled world still feels," Rich wrote, "at moments, wildly unmothered."[51] Rich called on women to explore a different possibility: to embrace their "deepest mutuality" in every area of life—in their daily dealings with friends and lovers, with their midwives, and with their partners in political struggle. Only by uncovering and sharing the knowledge of the original mother-daughter bond, she wrote, will we be able to "come to view our physicality as a resource, rather than a destiny."[52]

Rich's idea of the mother's identity does not begin in the shared experience of oppression. For a mother to expand her sense of possibilities "means more than contending with the reductive images of females in children's books, movies, television, the schoolroom. It means that the mother herself is trying to expand the limits of her life. *To refuse to be a victim*: and then to go on from there."[53] The refusal to be a victim does not arise, for Rich, from a wish to downplay the extent or consequences of oppression. But Rich thought that women must recover and cultivate a deeper source for their identities: women's shared ability to nurture life—whether or not they could in fact biologically exercise it, whether or not they decided to do so. Pregnancy and birth can enable, through the intimate, free, and loving interaction of women with one another, profound self-understanding and self-fulfillment. This is why, in Rich's telling, men took it upon themselves to police the "institution of motherhood"[54] in the first place. To solidify their power over women, they had to estrange women from their bodies, embitter them to their own capacities for nurture, and rob them of the knowledge of their potential self-sufficiency in community with other women. In order to wrestle power back from men, women would have to make motherhood *for women* once more.

THE TASK OF overcoming mother-daughter alienation, and cultivating in its stead deep, sustaining connections with other women, is made that much more difficult and necessary in the face of other, intersecting forms of oppression. The more a woman's self-conception is compromised by the distorting effects of discrimination and hostility, the harder it can be for her to feel solidarity with other women in a similar position. In her 1983 essay "Eye to Eye," the feminist poet Audre Lorde wrote that Black feminists will never achieve meaningful solidarity, let alone "sisterhood," until they work through their misdirected anger toward one another: "As Black women, we have shared so many similar experiences. Why doesn't this commonality bring us closer together instead of setting us at each other's throats with weapons well-honed by familiarity?"[55]

Lorde's analysis was born of personal experience: no one provokes her resentment and rage, she confessed, as much as other Black women. Lorde vividly conveyed the disdain and fury she often could not help feeling in her interactions with other Black women, which she interpreted as an externalization of the hatred and violence directed at her for being both Black and female throughout her life. But Black women do not just internalize the racism and sexism of which they are victims. Racism and sexism compromise the relationship that Lorde, like Rich, considered to be the foundation for all other forms of female intimacy and friendship: a woman's relationship with her own mother. "My mother taught me to survive from a very early age by her own example," she wrote. "Her silences also taught me isolation, fury, mistrust, self-rejection, and sadness." When she became a mother herself, Lorde learned that her mother's failure was not simply a personal shortcoming. Trying to protect her teenage daughter as she made

her first forays into a world hostile to young Black girls, Lorde discovered how powerless she was to protect and console her: "I lis-
tened, hiding my pained need to snatch her back into the web of
my smaller protections. I sat watching while she worked it out bit
by hurtful bit—what she really wanted—feeling her rage wax and
wane, feeling her anger building against me because I could not
help her do it nor do it for her, nor would she allow that."[56]

This original experience of disappointment and frustration—
the distressing realization that the mother you believed would
always protect you is in fact powerless to do so—is devastating,
and formative. The young daughter feels, to recall Rich's phrase,
"wildly unmothered." The estrangement undermines her trust in
women, and in particular other Black women. But, Lorde asserted,
it doesn't have to be that way. "We can learn to mother ourselves"—
cultivate tenderness, affirm one's worth, and treat other women
with the compassion and care they deserve: "If we can learn to
give ourselves the recognition and acceptance that we have come
to expect only from our mommas, Black women will be able to
see each other much more clearly and deal with each other much
more directly."[57] Lorde's call for women to work through their ambivalent relationship with their own mothers reflected the deep
longing of her generation to connect and redeem this originary
bond. One can hear it already in Alice Walker's 1972 paean to her
mother: "Guided by my heritage of a love of beauty and a respect
for strength—in search of my mother's garden, I found my own."[58]

The personal efforts of thinkers like Lorde and Walker
emerged against the background of a larger reckoning with the
historical role of mothers in Black American life and culture. By
the time white feminists in the 1960s and 1970s were calling to
"politicize the family," women in the civil rights and Black liberation movements had been grappling with the so-called motherhood question and its political dimensions for a long time.[59]

The recognition that motherhood was a political problem was at the root of a national debate about Black families, which traced to the 1939 publication of *The Negro Family in the United States* by E. Franklin Frazier. Frazier, a Black sociologist at Howard University, blamed the breakdown and dysfunction of the Black family on the uneven balance of power within Black homes—a "matriarchate," as he called it, wherein the wife was both breadwinner and the primary authority figure.[60] Frazier's analysis was used as the basis for the U.S. government's 1965 Moynihan Report, which attributed the social problems afflicting African American communities, including poverty, crime, and children born out of wedlock, to women's dominance within the home and an absence of "male leadership."[61] (Among other offensive proposals, the report, published at the height of the Vietnam War, notoriously tried to promote military service among Black men as a means of compensating for the absence of positive paternal influences.) At the same time, the idea that the blame for what Frazier called the "disorganization" of Black American society could be laid at the feet of Black mothers was taken up by the Black Power movement. In "The Allegory of the Black Eunuchs," Eldridge Cleaver alleged that the "myth of the strong black woman" had turned her into the white man's "silent ally" in a war against Black men.[62]

Writing from jail in 1971, Angela Davis confronted these critiques of Black women head on. In her essay "The Black Woman's Role in the Community of Slaves," Davis sought to discredit the myth of the matriarchate, and in particular the view that Black women were willfully dominating Black men and reaping the spoiled fruits of oppression at their expense. In Davis's analysis, Black women had indeed played a unique role in slave communities. As the primary caretakers of children and heads of family within the slave quarters, women had access to an arena of relative—though always highly circumscribed—autonomy and power. "It was only in domestic life—away from the eyes and whip of the overseer," Davis wrote, "that the slaves could attempt to assert the modicum of freedom they still retained." As a consequence, "domestic labor was the only meaningful labor for the slave community as a whole." Davis emphasized that this access to "meaningful labor" was granted to women only because under patriarchy it was they who were assigned domestic labor by default: "Precisely through performing the drudgery which has long been a central expression of the socially conditioned inferiority of women, the black woman in chains could help to lay the foundation for some degree of autonomy, both for herself and her men." Because of their a priori relegation to the inferior sphere of the household, women came to play vital leadership roles in their communities. This, Davis writes, constituted "one of the supreme ironies of slavery": the very system that kept Black women in bondage also "released [them] from the chains of the myth of femininity."[63]

Echoing Hegel's analysis of the master-slave dialectic, Davis recognized that Black women's oppression paradoxically exerted a leveling effect on gender relations within Black slave society:

> But out of this deformed equality was forged quite undeliberately, yet inexorably, a state of affairs which could unharness an immense potential in the black woman. Expending indispensable labor for the enrichment of her oppressor, she could attain a practical awareness of the oppressor's utter dependence on her—for the master needs the slave far more than the slave needs the master. At the same time she could realize that while her productive activity was wholly subordinated to the will of the master, it was nevertheless proof of her ability to transform things.[64]

Women's ability to effect change manifested also in instances of active resistance: in addition to the famed examples of Harriet Tubman and Sojourner Truth, Davis recounted the feats of women who attempted to poison their masters, set slave owners' homes on fire, and took part in slave rebellion.[65] But rebelling, she demonstrated, did not have to take such an overt form to be meaningful, or to shape the consciousness and self-understanding of the Black women who took part in it.

In light of this history, Davis warned, it was a grave error to place blame on Black mothers for the condition of Black people in America. It was the institution of slavery that deprived Black men of authority and dignity, warped Black families, and weakened community ties—not Black women. Black mothers did not benefit at the expense of Black men but rose to the occasion that extremely adverse circumstances afforded them. A year earlier, the Black feminist artist Fran Sanders expressed the same sentiment succinctly in an open letter titled "Dear Black Man." Sanders railed against the messaging in academia, Hollywood, Washington, and, worst of all, Black radical circles that suggested Black women had deliberately or inadvertently "de-balled" the Black man. "Now let's face it," Sanders wrote, "it was she who caused the race to survive. And if we are now all finally finding our voices to assert ourselves as a race, let it not be at her expense."[66]

The recognition that motherhood could be a source of power, a revolutionary force in its own right, gradually emerged as a prominent theme within the subsequent wave of Black feminist thought. In the Black liberation movement, women followed Davis and Sanders to find inspiration for their own feminist thinking and organizing in the stories of maternal resilience throughout Black history—from pre-slavery African villages to slave communities to their mothers and grandmothers' lives under Jim Crow.

WHITE FEMINISTS, TOO, were drawn to the idea that there was transformative power in the experience of motherhood—in the knowledge, emotions, and practices that were essential to bearing and caring for children. But while Black women writers reclaimed the mothers in their own ancestral lineages, white women were turning to societies and divinities that belonged to a barely retrievable past. The difference is not accidental: in part, white feminists' appeal to mythical matriarchs instead of actual ones reflected the ways in which the white feminist movement was, as American historian Lauri Umansky has observed, often based in intergenerational conflict.[67] (A central impetus for Adrienne Rich's call to rehabilitate the mother-daughter relationship was the disappointment and resentment she and other feminists of her generation harbored against their own mothers, who failed, as Rich writes, to "teach us to be Amazons," who "bound our feet or simply left us."[68])

Explorations of ancient matriarchies and religious worship of feminine, maternal divinities exploded on the feminist scene in the 1970s. This new feminist mysticism, which emerged during the heady days of women's liberation, preached the gospel of the mother divine.[69] The incense-laden currents of New Age culture carried the call for women to get in touch with their inner life-giving "goddess" and harness the sacred feminine energy that was every woman's birthright. The resurgent interest in the feminine divine coincided with the rediscovery of texts like Helen Diner's 1930 study *Mothers and Amazons* and the publication of revisionist historical accounts of ancient matriarchies like Elizabeth Gould Davis's 1971 *The First Sex* and Merlin Stone's 1976 *When God Was a Woman*.[70] Writers like Gould Davis and Stone argued that prehistory was ruled by women:

peaceful matriarchal leaders oversaw the worship of feminine divinities and conflict- and violence-free collective societies for many generations before they were deposed by male-led nomadic cultures that lived and died by the sword.

Even as the historical veracity of such accounts came under scrutiny, there was no underestimating their cultural and political impact: "Against all the works detailing woman's oppressed condition," Rich wrote of Gould Davis's book, *The First Sex* "stands out as the first to create a counter-image."[71] Such counter-images fed into feminist utopian thinking that advocated for literal or figurative matriarchy: wholesale revolutions of values and political structure that put idealized conceptions of womanhood and motherhood at their center. Perhaps the most famous of such attempts was made by Mary Daly, the radical lesbian feminist theologian. In her 1978 book *Gyn/Ecology: The Metaethics of Radical Feminism,* Daly argued that male society is a phallocentric cult of death and violence, rife not merely with "womb envy" but also with spiteful hatred of "female creative energy in *all* of its dimensions."[72] Radicalizing Rich, Daly claimed that powerful men "wage an unceasing war against life itself," directing their ire and violence at women because "female energy is essentially biophilic," or life-loving. Resentful of women's procreative capacities, men took to mastering *synthetic* processes—technological innovation, genetic engineering, nuclear science, medicine (and particularly gynecology)—that mimic and exploit the creative cycles of Mother Nature. These pale attempts at "male motherhood" mocked and tyrannized women, rendering them mute, supine, and dependent, while also causing irreparable damage to the earth. "Unable to create life, [men] are performing the most potent act possible to them: the manufacture of death." To find the antidote to the patriarchal death drive, it was necessary for women to establish a "Hag-ocracy" of cackling wild women in order to tap into more holistic ways of thinking and being: ecstatic, feral, and essentially female, whether literally maternal or otherwise life-giving.[73]

In the years to follow, Daly's project would come under harsh criticism. Some assailed her gender essentialism; others denounced her work as ethnocentric.[74] Both the significance and the limitations of *Gyn/Ecology* were encapsulated by Audre Lorde's 1979 open letter to Daly. Addressing her as "a sister Hag," Lorde thanked Daly for sending her the book—"So much of it is full of import, useful, generative, and provoking"—before excoriating her for leaving out all but white women from her analysis, which centered Western mythology and history: "What you excluded from *Gyn/Ecology* dismissed my heritage and the heritage of all other noneuropean women, and denied the real connections that exist between all of us."[75]

Today Daly is often remembered more for her eccentric wordplay and virulent anti-trans sentiments than for any of her larger theoretical and political ambitions.[76] Yet Daly's hope that the essential capacities of women could inspire a new ethical and spiritual revival did not end with her. A version of the same idea, though cast in a dramatically different style, can be found in the work of Sara Ruddick. Ruddick similarly advocated for the recovery and widespread adoption of unique, maternal perspectives and values, but did so in a far tamer and more analytic style. In her 1989 book, *Maternal Thinking*, Ruddick echoed both Rich and Daly in arguing that the women of her generation, in their eagerness to free themselves from the duties of wife and mother, had adopted masculine ways of thinking and seeing the world.[77] Like Daly, she insisted that surmounting the "masculine" outlook meant not just overcoming the hatred of women's bodies, aggression, and the cold pursuit of power but reconceiving "reason" itself.[78] For Ruddick, however, the counter-image to the calculating, destructive male was not the cackling, jeering hag but the loving, accepting mother.[79] In this way, Ruddick's project was more palatable than Daly's: unlike the separatist Daly, who deemed all men a danger to the feminist project (she was notoriously forced to retire from her academic appointment for refusing to allow male students into her classes), Ruddick believed the proliferation of maternal values could benefit all of humankind. And whereas Daly thought that the communication of her ideas demanded the resurrection of myth and an experimental overhaul of language, Ruddick, who was professionally trained as a philosopher, opted for plain (if at times dry and abstract) prose as she laid out her case for mothering as a valid, and potentially transformative, mode of thinking.

Though Ruddick herself presented her definitions, arguments, and prescriptions about motherhood and feminism coolly and schematically, she identified classic Enlightenment values like "objectivity, self-control, and detachment" as too paltry and impersonal to encompass the complex, fulsome reality of human existence. Her ambition was not just to overturn the "aesthetic" of reason but to warn against the active harm a commitment to "rationality" can bring about: prioritizing individual desire over the communal good, competition over cooperation, the pursuit of technological progress for its own sake over addressing real human needs, dominance instead of compassion, untrammeled acquisition instead of sacrifice and generosity. This constellation of values led humanity down a road of violence and destruction that culminated in two world wars, the A-bomb, and Vietnam. (Bringing Ruddick's arguments up to date would doubtless require adding climate change to this list.) To propose alternatives to values like autonomy and self-sufficiency, Ruddick reflected on her own experience of motherhood to identify "ideals more appropriate to responsibility and love": protectiveness, nurture, and moral education—principles and practices that constitute the mutual dependence of mother and child as well as the selflessness that characterizes the work of mothers. "I still treasured Spinoza's identification of the individual as the one who perseveres in its own being," she wrote. "But now my being was not my 'own,' nor did I want it to be."[80]

While Daly remained suspicious of males—particularly professionals like therapists and gynecologists—who tried to assume motherly roles, Ruddick maintained that the maternal orientation toward the world was a social identity that could, and should, be universally adopted. Ruddick defined a mother as any "person who takes on responsibility for children's lives and for whom providing child care is a significant part of her or his working life." Regardless of one's capacity to physically bear children, and indeed, regardless of sex or physicality altogether, Ruddick believed that *everyone* should think and live "maternally." Following the logic to its conclusion, she advocated for relabeling all men who take equal part in childcare as "mothers." The revolutionary potential of such a reorganization of values was, according to Ruddick, nearly limitless, stretching far beyond the reconstitution of traditional gender roles all the way to a new, more peaceful, global world order. There is, she wrote, "a contradiction between mothering and war":

> Mothering begins in birth and promises life; military thinking justifies organized, deliberate deaths. A mother preserves the bodies, nurtures the psychic growth, and disciplines the conscience of children; although the military trains its

soldiers to survive the situations it puts them in, it also deliberately endangers their bodies, minds, and consciences in
the name of victory and abstract causes.[81]

Ruddick was keen to avoid the implication that women were
necessarily more peaceful by nature—pointing out that they are
capable of anger and cruelty, and that men are not inherently
violent. But like Daly before her, she still came under attack by
other feminists for essentializing womanhood, seeing the traits
of "nurture," "love," and "social training" as fixed, natural, and
deeply ingrained rather than culturally, historically, and socially contingent.[82] Others dismissed Ruddick's maternal peace
politics as sentimental and criticized her extended reliance on
her own specific experience of motherhood as a theoretical resource.[83] The allegedly "universal" features of "maternal thinking" that Ruddick identifies, they warned, might just be rosy
extrapolations from her own fond memories of motherhood as
an upper-middle-class white woman.

When Ruddick addressed her critics, she defended the "feminist optimism" of her work. She traced the origin of her thinking
to a time of unprecedented opportunity for the women's movement, a moment of "splendid assertion" of women's rights, experiences, and capacities, which gave rise to a giddy willingness to
explore what made women different and better than men.[84] At
the same time, she was not able to answer the essential criticisms
levied against her. Ruddick insisted that practices of nurturing and emotional and moral education have enduring political value, but she acknowledged that characterizing them as
uniquely feminine qualities might be a dead end. And while the
celebration of motherhood continues to have purchase outside
of academic and activist circles today, for most feminists, pro-
motherhood positions have by now come to seem hopelessly

sentimental, woo-woo, or reactionary. The age of maternal optimism has ended.

BY THE 1980S, the motherhood debates had reached an impasse. If for several decades pro- and anti-motherhood positions were part of the lively interfeminist conversation, by the 1990s there were few self-identifying feminists left to sing the praises of the practice, much less the institution.

While a pro-motherhood feminist attitude was once evinced by groups as diverse as the 1970s communitarian lesbian feminists who wished to refound matriarchal society in our time and the Black feminists who criticized the racist, eugenicist agenda of the birth-control movement and celebrated mothers as a source of communal strength, today explicitly pro-motherhood positions are almost entirely the remit of conservatives. All the while, in the mainstream culture, diffuse motherhood-centric assumptions about the unique, even instinctual powers possessed by women, the indispensability of mothers' care to the well-being of children, and the larger societal benefits of allowing women to devote themselves freely to motherhood are sustained by various popular child-rearing ideologies that promote practices like natural birth, breastfeeding, and attachment parenting. Whatever objective benefits the actual practices may confer, the common tendencies of those who advocate their adoption—the idealization of the mother-child bond, the frequent conjurings of primordial forms of human life replete with casual references to "primitive societies," and their characteristically knowing mix of pop-science ("antibodies," "oxytocin," "sleep cycles"), folk wisdom (swaddling, castor oil, fenugreek), and New Age innovations (water births, amber teething necklaces, osteopathy)— all speak to a sentimental faith in the possibility of authentic existence invested in the figure of the mother and her young infant. Feminist critic Élisabeth Badinter identified a deep conservative undercurrent in this "new essentialist feminism," nowhere as evident as in the strident activism of the breastfeeding evangelizers of La Leche League.[85] Indeed, the onus of executing these programs—which are time intensive and often homebound—largely falls upon women, and the associated norms are enforced by more or less subtle forms of social pressure: hyperbole, competitive nudging, and guilt.

As for the choice to have children, progressives and liberal feminists are growing increasingly ambivalent. As we've seen, over the years, the impulse to liberate women from motherhood has been shared and amplified by radical feminists and queer theorists in the academy who have trained their aim on contemporary forms of social reproduction, the traditional family chief among them. Whereas feminist critics like Firestone and Lewis questioned biological reproduction as the basis of gender identity and social value, the queer literary theorist Lee Edelman went so far as to argue in his 2004 book *No Future* that procreation itself, as a symbol as much as a practice, was part and parcel of an oppressive heteronormative ideology.[86]

While such radical critiques remain largely unfamiliar outside academic and activist circles, skepticism about family and wariness of motherhood have found their way into the mainstream in subtler ways. Liberal and neoliberal feminists—from Hillary Clinton to Sheryl Sandberg—have equated the emancipation and advancement of women with equal opportunities for professional success. The animating ambition of many neoliberal feminist efforts, in particular, has been to clear the way for other women to get to the very top. Leaders like Sandberg and Clinton did not advocate for other women to abandon motherhood—many are mothers themselves, and much of their work has been dedicated to the enactment of policies to promote pre- and post-natal care and affordable childcare. But as women found the freedom to pursue education, careers, and social and romantic fulfillment, the hold of motherhood as a central source of identity and worth began to slacken. From the standpoint of highest distinction and success, motherhood might not just be far less necessary or urgent but a pragmatic obstacle to the achievement of heretofore impossible goals. Anne-Marie Slaughter's 2012 "Why Women Still Can't Have It All," which we discussed in the previous chapter, went viral because it named the achievements of women like Clinton and Sandberg as the exceptions that proved the rule: reaching the pinnacles of success, whether in politics or the corporate world, is rarely compatible with family life.[87] Of course, not all women, or men for that matter, wish to become heads of state or titans of industry. But Slaughter's conclusions suggest that having a family, under current conditions, may be at odds with even more modest career goals. Slaughter hoped that debunking the myth of "having it all" would force a rethinking of our idea of success, "so that we can make room for care and wellbeing alongside competition and ambition."[88] But the growing recognition of just how hard it is to pursue both career and family concurrently has hardly led to a revolution in the workplace. For many women today, the worry that it might be impossible for them to "have it all" is giving way to resignation, the sense that we no longer know what it would mean to wholeheartedly want any of it.

The inescapability of the forced choice between family and work—or glory, adventure, and self-fulfillment—is on full display in popular culture. For the sake of representing women as whole, complicated, autonomous beings, contemporary portrayals often sidestep the desire for and experience of motherhood. The idealization of the family in American TV—from

*Leave It to Beaver* (1957–1963) up through *Malcolm in the Middle* (2000–2006)—and with it the sequestering of women in the merely supporting roles of wives and mothers, has been supplanted by a very different standard of drama and interest. Mothers are increasingly portrayed as ambivalent and reluctant (*Succession, Homeland*), while some of the most memorable female TV protagonists of the past decade have been childless: stoners (*Broad City*), twentysomething hipsters (*Girls*), thirty-something manic-pixie dream girls (*New Girl*), modern-day Machiavellis (*House of Cards*), political operators (*Scandal*), superheroes (Captain Marvel, Wonder Woman, Black Widow, Lady Thor), corporate executives (*The Good Fight*). In these narratives, no line of work, vocation, or lifestyle is closed off to women—as long as they don't try to be mothers first.

The message is implicit but clear enough: even where reproductive choice is guaranteed, the costs of the choice are high. How is one to decide? Is the capacity to give birth a source of power and meaning, or is motherhood a cumbersome, potentially torturous, and at any rate unnecessary and overrated experience? An impartial examination of the past couple decades could easily lead one to conclude that the answer is, paradoxically, both.

A case in point: in 2004, the journalist Elizabeth Kolbert staged another iteration of the motherhood debate in the pages of the *New Yorker*.[89] Kolbert reviewed two books that touched on the "home-work problem"—the then-growing (and now more-or-less accepted) realization that allowing and enabling women to join the workforce had hardly ushered in a golden age of female empowerment and fulfillment.[90] The two books under review—by now mostly forgotten—Daphne de Marneffe's *Maternal Desire: On Children, Love, and the Inner Life* and Susan J. Douglas and Meredith W. Michaels's *The Mommy*

*Myth: The Idealization of Motherhood and How It Has Undermined Women*, made diametrically opposed arguments. De Marneffe, a clinical psychologist, described heeding the call of her "maternal desire" and putting her career on hold in order to raise her children.[91] Based on that experience, she claimed that contemporary ideology suppressed the expression of such longings and that, contrary to feminists' insistence, staying at home to raise children does not have to mean relinquishing one's adult identity. Motherhood, she argued, was a good way for women to forge a meaningful and fulfilling life and sense of self. At the very same time, Douglas and Michaels, professors of communication studies and philosophy respectively, lamented what they saw as the mainstream valorization of self-abnegating motherhood and called for more social support for women to pursue education and careers on a par with their male counterparts.

These split perspectives on motherhood persist to this day. If Kolbert were to write the article today, she could have picked recent titles like Angela Garbes's *Essential Labor: Mothering as Social Change* and Jessica Grose's *Screaming on the Inside: The Unsustainability of American Motherhood* (or Nancy Reddy's forthcoming *The Good Mother Myth*) to illustrate how the motherhood discourse gets polarized along the very same axis.[92] What is notable about the disagreement between books like *Maternal Desire* and *The Mommy Myth* is not that they advocate for different agendas. Rather, it is the stark contrast in their assessments of one and the same liberal and progressive society, which they presumably share. Both books warned of a discourse that oppressed women, but the discourses they had in mind seemed incompatible. De Marneffe described a society that demanded that women stifle their desires to spend more time caring for their children. "For a certain class of contemporary woman," she wrote, "it's almost as if the desire for sex and the desire to mother have switched places in terms of taboo."[93] Meanwhile, Douglas and Michaels observed almost the exact opposite: a society that idealized motherhood and required mothers to readily sacrifice any and all other aspects of their lives for the sake of their children. "Logically," wrote Kolbert in her review of the books, it was "impossible for both 'Maternal Desire' and 'The Mommy Myth' to be right about what constitutes the prevailing ideology."[94]

The reason why both analyses reached such different conclusions, Kolbert suggested, is that women insisted on measuring themselves against unreasonable and oftentimes contradictory standards. This process, she warned, sets women up to feel like personal and professional failures. For Kolbert, there was no way out of this trap: trying to clarify these conflicting standards through analysis or debate was a nonstarter. When it comes to motherhood, the only thing worth asserting is that all choices are more or less equally valid: "If a woman wants to take time off from her career to raise a family, and if she can afford to do so, what more can she reasonably desire? That everyone else act only in ways that validate her decision? Conversely, if she wants to work, and can find someone to care for her children, does that really mean Jodie Foster has to stop nattering on to *People* about her babies?" Everyone, in other words, should do what seems best to them and leave others be. At the end of her review, Kolbert went on to suggest that both parties to the debate should remain mindful of the privilege their dilemmas imply. "How worried should we be about what these women, which is to say ourselves, are feeling?" she wondered. "Choosing between work and home is, in the end, a problem only for those who have a choice. In this sense, it is, like so many 'problems' of twenty-first-century life, a problem of not having enough problems."[95]

Kolbert's suggested resolution of the motherhood impasse—minimize the concerns of women living in comfort as subjective and therefore less consequential—is a critical move that will be familiar to many readers today. But it is not new. Already in 1976 in *Of Woman Born*, Adrienne Rich considered a similar objection to her own work. She did not flinch in her response:

> As I write these words, most women in the world are far too preoccupied with the immediate effects of patriarchy on their lives—too-large families, inadequate or nonexistent child-care, malnutrition, enforced seclusion, lack of education, inadequate wages due to sex discrimination—to demand anything, or to ask this question; but that fact does not render the question either reactionary or trivial.[96]

Rich's point is that recognizing that progress is uneven doesn't render the concerns of the beneficiaries of uneven progress morally invalid or unimportant. And, as we've seen, worries about whether or not to have children, and how to raise them, are hardly just the preoccupations of the well-to-do. (To suppose otherwise might be its own form of prejudice.)

There is a still deeper reason to doubt the idea that, at the end of the day, the internal tensions in the dominant attitudes toward motherhood do not matter all that much. The sense that we are living in a world that is *both* pro- and anti-natalist, pro- and anti-motherhood—the sense Kolbert captured already twenty years ago and that we discovered for ourselves while researching this book—is not just a reflection of the subjective feelings of women who put too much pressure on themselves to excel both in and outside the home. The conflicting assessments of one and the same reality tell a far more interesting story. The attitudes toward mothers and motherhood need not be any more unified or consistent than the experience of motherhood itself—full, as Rich wrote, with "the potentialities for both creative and destructive energy."[97] But our demands of women and mothers may also be at internal odds: we hold mothers responsible, Jacqueline Rose has argued, for "both securing and jeopardising" our "impossible future."[98] It is possible, in other words, for the prevailing ideology itself to be disjointed and contradictory. This crisis of interpretation is the reason why in 2004 both *The Mommy Myth* and *Maternal Desire* could coexist side by side. And it is also why, a little more recently, so many commentators can confidently assert that we live in a pronatalist society at the same time that many women attest to no more external pressure to have children than having to listen to their mothers' fantasies about becoming grandmothers, or simply none at all.

It is understandable that, in the face of the kind of genuine emotional ambivalence, intellectual perplexity, and political enmity that motherhood raises, we find ourselves seeking exclusive refuge in the unquestionable value of free choice. But if the basic feminist goal is to liberate and empower women, then simply insisting on a woman's right to choose won't quite do. Embracing private deliberation and autonomous choice may seem like the only way to guarantee people's freedom to determine the course of their lives for themselves, but refusing to continue a conversation past the point of such affirmation can amount to a dodge of the issue, abandoning the uncertain to the existing—often conflicting—mores of their societies and social circles, or to the inertia of their lives. The fact that de Marneffe and Michaels and Douglas alike were not content with keeping their thoughts about motherhood to themselves but made a public case for their positions speaks to their shared intuition that at least some might benefit from seeing these questions thought through in public. Without this kind of public conversation, many of those who have not already made up their minds might simply be left adrift. Being suspended in ambivalence is stressful, but even worse, it can be disempowering; to remain stuck in indecision means forfeiting your agency to choose. In the end, exercising the freedom to decide what shape you want your life to take requires seriously thinking through the conflicts at hand.

To TAKE THE questions surrounding motherhood seriously does not necessarily mean just picking a side. Already in the mid-1980s, twenty years before Kolbert wrote her review in the *New Yorker,* the dynamics of the motherhood debates had grown so overdetermined that they became a subject of critique in their own right. In her seminal 1984 work, *Feminist Theory: From Margin to Center,* bell hooks condemned the opposition between those who sought to free women from the burdens of motherhood and those who wished to reclaim motherhood as a legitimate and empowering source of identity. All along, she forcefully argued, both sides had been missing something crucial: in hammering out the theoretical basis for their positions, they failed to seriously take into consideration how the women whose interests they were ostensibly promoting actually lived and what really mattered to them. This oversight was intellectually and ethically misguided, and politically counterproductive.

The norms of the institution of motherhood among the white middle classes, hooks pointed out, were quite distinct from how motherhood looked and what it meant elsewhere.[99] For example, while many feminists rued the fact that mothers were deprived of opportunities to work outside the home, motherhood had never prevented Black and poor white women from entering the work-force.[100] This, hooks observed, was simply because Black and poor white women had always worked. The underclasses didn't need any liberation into the workforce; what they needed was sometimes exactly the opposite: they needed, and wanted, more time at home. Echoing Angela Davis, hooks observed that Black women, in particular, have historically identified the work they performed in the context of their own families as "humanizing labor, work that affirms their identity as women, as human be-ings showing love and care, the very gestures of humanity white supremacist ideology claimed Black people were incapable of ex-pressing." For Black and working-class white women, the labors of care inside the home contrasted sharply with the "stressful, degrading and dehumanizing" work that they had to perform outside of it. Indeed, once middle-class women began entering the workforce in the 1960s, hooks noted, they, too, quickly found out how frustrating wage work can be. And even among those who enjoyed it, many came to feel that it demanded too much of their time and required them to spend most of it away from their families. The fact was that while work did grant women some sorely needed financial independence, for most women, work had "not adequately fulfilled human needs." The feminist movement, hooks argued, had failed to take this into account— that women valued the labor they performed at home and wanted the freedom to engage in it. Though feminists in the sec-ond wave of the women's movement had sought recognition for housework and childcare as forms of labor, they often refused to acknowledge the "significance and value of female parenting," of motherhood, in anything like the terms in which women them-selves understood those activities. The failure was both ethical and strategic: the early feminist attacks on motherhood, hooks wrote, "alienated masses of women from the movement, especially poor and/or non-white women, who find parenting one of the few interpersonal relationships where they are affirmed and appreciated."[101]

At the same time, hooks lamented the fact that too often the positive feminist reassessments of motherhood were inadvertently steeped in sexist stereotypes: when motherhood was honored it was romanticized, laden with stale images of sacred motherly love derived from the Victorian "cult of domesticity." The idea that women, and only women, are "inherently life-affirming nurturers" was plainly sexist, hooks argued—part and parcel of male-supremacist ideology. To maintain that caring for others is a woman's "truest vocation" suggests that it is ultimately her most, and perhaps only, worthy project. It implies that women who remain childless, and in particular those women who choose to dedicate their lives to their careers, creative efforts, or politics, are "doomed to live emotionally unfulfilled lives." Recognizing this did not entail dismissing motherhood as a source of identity and dignity. To feminists like Sara Ruddick, who insisted that motherhood was "more rewarding" and "more important" than any other role a woman could perform, hooks had a straightforward retort: "They could simply state that it *is* important and rewarding."[102]

For hooks, a comprehensive feminist outlook would be able to equally legitimize childbearing and childlessness as possible choices for women. But this was not just a matter of respecting every woman's personal choice; rather, it required acknowledging the intrinsic worth of both possible paths on their own terms. To do this, feminists would have to consciously leave behind the many myths of motherhood. Women are no more suited for the work of parenting than men, nor are they any more necessary. There were no duties of parenting—tenderness,

affection, care—or "maternal desires," that come more "naturally" to women than they do to anyone else.

Many women would no doubt hesitate to give up on the idea
of women's parental exceptionalism, hooks predicted. Women
take pride in the physiological feats of childbirth and mothering and are reluctant "to concede motherhood as an arena of
social life in which women can exert power and control." But
hooks insisted that it was necessary to relinquish these particular sources of self-worth, not only in order to enable women to
pursue their paths free of social coercion but also to secure their
equality with men: "As long as women or society as a whole see
the mother/child relationship as unique and special because the
female carries the child in her body and gives birth, or makes
this biological experience synonymous with women having a
closer, more significant bond to children than the male parent,
responsibility for child care and childrearing will continue to be
primarily women's work."[103]

To liberate women, we do not need to universalize "mothering" but must commit ourselves to sharing equal responsibility
in parenting between the sexes. Here, the key was reconceiving
the socialization of men. "Men will not share equally in parenting until they are taught, ideally from childhood on, that fatherhood has the same meaning and significance as motherhood,"
hooks wrote:

> Wishful thinking will not alter the concept of the maternal
> in our society. Rather than changing it, the word paternal
> should share the same meaning. Telling a boy acting out the
> role of caring parent with his dolls that he is being maternal
> will not change the idea that women are better suited to
> parenting; it will reinforce it. Saying to a boy that he is be-

having like a good father (in the way that girls are told that they are good mothers when they show attention and care to dolls) would teach him a vision of effective parenting, of fatherhood, that is the same as motherhood.[104]

Here hooks was echoing ideas found earlier in Rich, who argued that men ought to be recruited en masse into a comprehensive childcare system in order to overhaul the gendered socialization of boys and men. For both Rich and hooks, this equitable redistribution of parental responsibilities was not the demand of some abstract ideal of fairness. Rather, it was necessary in order to change the expectations that children—both male and female—have of women and men, and thus to break down traditional gender roles in and outside the home. The effect on men, in particular, would be profound: as long as men do not learn to nurture—to care for children as well as for their fellow men and women—they will continue seeking out women to provide them with comfort, support, and acceptance. "In learning to give care to children," Rich wrote, "men would have to cease being children." Until then, men will continue to demand that women satisfy their every infantile need: a man "learns contempt for himself in states of suffering, and can reveal them only to women, whom he must then also hold in contempt, or resent for their knowledge of his weakness." In a new world order in which men will not merely toy with fatherhood when it suits them but assume an equal share of the responsibilities of nurturing as a matter of course, both men and women will have "a greater chance of realizing that strength and vulnerability, toughness and expressiveness, nurturance and authority, are not opposites, not the sole inheritance of one sex or the other."[105]

In other words, finding a proper place for motherhood in women's lives requires that we disentangle parenting and women altogether. The so-called motherhood question would have to be not so much answered as transcended.

HOOKS AND RICH thought that broadening the question of motherhood to that of parenthood would make it possible for feminists to defend the legitimacy and worth of women's choice to mother without insisting that women are somehow *uniquely* endowed with a capacity to nurture. Only then could feminism avoid reproducing the kinds of unnecessary dimensions of difference between men and women that limit everyone's human horizons—their character, their aspirations, and their hopes of enjoying family life. Otherwise, they warned, feminism would be doomed either to lose contact with the real lives of women or impede the equal distribution of parenting duties between the sexes.

Both hooks and Rich, however, were writing at a time when the question *whether to have children at all* was rarely raised in mainstream society. Today, as ambivalence about having children spreads, their critique can be extended in yet another direction. It isn't only that we must acknowledge the capacity and responsibility to nurture children as common to both sexes, lest we inadvertently place an unfair burden of care on women. We must also reckon with the unequal distribution of the task of figuring out what one actually wants. For conceiving the question of family exclusively as one of "motherhood" is part of what can make it so hard to come up with a confident answer, for men as well as for women.

In center-left circles, the conviction that women ought to be able to determine their own reproductive fates and exercise as much autonomy over their bodies as men has transmuted over the years into the presumption that the question of whether to start a family is the purview of women alone. The duty to respect "women's choices" has morphed into something approaching the status of a prohibition on male involvement. (This is an impulse that the recent conservative attacks on women's reproductive rights are likely only to exacerbate.) As a result, men are often relegated to the role of passive, neutral observers—to the point that the suggestion that a man in a relationship with a woman in her late twenties or early thirties should make his desires known and express more than a passing interest in starting a family is increasingly seen as strange, if not intrusive or controlling. Decades of feminist gains in the arenas of theory, politics, and culture have shed light on the tolls motherhood takes on women. Once the price exacted by motherhood is acknowledged, how could a man ask the woman he loves to submit herself to such a fate? Wouldn't the expression of desire, one way or the other, constitute a form of illegitimate pressure? It's not just that men who fancy themselves progressive on gender issues feel they must take a supporting role in the decision; for many men, the question of children feels more or less off-limits.

To be clear, the problem isn't that men are unwilling to take part in raising a family. Many men today, especially those in the educated middle- and upper-middle class, have internalized the expectation that they ought to contribute more to running the household and taking care of the kids, if they end up having any. What's more, the persistence of disparities in the domestic sphere is due not only to lingering personal failings but also to structural ones. As the philosopher Gina Schouten observed in her 2019 book *Liberalism, Neutrality, and the Gendered Division of Labor*, "Many men now coming of age in liberal democracies support their partners' work aspirations and want, for themselves, a larger role in caregiving. But social institutions are still designed around the breadwinner/homemaker ideal; they have not evolved to accommodate the reality of dual-earner households."[106] Despite the psychological and systemic barriers, progress in the distribution of housework and childcare is undeniable: men today spend more time doing household maintenance and child-rearing than ever before, though still not as much as women, and, often, less than they themselves believe they do.[107] (How secure these gains are is also not entirely clear: research into the effects of the pandemic on the gendered division of household labor has so far delivered mixed results.[108]) Still, as some of the material burdens involved in maintaining a home and family have been lifting off women's shoulders, they have been replaced by a psychic burden that, for many, is no less heavy.

When it comes to deciding whether or not to have children, men are too often let off the hook. From the standpoint of many women struggling with the decision, it is not enough for men to acquiesce to their choices, standing by sympathetically but silently while deliberations are underway. How different would women's decision-making process be if their partners saw that their responsibility ought to extend beyond passively supporting them in "whatever you choose"? How much easier would all of our lives be if we all recognized that being a "good ally" to the feminist cause does not bar (or exempt) men from taking an active interest in the possibility of starting a family, its practical burdens, and the work it would necessarily entail?

The feeling, shared by so many women, that this decision is their cross to bear was presented in literary form in Sheila Heti's celebrated autofictional novel *Motherhood*. At the beginning of the novel, the unnamed narrator is about to turn thirty-seven and is caught in a thicket of ambivalence about whether or not she wishes to have children of her own. Her partner has a daughter from another relationship and does not especially want

another child. Despite this, she says, he "has said that the decision is mine": "*It's a risk*, he says, his daughter is lovely, but you
never know what you're going to get. If I want a child, we can
have one, he said, *but you have to be sure.*"[109]

Heti presents her protagonist's partner as someone who takes
himself to be supportive. But by pushing the decision onto her
alone while seeding feelings of reluctance and doubt, he has put
the narrator in a bind. What might at first seem like an act of
selfless deference (if you want a child, we can have one) functions more like an evasive maneuver. The choice is laden with
risks ("you never know what you're going to get") and yet she is
the one who has to make it ("you have to be sure"). The responsibility for anything that might go wrong is placed entirely on her.
This is why hearing "if *you* want a child, we *can* have one" from
one's partner and prospective co-parent will not move someone
already on the fence. ("The thing to do when you're feeling ambivalent is to wait," Heti writes shortly thereafter. "But for how
long?"[110]—or, for what exactly?) Lukewarm offers of cooperation can stand in the way of making the choice confidently and
without reservations. Who would want to bring a child into the
world with someone who, when asked whether he wants to be
a dad, has only a feeble "if you insist . . ." to offer in return? The
remark "whatever you want—it's up to you" is annoying enough
when trying to pick a film to watch or a restaurant to order take-
out from; it can feel unbearable as a response to the question
"Do you want to have a child with me?"

The dilemma in *Motherhood* is not merely a novelistic conceit. Dalia, a thirty-three-year-old who runs her own digital
marketing business in Vancouver, told us in an interview that
she had been violently "thrashing" between wanting and not
wanting to have children for several years, all while in a relationship with someone who was agnostic on the question of whether

he'd like to become a father. "He just wants to be with me, and so if that means having children, great, if that means not, that's fine, too." But the unreserved open-mindedness was hard for Dalia to bear. "I've said to him, you need to locate your own desire in this decision, and it doesn't mean anything to me for you to say you're going to do what I want. This isn't about what I want."

Like Dalia, many women don't need their boyfriends and husbands to simply defer to their judgments and acquiesce to their choices—they want something more: real partners with whom they can be mutually forthright about their own desires and conflicts, and with whom they can hope to achieve clarity together. A startling conclusion follows: men who seek to promote gender equality within relationships must do more than make sure they do their fair share of the chores. To meet women on an equal plane might mean taking their partners' worries, and the urgency of those worries, as their own. That is to say: what women need from their partners is not for them to leave them alone with the question "should I have children?" but to join them in asking it *together*. This is yet another reason why asking whether children are good or bad for women inevitably opens up the broader, and more essential, question of whether children are good or bad in the first place.

THE LONG ROAD of feminist struggle has brought us far: women have never before enjoyed as much freedom of opportunity when it comes to their education, careers, and personal lives.[111] While the repeal of *Roe v. Wade* has made painfully clear that, as with all political victories, these privileges cannot be taken for granted, for most young women in the developed world, their financial and political independence, as well as their sense of self-worth, is no longer bound to the prospect of finding a suitable match and bearing children. Against this background, the challenges of navigating the choice whether or not to have children open a new frontier for feminist thought and practice. Many of the women we spoke to who are undecided about having children expressed feelings of confusion, powerlessness, and, above all, loneliness. They felt the decision fell squarely on them, but they didn't know how to proceed. Often, they understood their lack of clarity and mixed feelings as aberrations before learning that others share similarly overwhelming feelings of uncertainty and doubt. This, too, should be of concern to those of us committed to addressing structural disadvantages faced by women. While many of the battles women waged before us—for reproductive freedom, egalitarian workplaces, and access to social support for mothers—are still ongoing, feminists must be willing to extend their vision further.

Feminism is not a checklist of a predetermined set of goals but an evolving movement; it should rise to respond to the challenges of the lives of women as they emerge, their very own problems with no name. Promoting women's interests calls for helping them to thoughtfully engage with the questions that preoccupy them. At this time, it means that children ought to become an acceptable and welcome topic of discussion, among women *and men*, and not only those in serious, long-term relationships. As thinkers like Beauvoir, Rich, and hooks argued all along, feminist commitments, fully thought through, point beyond themselves—from questions that relate only to women toward general ethical questions that implicate all human beings. After all, what could be more feminist than recognizing that "women's problems" are just one expression of the most fundamental human concerns?

CHAPTER 3

# Analysis Paralysis

While our grandmothers and mothers might have turned to feminist tracts like Friedan's *The Feminine Mystique*, Rich's *Of Woman Born*, or Kate Millett's *Sexual Politics* in order to critically explore their identities as women, the millennial women after them have often supplemented their feminist canon with literature. The relevant texts include formally daring, stream-of-consciousness novels like Lucy Ellmann's *Ducks, Newburyport* and Elisa Albert's *After Birth*; international favorites like Mieko Kawakami's *Breasts and Eggs*, Ariana Harwicz's *Die, My Love*, and Guadalupe Nettel's *Still Born*; magical-realist fantasies like Rachel Yoder's *Nightbitch*; and more traditionally plotted novels such as Jessamine Chan's *The School for Good Mothers*, Taffy Brodesser-Akner's *Fleishman Is in Trouble*, and Torrey Peters's *Detransition, Baby*. But some of the most celebrated examples are works of "autofiction" or memoir—Sheila Heti's *Motherhood*, Maggie Nelson's *The Argonauts*, Jenny Offill's *Dept. of Speculation*, Rachel Cusk's *A Life's Work*, Meaghan O'Connell's *And Now We Have Everything*, Rivka Galchen's *Little Labors*, Sarah Manguso's *Ongoingness*, Courtney Zoffness's *Spilt Milk*, and Kate Zambreno's *Drifts*. The deep personal ambivalence about the meaning and value of motherhood has become a literary genre unto itself.

These memoirs and autofictional novels, which dramatize the feelings of doubt and anxiety associated with parenting and family life, have become cultural touchstones for educated millennial women in the throes of uncertainty. The proliferation and popularity of this "literature of domestic ambivalence," as Kim Brooks called it in *New York* magazine back in 2016, attests to the avid hunger for serious and accessible treatments of pregnancy and motherhood among women today. And while it is by no means unprecedented for literature to take an interest in motherhood, it is remarkable just how common it has become for these titles to be treated not just as objects of art but as guides to navigating critical crossroads in their readers' lives.[1] Readers often characterize their experience of reading these narratives as therapeutic: book critics and Goodreads reviewers alike have described devouring these narratives with the urgency of one seeking answers to life's deepest questions and encountering the female protagonists' problems as their own. "I spent the year before freezing my eggs basically reading a lot of novels and articles about being a writer and having kids," Defne, a literary critic and university lecturer, told us. "I turned to it as a kind of self-help." These narratives have become for many women a shorthand for a persistent internal debate: bookmarking their pages, posting choice quotes, and referencing them in conversation with friends, they have given narrative structure and dignity to what many women experience as a private, solitary dilemma.

Experimental in form, and written in a distinctly ruminative register, motherhood ambivalence literature often combines fragmentary first-person narration with excerpted journal entries and letters, recollections of dreams, and occasional readings of works of literature or other art forms. Not much happens, but the topic is so weighty that it is presumed not much has to happen to keep our attention. A rough outline: the narrator is a woman, no longer young but not yet ready to settle into the anesthetizing rhythms of middle age. She is an artist—almost always a writer—who has achieved some measure of success, but she feels as though she's only just beginning: she's obviously good at her work but real greatness has so far eluded her. She is newly a mother, or about to become one, or trying to decide whether that is what she wishes to be. In any and all cases, motherhood is an unavoidable question for her. The overriding source of dramatic tension in her life is the simultaneous pull of the life of a mother, on the one hand, and the life of the artist on the other. These paths are presented as incommensurate if not incompatible. Her tone is direct but detached; she speaks in clipped sentences, at a dreamy remove, as if her life is not quite her own and she is being acted upon by cosmic forces far beyond her control ("fate," for Heti; the "black magic" of babies for Galchen; while breastfeeding, Cusk imagines herself "unbodied, a mere force, a miasma of nurture that surrounds [the baby] like a halo").[2] She wants to be in control. Writing is the means by which she can achieve this. "Stories impose order onto chaos. Offer control over our lives and destinies," Zoffness writes at the end of her memoir about the anxiety of motherhood. "And isn't control a kind of salvation?"[3] Likewise, Heti's narrator is driven to write in order to make sense out of her confusion: "I lived only in the greyish, insensate world of my mind, where I tried to reason everything out and came to no conclusions," she says by way of introduction. Her "only hope" is to somehow transmute that uncertainty into "a solid and concrete thing," "a powerful monster": the novel.[4]

The motor of the narrative progression is almost entirely internal to the speaker's mind, to the exclusion of anyone else's—except, of course, for the baby, real or dreamed of. The undulations of her thought process are the whole book. The plot, the characters, the narrative friction all exist *within her*—what she is thinking about, what she fears and desires, who she wants to become one moment and then the next. Other people make only fleeting appearances, more like extras than supporting characters. Their portrayals are brief, partial, and approximate. The narrator has a partner—sometimes a boyfriend, sometimes a husband—who lingers on the periphery of the narrative like an apparition. When he is mentioned, he is given to be reasonably kind and supportive, if mostly impassive and ineffectual. Friends are mentioned in passing, sometimes just in reported dialogue or as sources of advice. Their words serve to introduce a theme, an idea, perhaps a disagreeable suggestion, but it doesn't really matter who said what or why. This is not the story of the narrator's relationship with them, or anyone else for that matter. The thoughts expressed by these interlocutors get picked up by the narrator, who collects and lays out such interventions, collage-like, for her consideration and ours. When there's a climax (there isn't always), it involves giving labor, or publishing a book, or both.

This structure produces a very different kind of female protagonist than the famous heroines of the nineteenth and twentieth centuries. Today, it's relatively unusual for fiction to be written in the mode of the social novel, wherein characters who are shaped by their times and social conflicts struggle to pursue happiness in a hostile and unforgiving world populated by others whose interests clash with their own: family, rivals, objects of desire, figures of authority, friends and foes. Characters like Jane Austen's Elizabeth Bennet, Gustave Flaubert's Emma Bovary, and Leo Tolstoy's Anna Karenina falter under the weight of the expectation that they should start and maintain a family of their own, as is befitting of their social standing. In these novels, the

central conflict arises from the mismatch between this require-
ment and their own wishes, particularly their romantic desires.
The condition of the heroine's survival is the alignment of the
two: if she can successfully bring personal wants in line with expectation, she can flourish (Jane Eyre, Elizabeth Bennet, Doro-
thea Brooke); if she fails to make them coincide, she is doomed
(Emma Bovary, Anna Karenina). The narrator, speaking in the
third person, moves between their own omniscient point of view
and the limited perspectives of the characters. We come to identify our heroines' inner thoughts as only one limited part of a
larger narrative: our perspective on their lives always exceeds
their own.

With the advent of the twentieth century, novelists started
identifying subjects' consciousness as a site of drama in itself.
Virginia Woolf's Lily Briscoe, Doris Lessing's Anna Wulf, Renata
Adler's Jen Fain, Sylvia Plath's Esther Greenwood, and Elizabeth
Hardwick's Elizabeth also struggle to find a place for themselves
in the world, not primarily as feeling, desiring subjects but as
"thinking women." Nineteenth-century heroines are often ex-
ceptionally bright and even intellectually ambitious, but the
twentieth-century female protagonists are actively seeking to be
recognized as such by their peers, with varying degrees of success. They are highly educated and intellectually or artistically
inclined, and when these protagonists clash with their environ-
ments, they do so as free and sensitive minds who are painfully
aware of the ways in which they are alienated from the world
around them. Indeed, what distinguishes them most from their
literary precursors is the extent to which they are aware of the
forces that bind them. If one of the distinct pleasures of the classic nineteenth-century novel is the intimacy between narrator
and audience fostered by a sense of knowing communication behind the backs of the protagonists, in twentieth-century novels

the protagonists are in on the tragic irony of their circumstances and self-consciously reflect on it. No one knows better, because no one suffers more, the shallowness, vacuity, and incoherence of the societies these women live in. The frequent use of the first person allows such characters to retreat from the hostile world into their own thoughts, where we find them trying to dissect and comprehend the matter of their lives. The texts' fragmentary style mirrors the extent to which this matter is itself confused and contradictory. The female protagonists search for an uneasy resolution, a kind of synthesis, of the many disjointed elements of their identities and their already fragile social worlds. But even here, although the reader's point of view is restricted to that of the protagonists', the speakers' uneven narration betrays their vulnerability and lack of self-clarity. In their honest reports on their strained interactions with others, we glimpse their own reflections in other people's confused, concerned, and judging eyes.

In our time, the female protagonist's inward turn has been brought to its logical conclusion. As if taking Virginia Woolf's call for "a room of one's own" to be a formalist manifesto, the twenty-first-century motherhood novels isolate their narrators in an imaginative space that is free of psychic interference. In the works of Heti, Cusk, Galchen, and Nelson, the female artist's consciousness provides not just a privileged perspective on the action but also its domain. With her horizons entirely open, the narrator's task is only to choose a path: motherhood or art? No one can ultimately help her decide. How she will choose is a hidden fact that is within her power to discover and manifest. "Whether I want kids is a secret I keep from myself—it is the greatest secret I keep from myself," Heti's narrator says at the beginning of *Motherhood*.[5] But if the answers lie hidden within, the so-called real world is a distraction from the quest for self-understanding, which the female protagonist can attain only by tunneling deeper into her private experience and thoughts. (Though even if she wanted to have a serious conversation about her predicament with someone else, there would be few suitable interlocutors around.) Her reckoning will no doubt have repercussions beyond the confines of her own mind, but the effects it will have on her material circumstances and close relationships do not enter into her deliberations as such. The key to making up her mind is realizing what it is she actually thinks and wants *for herself*—as if one could clarify that "greatest secret" through yet more private contemplation and metacognition. Later in *Motherhood,* the narrator wakes up horror-stricken in the middle of the night and asks, "What if I've suppressed my desire for children so much that my desire is unrecognizable to me?"[6] In this way, the novels instantiate, in their very form, the ideal of the decision-making procedure as an exploration of one's own desire: as in the motherhood ambivalence course, so, too, in the motherhood ambivalence literature, the question of motherhood can only be truly worked out if one divorces oneself from one's so-called externals and captures the elusive being that is one's innermost personal desire.

One might expect the totalizing interiority that is the formal conceit of such novels to produce the ultimate degree of individuality. But this is almost never the case. Ironically, the deeper we go into the recesses of our narrators' minds, the less we can tell what they are like and who they are. The thought experiments, theoretical ruminations, and abstract expressions of feeling are not enough to provide us with the contours of concrete personalities. (Imagine trying to describe one person to another only by recounting their opinions and inchoate sentiments on one particular topic.) The fact that other characters are only incidental to the action amplifies the impersonal effect. Our protagonists are by and large untethered: no one (except for their babies) seems to demand much from them, and they are less concerned with how their decision will affect others than what it says about them—as women, as intellectuals, as artists. This does away with any prospect of recognition or misrecognition of the self the narrators have so carefully constructed: we rarely learn what anyone else thinks about them. When, in rare cases, they address their lovers and partners, as Maggie Nelson does in *The Argonauts,* the effect is less of a dialogue and more like a love letter one might never send.[7] "A life is just a proposition," Heti's narrator says; "you ask it by living it, *Could a life be lived like this, too?*"[8]

Living is indeed an experiment, a series of attempts to get things right, the actual results always up in the air. But the measure of a life—whether the experiment has succeeded, whether the answer to the question is yes or no—surely depends on more than just one's intentions and the satisfactions one has derived from contemplating it along the way. To say that in these books there are many questions asked and very little living portrayed is to say that in them there is nothing and no one to confirm or deny the narrators' propositions. The questions posed in these novels are not pointless, but they are raised in such a way that ultimately makes them seem like mere abstractions.

Even the minimal distinction between author and narrator is lost: there is little evident distance, ironic or otherwise, between the person composing the story and the person living it out on the page. (It's not incidental that the protagonists of these stories, whether explicitly marketed as memoir or as novels, either have no name at all or share their authors'.) Without such a distance, these protagonists are deprived of one of the basic signatures of human particularity: the infinitely many ways each of us can be opaque to ourselves, blind to our own weaknesses, deluded about our motivations. "Can it be that I am the subject?" asks the protagonist of Hardwick's 1979 novel *Sleepless Nights*.[9] For her, subjecthood is a fight that one can win or lose. But for the motherhood ambivalence narrators, their position as subject is more or less taken for granted. The narrators might consider a personal fault or failing, but these shortcomings are rarely grounds for them to doubt their authority as self-analyzers or decision-makers. They are almost never, in other words, grounds for real self-doubt or transformation. And so while there is a presumption that the protagonists are in a constant state of becoming, the person speaking at the end seems to be hardly different from the person they were when the story began. This is why, although the ostensible topic is a momentous decision (should I have children?) or a life-altering experience (having and beginning to raise children), the narratives are largely static, and many of their parts interchangeable.

The amorphousness of these works is crucial to understanding why they are so relatable to so many readers. Their protagonists' voices are easy to identify with, not despite but because the person behind the persona lacks a concrete form. They are pure thought and feeling: even though their subject matter involves pregnancy, nursing, and nurturing an infant—which are sometimes described in detail—the speakers are for the most part remarkably disembodied: we learn little about their physical characteristics; we almost never get a sense of how they look. With a few notable exceptions, they are also fairly disconnected from the surrounding social world, which is assumed to be one the reader is familiar with and largely shares. When social life makes its way into the narrative, it is as an intrusion or a temptation from the real domain of interest, which is the writer-speaker's mind. "The choice has presented itself," Heti's narrator says, "to make a change and run off to New York and have fun, or to *be a writer*."[10] Her boyfriend supports her decision to stay where she is: "Once a writer starts to have *an interesting life,* their writing always suffers." As a first-time mother to a newborn, Cusk experiences a similar crisis: "I am invited to a party, and though I decide to go, and bathe and dress at the appointed hour, I end up sitting in the kitchen and crying while elsewhere its frivolous minutes tick by and then elapse."[11] Not having a recognizably "interesting life" becomes an ethos, and the stream of consciousness of the incorporeal, socially unmoored writer is a script that any reader from a similar-enough cultural milieu can use to play out her own particular desires, confusions, and dilemmas. In the absence of any individualizing distinctions, the audience's connection to the narrator becomes increasingly immediate: the thoughts are so abstracted they might as well be the reader's own.

DUE TO THEIR intimate nature and immediacy, these works have acquired a reputation for particular candidness about the predicaments of motherhood. "A tortured, honest novel," commended Maggie Doherty in her review of Heti's *Motherhood* in the *New Republic.*[12] Cusk's *A Life's Work,* wrote Jennifer Szalai in the *New York Times,* evinces "an honesty and clarity that makes this memoir feel almost illicit."[13] "An honest, joyous affirmation," *Publishers Weekly* said of Nelson's *The Argonauts.*[14] Cusk herself claimed, some seven years after publishing her memoir, that one of her motivations for writing *A Life's Work* was to dispel misleading ideas surrounding motherhood: "In motherhood the communal was permitted to prevail over the individual, and the result, to my mind, was a great deal of dishonesty. . . . My own struggle had been to resist this mechanism. I wanted to—I had to—remain 'myself.'"[15] This task of resistance entails, in the first place, being willing to say what others will not:

"I often think that people wouldn't have children if they knew what it was like," Cusk announced in her memoir. (In this case, she was not speaking from personal experience: Cusk wrote the book about having her first child only after she was pregnant with her second.) And: "One does not, it is true, often hear a woman observe with incredulity that her baby won't seem to go away, not even for a night so that she can get some sleep, but that doesn't mean she doesn't think it, hasn't always thought it."[16] In contrast to the gauzy myths peddled by advertisers and mommy blogs, the ambivalent narrator promises to puncture through the veil of illusions about motherhood and femininity. Far from the distorting influences of other minds, she is liberated to finally express, finally confess, hitherto unspoken truths.

What truths, then, do these books tell? In their representations of motherhood, certain themes recur: temporary body changes and permanent bodily disfigurement, the agony and ecstasy of childbirth, exhaustion, the way the days and hours meld together until they can no longer be distinguished, the drudgery of breastfeeding but also its occasional eroticism, how boring it is to be with children. Chief among these motifs, however, is the loss of self—the threat that motherhood will annihilate the narrator's identity. For O'Connell, imagining her life after giving birth "feels like an oblivion": "I don't even know who I will be after him. . . . If I let him, my son will be the reason I don't do all sorts of things."[17] Burying herself "in the small successes of nurture," Cusk reports that the rest of her life comes to resemble "a deserted settlement, an abandoned building in which a rotten timber occasionally breaks and comes crashing to the floor, scattering mice."[18] Galchen recalls that she couldn't think straight during her first months of motherhood, and though she planned to write after her daughter was born, it was "as if every three minutes I had fallen asleep, curtailing any thought, morphing it into dream, which, when I woke, was lost altogether."[19] In these books, motherhood involves a kind of abnegation that extends into the farthest reaches of the self: babies don't just steal what little precious time you had for your art and social life, they re-wire your mind, your priorities, your most basic instincts, until you are a stranger not just to the world but to yourself. This "rival consciousness,"[20] as Cusk calls it in *A Life's Work*, takes over a mother's own, ineluctably, almost parasitically: "When she is with them she is not herself; when she is without them she is not herself; and so it is as difficult to leave your children as it is to stay with them. To discover this is to feel that your life has become irretrievably mired in conflict, or caught in some mythic snare in which you will perpetually, vainly struggle."[21] The fear of loss of self is foregrounded in the repeated references to famous female artists who did not have kids—as if to show how unwise having children might turn out to be, given that for such women living unencumbered was a basic condition of creative freedom and distinction.[22]

And yet, perhaps here lies artistic potential. As the narrators try to capture the enormity and strangeness of their experience of becoming a mother, or actually being one, or deciding to leave the path of motherhood behind, their rational and descriptive powers are extended to their very limit. "All the banal (or not) objects and experiences around me were reenchanted," Galchen writes. "The world seemed ludicrously, suspiciously, adverbially sodden with meaning. Which is to say," she continues, that the baby made her "more like a writer (or at least a certain kind of writer) precisely as she was making me into someone who was, enduringly, not writing."[23]

Despite their best efforts to master the narrative of their lives, the protagonists all seem to realize that there is a "mythic" quality to their struggle, something about it, great and terrible, that far exceeds their grasp. "I wanted keeping [the baby] to feel inevitable, like fate, but also, somehow, for it to be a choice," O'Connell writes.[24] When words fail, they resort to mysticism and occasionally magical thinking. Heti's narrator uses a technique from a classical Chinese divination guide, the *I Ching,* to perform and work through her uncertainty: she asks yes-or-no questions and flips three coins for answers. She reports on her dream symbolism and envisions the decision she is confronting to be akin to Jacob's wrestling with the angel. Zoffness, for the first time in her life, visits a mikvah (a Jewish ritual bath) with a friend who is about to become a surrogate, out of reverence for and astonishment at her friend's decision to carry another couple's child: "You are here, in Massachusetts, getting naked in the bathroom of this religious center because of Carrie, but also because of another kind of faith: Pregnancy. Parenthood."[25] Galchen researches crystal children—a New Age theory about babies that get born on earth but come from other cosmic dimensions. When she became a mother, she writes, everything becomes at once charmed and haunted. Soon after giving birth, she is hit with "an unsettling, intoxicating, against-nature feeling. A feeling that felt like black magic."[26]

The forays into spiritual seeking and surrealism that punctuate these books are meant to express the ways that both the decision and the experience of having children exceed the ordinary. These allusions to the supernatural remind us that, for many in secular society, parenting—with its unavoidable implications of identity, sacrifice, and destiny—offers the closest approximation of genuine religious contemplation and doubt available to us. But a quasi-religious transfiguration of motherhood—redeeming motherhood as a series of signs from another realm of meaning—testifies at the same time to how difficult it is for these books to grapple with the decision and its aftermath on its own terms. Motherhood can be a worthy subject of literature, and so a worthy choice in a creative life, only as transfigured into something else, something higher, something more interesting.

One notable exception underscores some of the genre's greatest limitations. Though Torrey Peters's 2021 *Detransition, Baby* is not often classified as a "motherhood ambivalence" novel, in its restaging of the motherhood question it is arguably one of the best. Like Nelson's *The Argonauts,* the book is an attempt to think through the possibilities of queer family in American life. But in doing so, it provides a profound exploration of the promises of motherhood and its uncertain and unstable role in constituting womanhood.

The story centers on three characters: Ames, who lived for many years as a trans woman but has since detransitioned and now lives publicly as a man; Katrina, Ames's cis-female boss and lover, who unexpectedly gets pregnant with his child; and Reese, Ames's ex, a trans woman who badly wants a baby. Unlike the standard motherhood ambivalence novel, the narration is relayed in the third person, with each chapter told from the point of view of one of the three main characters. Their personal histories, social lives, and idiosyncrasies are so precisely drawn that the novel frustrates any simple identification with the protagonists. Instead, each of the three perspectives offers the reader a different lens through which to examine the meaning of motherhood.

The action of the novel is concentrated in the three characters' attempt to decide, together, whether or not to have the baby. It is, they agree, ultimately Katrina's choice, as she is the one carrying the pregnancy, but they all likewise recognize that the condition for having the child is their ability to raise it in one family, which means that they must all want to do so. The novel thus takes the form of a love triangle, a love that is both erotic and, potentially, familial. Together the trio indulge their fantasies of parenthood, developing "mom-crushes"[27] on one another, making dinner, and shopping for the nursery. Through their interactions and hesitations, their illicit desires and explicit disagreements, we learn what the concepts of "family," "mothering," and "femininity" mean to each of them, how they came to form them, and why they feel about them as they do. No one character has a monopoly on thinking about motherhood—each position is rendered as potentially flawed and incomplete. And, crucially, Reese and Katrina both directly confront the question, "Why do you want to be a mom?"—sometimes warily and with mutual suspicion or contempt, but with the full knowledge that this question is not one they can dodge or talk their way out of.[28]

Because "family" is not a given for the trans and queer characters in the novel, wanting a family raises questions for them that most of the cis white "motherhood ambivalence" female narrators do not venture to ask: What about motherhood is unique, and uniquely desirable? For all the costs of assuming this new identity, what new joys or freedoms might one gain? Is there anything that might be lost if one failed to attain it? For these characters, such questions are not merely hypothetical; they have real stakes. And it is because the characters must face them together that the novel manages to escape the subjectivity trap that renders many of the other ambivalence novels and memoirs inert as works of imagination and ineffectual as commentaries.

Their vision of a new and different kind of family eventually falls apart, but this does not speak against its intensity or attraction. This turn of events is presented as a tragedy of circumstance, in the traditional novelistic sense—a tragedy rooted in the protagonists' imperfections but neither foreordained nor entirely under their individual control. Forbidding social conditions, combined with the protagonists' incompatible desires and shortcomings (Ames's passivity and confusion, Reese's impetuosity and self-loathing, Katrina's rigidity) prove to be an untenable combination. And the clash is as much between worldviews or forms of life as it is between the individuals. When it becomes clear these are incommensurable, the possibility of a happy ending for the three of them quickly recedes. Yet, even though things don't work out—Katrina has an abortion—the book does not despair of the very idea of such happiness. On the contrary: by permitting her erring, eminently human characters to want and dream of family, even in its existing bourgeois forms, Peters has produced an effective, critical intervention into the sort of radical discourse that posits the family as hopelessly irredeemable. Ambivalence, Peters shows, isn't exhausted by a willingness to be honest about disappointment, anger, and sadness; it means a capacity to accept that one and the same experience might elicit genuinely contradictory emotions, genuine yearning as well as aversion or fear.

STARTING WITH FREUD, early psychoanalysts conceived of "ambivalence," the state of having both positive and negative feelings toward the same object, as a constituent of pathologies such as obsessional neuroses and melancholy. The son who both reveres and abhors his father, or the mourning lover crushed at one and the same time by the weight of his love and grief—such figures demonstrate how the inability to resolve emotional conflict can produce its own unique kind of suffering. Melanie Klein radicalized Freud's idea: in her psychoanalytic narrative of the child's development, ambivalence mattered not just as the ground of a pathological failure to clarify one's emotional attitudes toward an object but as a necessary step in the maturation of every human being. It was an accomplishment, and always a tentative, temporary one at that—an aspirational goal more than an actual destination.

In the child's very first relationship, in most cases their relationship to their mother, they are confronted with the alarming fact that the sources of their pain and pleasure, their comfort and distress, are all one and the same. The infant copes with this intolerable inconsistency, Klein conjectured, by unconsciously splitting the one object into two: Klein's infamous "good" and "bad" breasts—two objects that the child can love and hate separately, without any reservation or guilt. But growing up requires the subject to try to synthesize these opposed qualities into one whole object. This isn't easy. It is so hard, in fact, that it lurches children into what Klein calls "the depressive position," a state in which the subject must learn to accept and tolerate the complexity of the objects of their desires and the mixed feelings this complexity evokes.[29] To learn to mitigate ambivalence requires the acquisition of a host of basic psychological capacities, chief among them the ability to recognize other subjects as thinking, desiring beings like oneself, and to accept the ways in which others' choices might adversely affect one without intending to do so. But ambivalence can never be eradicated in its entirety. Psychic health involves the capacity to tolerate imperfection and compromise—in our loved ones, in our goals and aspirations, and in ourselves. Extrapolating, we may say that the highest form of happiness we may wish for involves not unqualified bliss but the ability to enjoy satisfaction in the face of inevitable, constitutive ambivalence.

In light of this, it is not obvious that the name of the genre— "motherhood *ambivalence*"—is entirely apt. In the first place, the impressions and emotional states expressed in these novels are often more plainly negative than genuinely ambivalent. This is inscribed in the basic formal features of the books. For one thing, their narrow focus on the decision process, and then pregnancy and its immediate aftermath, abstracts from "motherhood" its bulk share: we hear almost nothing of the many possible satisfactions—as well, of course, of the many misfortunes—to be had while caring for toddlers, raising maturing adolescents, or leading lives alongside adult children. But while pregnancy and nurturing newborns and infants can occasion some of the most emotionally intense, physically demanding, and psychologically formative experiences for both children and parents—it is nevertheless the case that those early days are numbered. That experience is intense, but it does not last forever.

How skewed a perspective on motherhood can be when it restricts itself to the harrowing first months with one's first child becomes apparent when speaking to older mothers about their experience of raising children. Sharon, a seventy-two-year-old retired diplomat and mother of two grown sons, told us that she decided to have children in her early thirties when she "realized that my parents really enjoyed having adult children to be interested in, to see life through younger eyes." She wanted adult children "to connect with as I aged" and confessed to encouraging her own sons to have children "so that they, too, will have adult children to connect with when they are old." Reflecting on the experience as a whole, Sharon said that she "*loved* having children, at *every stage* of their lives." The point is not simply that things eventually get better—which, though fortunate, would not necessarily redeem the challenges of the beginning. The point is that the experience of motherhood is an evolving process, and it is impossible to evaluate any one part of it out of the context of the whole.

But in the motherhood ambivalence novels, the early days of motherhood are not something one moves through; they are a sinkhole. The books usually end before we can find out whether our protagonists will manage to climb out. And while "ambivalence" connotes a vacillation between options, the motherhood ambivalence narrators do not ultimately have much to say that is genuinely compelling *for* the decision of having children. This is true even of those who decide to have them. In *Motherhood,* the novel ostensibly presents Heti's narrator as trying to reach a decision about whether or not to become a mother, yet it is hard to shake the sense that the conclusion she finally arrives at is foregone. She never really seems all that tempted by motherhood. Her decision is not easy, but this has relatively little to do with the fear of losing out on something truly valuable. The problem for Heti's narrator is that not having children will mark an unmistakable departure from mainstream ways of life: "There is a kind of sadness in not wanting the things that give so many other people their life's meaning," she writes. "There can be sadness at not living out a more universal story—the supposed life cycle."[30] In Cusk's *A Life's Work,* the question of motherhood fascinates and repels her in equal part. "If at any point in my life I had been able to find out what the future held," she confesses in the opening lines of the memoir, "I would always have wanted to know whether or not I would have children. More than love, more than work, more than length of life or quantity of happiness, this was the question whose mystery I found most compelling."[31] But Cusk says nothing about why she chose as she did, even though she did so twice, and pregnancy and the early months of motherhood are characterized, for her, primarily by their life-destroying potential. Seven times Cusk uses the figure of an unexploded bomb as a metaphor for her or other people's babies. (A midwife's bag portends horror "like a bomb"; Cusk lays out bottles and formula on the counter "like someone preparing to assemble a bomb"; new life arrives "like a letter-bomb";

the "object of the baby" functions "like an unexploded bomb in a Hitchcock film"; a short-lived nanny holds her baby "as one might hold a small bomb"; as the baby grows and the risk of injury increases, their family life "was like a drama in which a bomb is being disabled against the clock"; a friend seems to expect her son to "go off like a bomb in a public place."[32]) When babies do not threaten to blow up, they rob you of your freedom. Only six months after giving birth, Cusk gets pregnant once again: "I greeted my old cell with the cheerless acceptance of a convict intercepted at large."[33] In one of her only attempts to speak in favor of the experience, Cusk muses about the way in which the shackles of motherhood can have their own ennobling effects: "The harness of motherhood chafes my skin, and yet occasionally I find a predictable integrity in it too, a freedom of a different sort: from complexity and choice and from the realms of unscripted time upon which I used to write my days, bearing the burden of their authorship. The state of motherhood speaks to my native fear of achievement. It is a demotion, a displacement, an opportunity to give up."[34] This isn't much of a positive endorsement: motherhood permits Cusk to succumb to her own fear of ambition; it is an "opportunity to give up."

On its face, Galchen's memoir *Little Labors* seems to present a more positive portrait of motherhood. In her telling, motherhood is full of wonders. Having a child doesn't just rob Galchen of a self, it is also a poetic portal to a new, numinous experience. The narrator is so awestruck and overwhelmed by the arrival of her child that she calls her not by her name but instead refers to her as various kinds of exotic animals. "In late August a baby was born, or, as it seemed to me, a puma moved into my apartment, a near-mute force, and then I noticed it was December,"[35] the memoir begins. The baby later shapeshifts into a cat, a sloth, and a chimpanzee. Not quite human, nor something that will one day become human—the baby remains alien to her and an object of heedful fascination. Being around the baby, Galchen says, is like taking a drug: "One day I decide that she is an opiate: she suffuses me with a profound sense of well-being, a sense not attached to any accomplishment or attribute." But the full effects of the drug recall Cusk's own biting endorsement: "that sense of well-being is so intoxicating that I find myself willing to let my life fall apart completely in continued pursuit of this feeling."[36]

Galchen's attempt to reveal the possible attractions of being a mother depends, as it does for many of the ambivalence-literature writers, on sublimation, on recognizing it as something that transcends ordinary experience as well as our humanity, our consciousness, and our willpower. When Galchen tries to use more ordinary terms to capture how motherhood makes her feel, her metaphors, tender as they are, convey a certain emptiness. "My life with the very young human resembles those romantic comedies in which two people who don't speak the same language still somehow fall in love," she writes, on one of the few occasions she refers to her daughter as a human being.[37] But even here, in calling the girl "the very young human," Galchen places the child in the orbit of humanity with the remoteness of an alien reporting on life on earth. Her estrangement is preserved, just by other means. To cross the divide, Galchen employs the image of falling in love across a language barrier. It is an effective figure, one that communicates the primary mutual attraction of two radically different individuals. But comparing falling in love with your child to the plot of a romantic comedy—something you'd watch on an airplane, or on the sofa with a glass of merlot—suggests that the gratification one derives from seeing this relationship unfold is something of a guilty pleasure. It also implies that it might be a fantasy: a preordained, or scripted, encounter defined by a set of genre conventions, its own distinctive tropes and refrains. In turn, this hints at the worry that the satisfactions it confers aren't fully authentic or believable. On most days, Galchen is "wiped out"; on the best ones, she is dazed.[38] Never quite content with the experience in its ordinary manifestations, she is always searching for new language to describe what has happened to her.

Again, Peters's *Detransition, Baby* provides an instructive contrast. By getting out of her characters' heads and putting their ideas and feelings about motherhood into dialogue with one another, Peters manages to avoid both Cusk's fatalism and Galchen's romanticization. In a pivotal scene midway through the novel, a pregnant Katrina auditions Reese for a seat at their family table. Reese has spent most of her life and certainly all of her transition contemplating the requirements of womanhood and femininity. Preoccupied by the desire not just "to pass" but to be a woman in the deepest possible sense, Reese identifies pregnancy and biological motherhood as the sole components of womanhood that remain closed off to her. All the while, mother*ing* comes naturally: she takes a maternal role with everyone in her life—other trans women, the children she babysits, the men she dates. Katrina, on the other hand, is a cis woman who is far more hesitant about the prospect of motherhood, especially in the context of a nonnormative family arrangement. She interrogates Reese about why she wants to be a mother. Reese pointedly observes that if she were not trans, she would not be forced to answer this question. Most people, Reese says, recognize an intrinsic connection between being a woman and desiring to be a mother: "Until the day that I am a mother, I'm going to have to prove that I deserve to be one. That it's not unnatural or twisted that I want a child's love."[39] Katrina pushes back that motherhood is not so simple for straight cis women either. Besides, Katrina is not interested only in why Reese wants to be a mother as a trans woman: "Tell me why you, specifically, you, Reese, want to have a baby," she says again.[40] The narration lets us into Reese's whirring associations as she tries to assemble a proper response:

> There are so many reasons, but most of them are so simple, so embodied, that they feel inadequate to the question. She likes to hold children. To smell a baby's hair. To soothe a crying infant and feel his little frame let go of rigid fear to settle in her arms, the weight go slack and calm so that for a moment she both gives and receives a rare peace. To rock a baby and communicate with your body: *You're safe.* When she worked at the daycare she liked the thoughtless way a child would reach to take her hand. She liked watching kids puzzle out something new, their wonder, their awe and excitement, which was, when she let it be, contagious. She liked their sudden acts of altruism. She recalled this one kid at the daycare, maybe four years old, who built a tower out of blocks then tugged on her sleeve with the offer, "Do you want to kick it down?" He understood that the knockdown was the best part of building and he wanted to give it to her. Who else could give you something so pure but a child?[41]

Of all the motherhood-ambivalence narratives discussed so far, no other contains a passage that tries to describe the desire to be a mother in such straightforward terms. When Reese states these feelings aloud, Katrina is disarmed and her skepticism begins to soften.

FOR FANS OF authors like Cusk and Galchen, the absence of praise of motherhood in its most mundane aspects can hardly

qualify as a fault. To complain that books like these do not sufficiently address motherhood's familiar attractions would seem
to misconstrue their central virtues: the sincere revelation of
those aspects of the experience of motherhood that have been
ignored and gone unvoiced. Family and motherhood have
been dogmatically celebrated for long enough; a correction is
overdue. And if the strain and pain of motherhood were what
was most salient to their authors in those early months, who
would want to deny them the right to say so?

But the point is not that writers like Cusk and Galchen ought
to have written differently; it is only that one could. In her novels and letters, Elena Ferrante, author of the celebrated Neapolitan novels, is unsparing in her evaluations of the pain caused
by family and the unique trials involved in motherhood. At the
same time, she is able to acknowledge something more: the experience of motherhood is not only vexing or otherworldly but
can afford physical, emotional, and spiritual satisfaction for the
most intelligent, creative, and ambitious of women, on its own
terms. Indeed, it is in the ordinariness and familiarity of motherhood that Ferrante discovers depth.

In a short personal essay for *The Guardian,* Ferrante named a
wide array of conflicting emotions that motherhood can evoke,
a range of feelings that forms the backbone of much of her literary output:

> The first time I got pregnant, it was difficult to accept. Preg-
> nancy was an anxious mental struggle. I felt it as the break-
> down of an equilibrium already precarious in itself, as a
> revelation of the animal nature behind the fragile mask of the
> human. For nine months I was on a seesaw of joy and hor-
> ror. The birth was terrible, it was wonderful. Taking care of a
> newborn, by myself, without help, without money, exhausted

me; I hardly slept. I wanted to write and there was never time.
Or if there was some, I would concentrate for a few minutes
and then fall asleep fretfully. Until slowly everything began to
seem to me marvellous. Today I think that nothing is comparable to the joy, the pleasure, of bringing another living creature into the world.[42]

Ferrante does not gloss over the difficulty of pregnancy or early
motherhood. The challenge of motherhood consisted for her—as
for writers like Cusk and Galchen—not only in the personal
sacrifices it demanded but in how it forced her to confront "the
animal nature behind the fragile mask of the human": her mor-
tality, materiality, the limits of her autonomy. But nor is she embarrassed to describe "the joy, the pleasure" of it. These joys and
pleasures are not otherworldly but are of *this world, this life*. Here
Ferrante captures the sense of motherhood not as the highest
form or final end of a woman's existence but as one elemental
possibility for her time on earth—neither obligatory nor com-
mensurate with others. Though she was not always so certain she
wanted to be a mother, she says, now she can see that "the most
extraordinary thing in my life was to conceive and give birth."[43]
And this is not just because motherhood revealed to her a special
capacity to nurture or gave her access to a previously unknown
delight in children. The joys and pleasure of motherhood are not
concentrated strictly in her subjective experiences. They derive,
instead, from the act of "bringing another living creature into the
world"—a fact that involves another human being coming into
existence, and as such exceeds all the acts and experiences of the
mother, however rewarding or degrading. Ferrante is not simply
comparing child-rearing to other possible pursuits and accomplishments. She is reminding us that what is at stake in the decision to have children is not just a series of personal experiences to

be enjoyed and suffered but the possibility of human life, which is infinitely concrete but never reducible to its significance for anyone else.

In Ferrante's fiction, the presence of children is never impersonal: the children in her novels do not merely make generic demands on their mothers' bodies and time. From the earliest age they confront their mothers with distinct personalities and individualized needs. They do not exist solely for their mothers, they are not only inscrutable hindrances or magical presences; they are already on their way to becoming fully realized human beings, with whom one finds oneself bound in the most intimate relationship possible. The love of a child for her mother is "the single great tremendous original love, the matrix of all loves, which cannot be abolished," Ferrante says in her letter collection *Frantumaglia*. To fear and recoil from such love is an appropriate response, not just to the challenges it presents but to its intensity. "Love," she asserts, "should be troubling."[44]

Ferrante captures the simultaneous push and pull of motherhood nowhere as dramatically as she does in *The Lost Daughter*. In the novel, Leda Caruso, an English literature professor, faces the figurative loss of her daughters, both in their early twenties. Nearing full adulthood, they have both left Italy to join their father who has been living in Canada. This separation is not the first time she has faced losing them. When they were four and six, Leda committed the ultimate act of maternal betrayal and walked out on the family, returning only three years later. Now middle-aged, Leda takes a vacation in southern Italy and becomes fascinated with a fellow beachgoer, Nina, the young Neapolitan mother of a child of almost three named Elena. A series of disappearances—of the girl and then her doll—provokes Leda to interject herself into Nina's life. In the first instance, Leda retrieves the wandering child. In the second, she finds the child's lost doll, but keeps it to herself. For the rest of her stay in the resort town, Leda watches as the loss torments the child, who, inconsolable, clings violently to an increasingly exasperated Nina. Leda's abduction of the doll is inexplicable, even to herself. When she finally returns the doll to Nina, the young mother, stupefied, asks her, "Why?" Leda says she doesn't know. Leda's eventual response to Nina's demands for an explanation seems almost like a non sequitur: "I'm an unnatural mother."[45]

The strange plot of the doll's abduction is punctuated by descriptions of Leda's past as a young mother to two small girls. An exhausted Leda, then a graduate student and budding literary translator, is besieged by the children's demands, their violent outbursts (at one point, significantly, they destroy her favorite childhood doll). Her relationship with her husband—too busy with work to help—is strained; their sex is bad. Everything changes when a prominent English-literature scholar praises Leda's work publicly at an academic conference, giving her a first seductive taste of intellectual validation and professional success. An affair ensues. But this is not enough. Not long after, Leda leaves.

Nina is stunned when she learns of the betrayal. Up to this point, Nina has lavished Leda with admiration, and the urbane older woman has encouraged the younger, simpler Nina to turn to her for advice and support. After Leda tells Nina that she left her children behind, Nina asks Leda the very questions that her own daughters could never pose: Why did you leave? Why did you return? In response to Nina's prodding, Leda is finally able to speak truthfully of her past, giving expression to an irresolvable ambivalence:

"Why did you leave your daughters?"
I thought, searching for an answer that might help her.

"I loved them too much and it seemed to me that love for them would keep me from becoming myself."

I realized that she was no longer laughing continuously, now she was paying attention to my every word.

"You didn't see them for three years."

I nodded yes.

"And how did you feel without them?"

"Good. It was as if my whole self had crumbled, and the pieces were falling freely in all directions with a sense of contentment."

"You didn't feel sad?"

"No, I was too taken up by my own life. But I had a weight right here, as if I had a stomachache. And my heart skipped a beat whenever I heard a child call Mama."[46]

This exchange—at once cathartic and confrontational—marks the emotional climax of the novel and inaugurates its final movement. Here Ferrante captures genuine maternal ambivalence: how the sacrifices and frustrations of motherhood are coeval with its pull and rewards. Struggling with her own child, Nina wants Leda to confirm that leaving the children was a mistake, that Leda suffered having left them behind, that her maternal affection was so great that she couldn't keep away, that the world had nothing better to offer her. But the reality is more complicated. The possibility of escape enthralls Nina, but Leda refuses to endorse it. Nina is confused: "You felt bad, then, not good." She wants to pin Leda down, but Leda won't let her: "I was like someone who is taking possession of her own life, and feels a host of things at the same time, among them an unbearable absence."[47] No part could be summarily explained away, and a certain necessity attends to the complex movement as a whole: leaving, suffering, returning. The young Nina is troubled:

She looked at me with hostility.

"If you felt good why did you go back?"

I chose my words carefully.

"Because I realized that I wasn't capable of creating anything of my own that could truly equal them."

She had a sudden contented smile.

"So you returned for love of your daughters."

"No, I returned for the same reason I left: for love of myself."

She again took offense.

"What do you mean?"

"That I felt more useless and desperate without them than with them."[48]

Leda's answer that she "wasn't capable of creating anything" of her own that could equal the children echoes an earlier, pivotal moment from her encounter with two traveling hitchhikers who had abruptly left their jobs and families to be together. Before leaving, the woman asks Leda for something of hers to read. "Of mine," Leda reflects, "I savored the formulation—*something of mine*."[49] In telling Nina that she realized she could not create anything of her own that could equal the daughters, Leda signals that what made it possible for her to return was the discovery that her daughters, too, were her creation, perhaps the best creation she was capable of. Leda is finally able to return home not because her love for her children wins out in a battle with her selfishness or because she is disappointed by what the world had to offer her. Leaving them does not free her from feelings of uselessness and desperation; it augments them. She returns when she is able to incorporate her love for her daughters as an inalienable part of her own identity, alongside the others; when loving them becomes not what would keep her from "becoming herself" but a

necessary condition of coming into her own. (And this is a statement that remains true for Leda even though the relationship
she returns to, a difficult one to begin with, is obviously complicated and strained by the act of abandonment.)

*The Lost Daughter* hinges on the mirroring of two inexplicable acts: the original abandonment and the confiscation of the
doll. In the first place, a haunted Leda projects her own guilt
and self-hate on the restless and discontented young mother.
In taking the doll, Leda turns the screws on the relationship of
young mother and toddler, which begins to resemble the relationship Leda felt she had with her own daughters. Withholding
the doll from Nina, from this perspective, is a form of symbolic
self-punishment: Leda makes the young mother suffer for her
disaffection and inattentiveness, for her self-absorption and im-
patience, as she, Leda, deserves to suffer for her own. But the
story cannot find meaningful resolution here. By using Nina in
this way, Leda repeats her original transgression: once more, she
is making a young child endure a painful loss and in turn causes
a young woman—who is all the while treating her as a mother
figure—to suffer. A merely symbolic self-punishment turns out
to be just another act of selfishness. On some level, Leda seems
to know this: throughout the story she keeps neglecting to prop-
erly hide the doll, risking its discovery. The return of the doll is,
we can now see, a staging of what Leda needs most, namely, to
encounter her daughters' crushing disappointment, to face their
hurt and their rage.

The lost daughter must have her revenge. In the last pages
of the novel, taking hold of the restored doll, Nina makes a
move to leave. But Leda tries to reconcile with her—offering
her apartment up, blurting she's sorry. It is at this point that
Nina erupts into a violent rage, stabbing Leda in her side with a
hat pin. The stabbing leaves only a drop of blood on Leda's skin;

seemingly ignoring it, Leda packs her things for the road—it is time for her to go. At that moment, her daughters call her. Their words echo the very same demands they might have voiced when they were abandoned in their early childhood, and have barely managed to express since:

> "Mama, what are you doing, why haven't you called? Won't you at least let us know if you're alive or dead?"
> Deeply moved, I murmured:
> "I'm dead, but I'm fine."[50]

Leda is "deeply moved" because the questions the daughters ask mark just how far they have come since their days of abandonment. Now, they can ask her why she hasn't called, whether she is okay—now that they know not to fear the answer. Leda's response, and the final line of the novel, recalls her first hasty attempt at explaining why she left: "Sometimes you have to escape in order not to die."[51] Submitting herself to Nina's punishment, Leda does not try to run, and she does not try to save herself. Herein lies the key to Leda's decision to return: sometimes you do not have to escape in order to live, after all. Sometimes, it is alright to die.

It would be easy for a reader to assume that the story ends here, with Leda wounded, maybe fatally. But in fact, in a literal sense, it's where it begins. The very first scene of the novel introduces Leda while she is on the road, starting to feel the burning in her side again, deciding to persevere, losing her grip on the steering wheel. She imagines a calm sea, but she's afraid to enter it: there's a red flag, her mother is shouting warnings. When she wakes in the hospital, Leda is visited by friends, her daughters, her ex-husband. The violence Leda suffers at the hand of the young Nina, whom she had refused to deliver from misery, doesn't just precipitate a family reunion, it's also the occasion for the reflection that composes the story, a reflection on the origin of the mysterious wound in her left side: "a gesture of mine that made no sense, and which, precisely because it was senseless, I immediately decided not to speak of to anyone."[52] The senseless gesture is at once the abduction of the doll and the abandonment of the children. When Leda later tells Nina, who is demanding an account of the doll's disappearance, that she's "an unnatural mother," she is explaining both.

The novel demonstrates a point that lies at the very heart of Ferrante's entire oeuvre: the challenges of motherhood are no doubt exacerbated by adverse social conditions—economic hardship, sexism—but the deepest ambivalence that accompanies the experience of motherhood can only be eased, never eliminated. It is no more possible to escape it than it is to escape the mother-child relationship itself. To give life to someone else is always to give away something of your own and to saddle yourself with a love—yours, theirs—that can be almost unbearable. A child's life comes at the cost of yours. But Ferrante's novels, which cover decades and span multiple generations, remind the reader that no matter how hard we might try, life cannot be hoarded. Every life is a life that will be lost. We grow up, we grow old, we lose our youth and strength, and eventually we lose the sources of creativity and inspiration that make it possible for us to create something new of our own. This is true whether or not we have children. If we have them, along the way, we can at least pass on something of what we lose to someone else. This possibility—of sharing our life with those who will outlive us—may be one good reason not to try to escape it after all.

Ferrante's story, like Peters's, presents a model of maternal ambivalence that breaks out of the claustrophobia of one singular consciousness. *The Lost Daughter* shows—not via a monologue but through the confrontation between two women, two mothers—that the truth of motherhood, the core of ambivalence, can be aired and that, by facing it squarely, the cycle of suffering can be broken. Dealing with one's fears and inevitable failures as a parent is not something that can be accomplished strictly from within the confines of one's mind. It is an interpersonal achievement.

In Ferrante, the notion that children are a threat to a woman's independence, possibly even her life, is central. This anxiety dominates the outlook of Leda in her younger days, and it is one that Nina feels pulled by as well. But it is notable that, for Ferrante, what counts as accomplishment is not just developing this perspective but moving through it, surviving it. During the critical exchange between the two protagonists, Nina conjectures that Leda must have been disappointed by whatever she was looking for outside the family home. Leda resists this interpretation: "Nina," Leda says, "what I was looking for was a confused tangle of desires and great arrogance. If I had been unlucky it would have taken me my whole life to realize it. But I was lucky and it took only three years. Three years and thirty-six days."[53]

*The Lost Daughter,* then, isn't more successful as a depiction of motherhood because it paints a sunnier picture than the motherhood-ambivalence narratives we've discussed so far. In many ways, its portrait of ambivalence is darker and more tragic: the demands children make on one's time and creative capacities are dwarfed by the threat that the children—suffering, loving, hating—pose to the very self-understanding of their mother. To face one's child's shortcomings is to risk self-loathing, to recognize her virtues is to confront the fact of one's own beauty, talents, and power being sapped away. But Ferrante also has the courage to affirm the possibility of choosing motherhood, for all its sacrifices, without having to redeem it by the power of metaphors, and without suggesting that the women who are capable of such choices are little more than innocents.

Concluding a favorable review of a slew of books dedicated to the exposition of the historical and contemporary challenges of motherhood in 2014, the literary critic Jacqueline Rose wrote:

> As I was reading the outpourings of all these recent books on motherhood, it occurred to me that we need a version of this story for mothers, a version in which, without any need to deny everything else talked about here, the acute pleasure of being a mother would be neither a guilty secret, nor something enviously co-opted by bullies—"You *will* be happy!"—but instead would be allowed to get on quietly with its work of making the experience of motherhood more than worth it.[54]

It's hard to think of a better description of Ferrante's ambition in depicting a mother walking the path of abandonment and return. When Nina asks Leda why she went back to her daughters, Leda responds not with a well-reasoned defense but with a modest, quiet memory: "One morning I discovered that the only thing I really wanted to do was peel fruit, making a snake, in front of my daughters, and then I began to cry."[55]

THE HALLMARKS OF motherhood ambivalence literature attest to a unique contemporary predicament. As we've seen, the feminist dialectic of motherhood ended in an apprehensive stalemate: regarding the decision to have children, the only thing that could be meaningfully agreed upon was the inviolable right of each woman to choose her own romantic, social, and procreative destiny. Yet placing so much weight on individual autonomy—important as it is—has had some unintentional drawbacks. For one, it has too often made women feel that navigating this choice is something they must do alone; deciding whether or not to have children is a trial with life-or-death stakes, but one they must endure in isolation. Their friends, family members, dates, and partners leave them, for the most part, to their own devices and deliberations, waiting for them to bring up the subject and declare their position. At the same time, for many women it can feel dangerous to even acknowledge the pain and difficulty that attends the choice to become (or forgo becoming) a mother. Believing the choice comes easily to everyone else and that therefore they, too, ought to "just know," they perceive their struggle to make up their mind as abnormal. Something must be wrong with them to be so confused.

Perhaps the greatest combined achievement of the recent literary avatars of motherhood ambivalence is their ability to throw into sharp relief the experience of confronting the magnitude of this decision in some combination of solitude and bewilderment. Heti finds herself shouldering the burden of the choice more or less on her own; in Cusk's and Galchen's memoirs, mothering an infant takes the form of a lonely, introspective journey through the earliest days of their first child's life. But while they display, often arrestingly, the ways in which one can get stuck in indecision, in anxiety, in loneliness, such novels do not offer solutions. In giving a window into the interior life of ambivalence, they can offer little by way of guidance to those who turn to them for help. Though this has sometimes galled readers and reviewers, it is hardly a literary failure. It has never been the task of novels, or even memoirs, to help other people make choices by recommending one course of action over another. The fault, such as it is, lies no more with the books than with the readers who turn to them for self-help: we cannot demand of literature what it cannot give us.

In ways both subtle and overt, however, these books create and elevate a very particular vision of what it might mean for a woman to live her life without illusions. The marks of the intellectual and artistic soul are the refusal to be dependent on others' estimation, isolation in introspection, and robust suspicion of children as potentially grave threats to one's identity. Above all, the books represent thinking not as an end-oriented process but as a form of endless recursive activity.

Motherhood ambivalence is no longer just an intellectual or literary concern—and it isn't just a feminist issue, either. Many people, regardless of gender, respond to the prospect of family with uncertainty, hesitancy, and incomprehension. The motherhood ambivalence novelists are prescient insofar as the broader mood about parenting today is one of doubt. But this doubt does not call merely for validation—people do not just want to know it is okay to feel the way they do; some also wish to feel differently. This task requires stepping outside the frame of our own interiority: giving up on the hope of being able to settle the question of how we should lead our lives by tracking down our elusive internal desires. If we are to try to answer the question "Is having children good for me, personally?" we must learn to ask, "Is having children good as such?"

CHAPTER 4

# To Be Or . . . ?

"One cannot bring children into a world like this. One cannot perpetuate suffering," thinks Septimus Smith, the shell-shocked World War I veteran in Virginia Woolf's modernist classic *Mrs. Dalloway*. His wife of five years badly wants children, but the very idea of adding to the sum of humanity produces in him reflexive disgust. His resistance to her pleas is not just altruistic: Septimus sees all too clearly that the torments human beings endure are self-inflicted. Humans, he observes, are by nature selfish, opportunistic, and cruel. One ought not "increase the breed of these lustful animals, who have no lasting emotions, but only whims and vanities, eddying them now this way, now that." Having looked into the abyss that gapes beyond the boundaries of civilized life, he concludes, "Human beings have neither kindness, nor faith, nor charity beyond what serves to increase the pleasure of the moment."[1] Septimus refuses to have children, and by the end of the novel takes his own life.

Today, nearly a century after *Mrs. Dalloway*'s publication, a strikingly similar image of humankind haunts the horizon of parenthood. In Septimus's time, it was the Great War that forced a reckoning with the possible inevitability of human suffering

and evil. Cursing humankind, Septimus invokes the unprecedented bloodletting he witnessed: "They hunt in packs. Their
packs scour the desert and vanish screaming into the wilderness. They desert the fallen."[2] In our time, the threat appears under different guises—none so familiar to us, or so unsettling, as
man-made climate change. Still, it is not hard to recognize our
own reflection in Woolf's description of ravenous animals that
plunder and appropriate with no higher principle than their own
acquisitive desire. And it is not hard to see why someone might
reach the conclusion that it would be better for such a life form
to cease to exist.

The damage caused by humankind is no longer possible to
deny. "It is, I promise, worse than you think," the climate reporter
David Wallace-Wells warned in his 2017 essay for *New York* magazine, "The Uninhabitable Earth," subsequently expanded into a
best-selling book of the same title. "If your anxiety about global
warming is dominated by fears of sea-level rise," he wrote, "you
are barely scratching the surface of what terrors are possible,
even within the lifetime of a teenager today."[3] He proceeded to
list a cascade of biblical horrors that would be visited upon us
in the coming centuries—many as soon as this decade—if we
were to continue on our current fossil-fuel-burning trajectory.
Wallace-Wells's conjectures have since come under criticism
from climate scientists for being misleading as well as unpro-
ductively alarmist.[4] But while actual apocalypse might not be
in the cards, experts nevertheless agree that massive environmental degradation is already inevitable.[5] Writing in April 2023
for *Harper's,* Kyle Paoletta offered a corrective to the dystopian
doomerism of the late 2010s:

> It is, I promise, not quite as bad as you once imagined, but it
> is worse than you've lately been led to believe. The seas will

rise, the summers will get hotter. There will be more red-sky days, more storms, more jungles turned into savannas and savannas turned into deserts. Global emissions may peak in a few years, but the subsequent decline will probably be too gradual to limit warming to even 2.5 degrees Celsius—the level that the United Nations projects the world's net-zero pledges currently put it on track to reach. None of that constitutes an apocalypse, but it does suggest a world destabilized by hundreds of millions of people going hungry and being forced to flee their homes.[6]

More recent calls for optimism, Paoletta warned, were hardly more justified than the apocalypse mongering. For all the excitement about the rise in climate-change awareness and activism, especially among the young, we remain far from reaching the baseline of public interest and political engagement necessary to undergird the immense global effort required to avert the trend.[7] Realistically, even if we are likely to avoid the worst-case scenarios, the task now is to mitigate the harm done to our environment and fellow human beings, not prevent it. The end of times might not be around the corner, but what awaits us—slow, sluggish decline—offers little to look forward to, let alone celebrate. At least Armageddon would have been an event.

Can we justify subjecting unsuspecting others to such a fate? If human life is what got us into this trouble to begin with, do we really need more of it? Among the philosophers who, over the millennia, have tried to grasp what it is that makes us who we are, perhaps no one has bestowed a more double-edged verdict than Hegel. In his *Philosophy of Right*, an investigation of human freedom, Hegel remarked that "the animal cannot mutilate or destroy itself, but the human being can."[8] Hegel's appraisal is ambiguous: to say that we can bring about our own deaths implies that we are never determined solely by our biology. We are not simply programmed to do only that which will ensure our survival, and so, even under a threat to our well-being, indeed to our very lives, it remains in our power to refuse wrongdoing and do the right thing. But to say that human beings can mutilate and destroy themselves also means that we can sabotage our own aims and self-destruct without a higher purpose, perhaps even just out of spite. Ours is a moment that has made the truth of Hegel's observation all the more stark, and chilling.

"IF I WAS ever going to actually start a family," the climate activist and writer Daniel Sherrell writes early in his memoir *Warmth: Coming of Age at the End of Our World,* "then I'd owe you an honest account of why."[9] The book—a sustained meditation on the meaning of having children during the ongoing climate crisis—is addressed to a child not yet conceived, a child he wants one day but to whom he feels he owes an explanation now. For Sherrell, explaining how he could contemplate bringing a person into a rapidly degrading world requires telling the story of how he has come to terms with "the Problem," as he calls it: how he tried "to tread the liminal ground between denial and resignation, not always buoyed by hope so much as the terror of what giving up would force us to admit to ourselves."[10] To this effect, he recounts in detail his path to becoming an environmental activist, culminating in the arduous and uncertain—but ultimately successful—campaign to pass the 2019 Climate Act in the state of New York. Sherrell's message to his reader is, strictly speaking, political. If we wish to address climate change, he writes, we must revolutionize the way we extract, use, and exchange energy. This will require not so much persuading people to make better individual choices—whether by practicing so-called ethical consumerism or refraining from having children to reduce their carbon footprint—but amassing the political power necessary to pass far-reaching legislation.

But over the course of the book another line of thought breaks through. Sherrell traces the roots of climate change not just to a particular mode of production or political system but all the way back to human nature itself. While reflecting on the petty political squabbles that threatened to kill the bill he labored to get passed, Sherrell laments the "weight of human frailty" that always stands in the face of any remedial change. The inescapable fact of human weakness, he writes, "seemed to point at some compounded inevitability, something fundamental about our nature that not only predicted but *necessitated* the Problem. As if the Problem was just a part of who we were, an individual property emergent only at the scale of civilization." It is something deep in our core, our very humanity, Sherrell suggests, that is to blame. From this perspective, climate change isn't just a bad outcome. The phenomenon, he speculates, "doesn't simply adhere to the cascading rules of physics, but is additionally propelled by something deliberate and retributive, like a biblical plague." Biblical plagues served to warn and punish; they were deserved. Reflecting on the "incalculable damage" caused and predicted to be caused by climate change, Sherrell writes, "Sometimes . . . I feel so guilty in my humanity that I'm tempted to recuse myself entirely."[11] Perhaps climate change is so hard to solve because the Problem is not just a problem; it is also a solution.

Sherrell is giving voice to a set of sentiments that have become increasingly conspicuous in our culture. The speculation about *why* people are not having children today, as we've seen, is remarkably pluralistic. Declining birth rates are attributed to everything from lower sperm counts to historical trends like rising levels of secularism, wealth, education, and female advancement.[12] But when the question is *whether* to have children, the dilemma is most frequently couched in terms of the threat of climate change. In all arenas of public discourse, from the mainstream to the niche and rarefied, people are asking whether the proper response to the climate crisis might involve not just changing the way we live, individually or collectively, but reconsidering our attitude toward human life and the legitimacy of its future wholesale.

The signs are everywhere, from art-house films like Paul Schrader's *First Reformed*—in which a despairing climate activist commits suicide, abandoning his pregnant wife—to TV documentaries on *The Climate Baby Dilemma* and viral trend pieces and op-eds with titles like "We Need to Talk About the Ethics of Having Children in a Warming World," "Want to Fight Climate Change? Have Fewer Children," and "Your Kids Are Not Doomed."[13] In the winter of 2019, a year after she took office, Alexandria Ocasio-Cortez caused a stir by announcing to her 2.5 million Instagram followers: "There's scientific consensus that the lives of children are going to be very difficult. And it does lead young people to have a legitimate question: Is it okay to still have children?"[14] Now pop culture celebrities routinely express concern in puff pieces and tabloids about the ethical consequences of reproduction. "We're getting handed a piece-of-shit planet, and I refuse to hand that down to my child," the pop star Miley Cyrus told *Elle* in 2019. "Until I feel like my kid would live on an earth with fish in the water, I'm not bringing in another person to deal with that."[15] Even Prince Harry vowed, in an exchange with the legendary primatologist and conservationist Jane Goodall in British *Vogue,* that he would cap his family at "two, maximum!"[16] And in a 2021 interview with Howard Stern, the comedian and director Seth Rogen defended his choice to remain childless in the following terms: "Who looks at the planet right now and thinks 'You know what we need? More fucking people.'"[17]

Worries like these are becoming ever more common. In the largest global study of its kind about the effects of climate anxiety on young people today, published in *The Lancet* in 2021, researchers asked ten thousand people aged sixteen to twenty-five from ten different countries about the effects of climate change on their emotional lives. Among those surveyed, 75 percent said that the "future is frightening," and 56 percent agreed that "humanity is doomed." As for how these concerns affected the respondents' attitudes toward parenthood, 39 percent identified with the statement that climate change had made them "hesitant" to have children.[18]

Such flash surveys of the public mood, however, tell us little about how people are navigating this uncertainty in their own private lives. How do environmental worries find expression in the practical deliberations of ordinary people? Just how influential is the specter of climate catastrophe on their family planning? Here the findings are less conclusive. Out of a demographically representative sample of 3,866 eighteen- to forty-nine-year-old Americans surveyed by the Pew Research Center in 2021, 42 percent had yet to have children. Of those, 44 percent said that it is "not too likely" or "not at all likely" that they will one day have them—an increase of seven percentage points from 2018.[19] But very few respondents claimed that ecological concerns were the reason. Fifty-six percent said they "just don't want to have children," while other, more concrete explanations included: medical reasons (19 percent), finances (17 percent), lack of partners (15 percent), their own age or the age of their partner (10 percent), and more general worries about "the state of the world" (9 percent). Climate concerns, at 5 percent, came almost last in the list of explanations, second only to "partner doesn't want kids."[20]

The results preliminarily suggest that while climate change pre-
dominates in the public conversation about the choice to have
children, it is still rarely the decisive factor in shaping people's
actual reproductive choices. At least for now.

Despite its ubiquity in the discourse, the topic of climate
anxiety also came up rarely in the "Motherhood—Is It for Me?"
course. Of all the topics covered in the program—family dynamics, romantic relationships, creative and professional aspirations—
climate was one issue that remained largely outside the scope of
the conversation. Participants were more focused on how having
children would affect their relationships, their sense of independence, and their personal identity. On the few occasions that
politics and climate did come up, they were not presented as the
main obstacles to making the decision. The same was also true
among the men and women we surveyed about their attitudes toward having children. Even for those who had decided not to have
children or described themselves as ambivalent, climate concerns,
when mentioned, were in all but one case not given as the reason
for the choice.

How might we explain the apparent discrepancy between the
centrality of climate change in public discussions of the ethics of
having children and the actual role it appears to play in people's
lives?

In an interview with a Sierra Club journalist about whether
one should have children amid climate change, parenthood-
ambivalence counselor Ann Davidman suggested that raising
climate concerns may have a special function in discussions
about having children. "It's easier and more socially acceptable to
say 'climate' than 'I'm really ambivalent about having children,'"
she said. "We often get judged and shamed for not knowing. But
the climate argument shuts people right up."[21] In Davidman's
experience, these accounts of climate anxiety didn't just convey

people's pressing preoccupation with the material future of humanity; they also helped to legitimize the murkier ambivalence they were already feeling.

There's an important insight in this observation. Among the many reasons one might be reluctant to have children, being concerned with the fate of the world and the people one would doom to live in it is perhaps the only one that advances a widely recognizable moral claim. It's understandable that this moral register would appeal to the ambivalent, especially when you consider that a common worry among those who choose to remain childless is that they will be perceived as "selfish, shallow, and self-absorbed," to quote the title of a best-selling 2015 essay collection on the choice not to have children. And at any rate it can be difficult to know for sure what is actually motivating you, especially when faced with such a consequential decision. While Seth Rogen suggested in his Howard Stern interview that the last thing the planet needs right now is "more fucking people," he also said that not having kids was the key to his and his wife's happiness: "I don't know anyone who gets as much happiness out of their kids as we get out of our non-kids. Like, we're fucking psyched all the time! We're lying in bed on Saturday mornings smoking weed, watching movies naked. If we had kids, we could not be fucking doing this." When Stern said that when you're a parent the kids are the priority, Rogen responded matter-of-factly, "I don't want that. That does not sound fun to me."[22]

But listing climate change among one's reasons for hesitating about having children isn't just a way of cloaking a self-motivated decision in the trappings of righteousness. Naming climate concerns among the deciding factors is increasingly recognized as an act of moral and political significance in its own right. In a study published in 2021, the environmental humanities researcher

Matthew Schneider-Mayerson examined how climate-change politics influence reproductive choices. After surveying 607 "climate-concerned Americans" between the ages of twenty-seven and forty-five, he found that while "for a subset of Americans, political considerations are reported as being critical to their reproductive plans and choices," climate change is rarely the sole reason individuals choose not to have children, even among activists.[23] Nevertheless, environmentalists who were childless or already leaning against having kids often recognized the political potential in representing climate change as a decisive consideration. For that reason, they might exaggerate or place extra emphasis on its influence on their decision-making, especially in front of family members. Such young people, Schneider-Mayerson noted, are "leveraging the familial desires and expectations that are attached to their reproductive potential . . . to influence environmental politics at a micropolitical, interpersonal level." In doing so they were engaging in what he called the "socio-political weaponization of fertility."[24] One of the study subjects, a twenty-eight-year-old journalist in California, told Schneider-Mayerson that she saw her decision to not have children "as a political tool":

> I tend to prioritize the climate change component because I think it is important to make people think about that more. I don't think I'd want children regardless, but climate change makes it a hard no. . . . My mom and grandma have expressed dismay at my decision. I told my grandmother if she felt that way that she should vote for a Democrat in 2020.

A thirty-seven-year-old policy expert who participated in the same study reported that he and his partner told their families that climate change was their reason for not having kids in order to "help them understand the consequences of inaction." Such individuals, in Schneider-Mayerson's words, "saw their conversations with family members as an opportunity to strategically wield their fertility to convey the depth of their anxieties and fears about the future."[25]

To state the obvious, Schneider-Mayerson was not suggesting that the activists did not actually care about the future. Rather, what his study reveals is that one way of acting on that concern is to publicly link one's reproductive choices to the threat of climate catastrophe. Broadcasting the effects of environmental threats on personal reproductive choices has become a way for people to display and make tangible the destructive consequences of climate change in the present moment. To similar effect, commentators have started to deploy declining fertility in the service of climate activism in the media and online. Activist groups like BirthStrike and No Future No Children have tried to draw an explicit link between individuals' procreative choices and large-scale environmental inaction, with the organization Conceivable Future proclaiming that "the climate crisis is a reproductive crisis."[26] In 2021 the journalist Liza Featherstone opined in the *New Republic* that "If Politicians Want to Raise Birth Rates, They Should Pass Climate Policy," and, the following year, *Marie Claire* published an article with a headline that blared, "Women Are Deciding to Have Fewer Children, and Global Warming Is to Blame."[27]

Talking about how global warming affects reproductive choices, personally or collectively, serves a function: it helps concretize the abstract threats of climate catastrophe. Indeed, it is often said that one of the greatest obstacles to making people care about climate change is the intractability of the problem: the concrete causes are almost impossible to pin down, there's no single person or entity to blame, and all of the proposed solutions will require collective mobilization on a vast, never-before-seen scale. If that's not enough, the consequences loom in a future just distant enough to recommend the poisonous comforts of indifference. The environmental thinker Timothy Morton tried to capture this difficulty by classifying climate change as a "hyperobject," the kind of problem "you can study and think about and compute" but can never "see directly."[28] Following Morton's lead, the writer Amitav Ghosh has suggested that the unfathomable enormity of the problem renders it impervious to figurative representation. "Climate change events," Ghosh writes, are "peculiarly resistant to the customary frames that literature has applied to 'Nature': they are too powerful, too grotesque, too dangerous and too accusatory."[29] Inspiring action on climate change requires making the problem feel real, for oneself as much as for others—an incredibly difficult task. Against this backdrop, we can begin to see why there might be a heightened focus on the link between the climate threat and the ethics of reproduction: reporting on how climate change is—and should be—influencing the decisions of actual young people today serves to prove that it is not a far-off danger that will impact the lives of people we will never meet but a present, unfolding catastrophe.

The fact that climate worries and ambivalence about having children often work to reinforce each other does not do away with the question of whether climate concerns have a place in our thinking about the future of human life. The question is serious—and important. And though it might be tempting for some to see its emergence as the unique expression of a modern—perhaps even liberal or progressive—sensibility, it has a history that long predates our present predicament. The contemporary anti-natalist sentiments are merely the latest guise of an ancient set of questions that the prospect of parenting has always raised. While the current circumstances—climate change, political degradation, a recent global pandemic, late capitalism—are more or less new, the suspicion that humanity is too corrupt and too miserable to justify its perpetuation is not.

As UNPRECEDENTED AS our contemporary existential crisis might seem, its roots run deep. From the earliest ancient Greek writings to the foundational texts of the Abrahamic faiths, we see everywhere the traces of the idea that it would have been better had human beings never come into existence.[30] Historically, this claim has taken the form of two distinct arguments. There is, first of all, the inescapable fact of the suffering human life entails. What if life is so torturous that it is simply not worth the trouble? How could one justify bringing children into the world if it is impossible to guarantee not just their safety and happiness but ultimately, considering all possible risks, even their basic well-being? The second line of argument begins not from the fact of suffering but from the presumption of human evil. It holds that human beings, happy or otherwise, are so morally fallen that it would be better for them—as well as for the rest of creation—not to exist. The first kind of argument suggests that life is an evil imposed on humankind; the other, that humankind is itself an evil imposition on the world. Both versions have been present for almost as long as humans have been asking, Why are we here? And what ought we do while we're at it?

In what is perhaps the earliest extant formulation of the claim, found in the poems traditionally attributed to Theognis of Megara and dating to roughly the sixth century BCE, the Greek poet counsels his beloved:

> The best lot of all for man is never to have been born nor seen the beams of the burning Sun; this failing, to pass the gates of Hades as soon as one may, and lie under a goodly heap of earth.[31]

Theognis does not give an explicit reason for his judgment, but the lines that immediately follow speak of the unpredictability and unchangeability of the bad character of human beings. Giving life is straightforward, Theognis writes, but cultivating goodness—and hence leading the sort of life that is worth the trouble—is precarious and elusive.[32]

Perhaps the most famous articulation of the claim that not being born is preferable to its opposite appears in the ancient tale known as the myth of Silenus. The first reference to this story can be found in Aristotle's early, and now lost, dialogue *Eudemus, or on the Soul,* and it owes its survival to Plutarch's quoting approvingly from it in the first century CE.[33] The dialogue reveals that the anti-natalist line was something of a familiar truism at the time and, at least as a piece of folk wisdom, widely held. "That not to be born is the best of all, and that to be dead is better than to live," Aristotle's speaker declares, is a saying "on the lips of all men," one that "has been passed from mouth to mouth for many years." Its origin: the ancient legend of the great King Midas and the satyr Silenus, who discloses to the king the tragic truth about human existence. The myth of Silenus continued to inspire philosophers for millennia to come.[34] In his *Birth of Tragedy,* a young Friedrich Nietzsche would recount the ancient myth of the wise king hungry for knowledge who insisted on learning what would cause him the greatest pain—that the very best thing for him would have been not to have been born.[35] For Nietzsche, the Silenic truth could not be refuted, but it could be withstood. The task he undertakes in this youthful essay is to figure out how the Greeks succeeded in doing so. And in our own time, the prominent anti-natalist philosopher David Benatar, to whom we will soon return, alludes to the Silenic pronouncement in the title of his 2006 book, *Better Never to Have Been: The Harm of Coming into Existence.*[36]

The Jewish religious tradition was founded on the idea that God saw great goodness in his creation, not least of all in man, who was created in His image. In Genesis, God commanded human beings to "be fruitful and multiply."[37] It would be natural to assume, then, that Jewish thought would leave little room for doubt about whether it is good to bring more humans into the world. But though the question is not raised frequently, it is not ignored. In Ecclesiastes—a text in the Hebrew Bible traditionally attributed to the sagacious King Solomon, though dated by scholars to sometime between 450 and 180 BCE—the weary monarch Kohelet declares, "Vanity of vanities! All is vanity!"[38] Bearing witness to human beings' sorry state, the king concludes: "Therefore I praised the dead who were already dead, More than the living who are still alive. Yet, better than both is he who has never existed, Who has not seen the evil work that is done under the sun."[39]

This idea—that the dead are better off than the living but most fortunate of all are the unborn—is reprised in the Babylonian Talmud, the central Jewish record of laws, pronouncements, and rabbinical debates, written between the third and sixth centuries CE. According to the Talmud, the two great rabbinical houses, the House of Shammai and the House of Hillel, were locked in a years-long debate about whether it would have been preferable for man if he had never been created.[40] Eventually, no closer to consensus, they put the question to a vote. This settled the matter once and for all: it would have been better for man not to have been created. Now that he's here, it is incumbent upon him to judiciously examine his actions.[41]

Christianity is a more complicated case. Within early and medieval Christian writings the question was not, as it was for the classical philosophical tradition, how to affirm human life in spite of the evils of existence.[42] Rather, starting most famously with Augustine of Hippo's "On Holy Virginity" and "On the Good of Marriage," the question of the legitimacy of human reproduction came up primarily in attempts to clarify the status of procreation within Christian doctrine. Can we justify bringing more human beings into the world, fallen as they are? How can human procreation be anything but sinful? Considering the virgin birth of both Mary and Christ, would it not be better to imitate Christ in celibacy, too? (Significantly, of all miracles performed by Christ, he never helps a barren woman conceive.[43]) As a rule, despite the undisputed holiness of virginity, official Church doctrine insisted upon the legitimacy of human procreation and condemned attempts to proscribe marriage and sex as heresy. Nevertheless, a wide array of apocryphal texts as well as various writings of adjacent heretical sects repeatedly asserted that humans' sinful condition renders sex and procreation an evil from which they ought to abstain.[44] Occasionally, the residue of such attitudes could be found closer to the center of Christian religious authority and established dogma. "The bodily procreation of children . . . is more an embarking upon death than upon life for man," wrote the fourth-century Byzantine bishop Gregory of Nyssa in his encomium "On Virginity."[45] Eight centuries later, in his tract "On the Misery of the Human Condition," Lotario di Segni, who would come to assume the papacy as Pope Innocent III (1198–1216), claimed that "Man was formed . . . of the filthiest seed." He was, Lotario wrote, "born only to die." Though he never drew the conclusion that procreation is strictly forbidden, he came as close as Church doctrine would allow: man, he wrote, is "conceived in guilt, born to punishment. What he does is depraved and illicit, is shameful and improper, vain and unprofitable. He will become fuel for the eternal fires, food for worms, a mass of rottenness."[46] And if the official party line could not prevent Christian thinkers from suggesting the theological superiority of celibacy, it could do even less to prevent later thinkers from attributing celibate asceticism as the necessary, core teaching of the Christian faith—whether in celebration, as in Schopenhauer, or in disgust, as in Nietzsche.[47]

With the advent of modernity, the idea that life is simply an evil, best avoided and spared of others, finally assumed its place on the main stage. It is no coincidence that probing the truth of Silenus's dictum is arguably the main theme of Shakespeare's *Hamlet,* widely considered the greatest early modern tragedy. In a sardonic play on the Renaissance genre of treatises extolling the wonders of humanity,[48] Shakespeare's Hamlet rages against humankind: "And yet to me what is this quintessence of dust?"[49] He evinces disgust at the prospect of procreation, famously barking at Ophelia, "Get thee to a nunnery. Why wouldst thou be a breeder of sinners?"[50] The consummation "devoutly to be wished" for is not heirs, but death.[51] Ophelia complies. Two hundred and seventy years later, in 1872, Nietzsche would write in his *Birth of Tragedy* that what keeps Hamlet from carrying out his decision to avenge his father by killing his uncle is not, as was sometimes assumed, his epistemic uncertainty or tendency to overthink things. Hamlet's problem is, rather, "true knowledge, an insight into the horrible truth." According to Nietzsche, Hamlet sees "everywhere only the horror or absurdity of existence," and "he is nauseated."[52] What is at stake for Hamlet is not merely his resolution to act in one way or another; it is his very will to live.

It was not until the nineteenth century that the opposition to human life became a philosophical cause célèbre, as stirrings of discontent started to break through the optimism that had defined the Age of Reason.[53] Two and a half millennia after Theognis claimed it would be best never to have been born, pessimism about human life received what remains one of its clearest and most systematic expressions to date in the work of the German philosopher Arthur Schopenhauer. Schopenhauer argued that suffering was not merely a contingent fact of life but an absolutely necessary consequence of human existence. It was our self-centered and self-promoting grasping, our endless striving to actualize the objects of our desires, that was the root cause of our misery, as well as of our wickedness. The only possible solution, Schopenhauer claimed, drawing on Hindu and Buddhist philosophies, is to lift "the veil of Maya": overcome the illusion of the distinction between us and other people—us and the world. The path to freedom from suffering requires one to turn away from one's personal life and all its pleasures. A person must guard against any attachment of the will and establish "the greatest indifference to all things."[54] In other words, living in truth requires denying one's own will to live. The first step in such asceticism? Total chastity. Anything else would be wicked and cruel:

> If children were brought into the world by an act of pure reason alone, would the human race continue to exist? Would not a man rather have so much sympathy with the coming generation as to spare it the burden of existence? [Or] at any rate not take it upon himself to impose that burden upon it in cold blood.[55]

Schopenhauer gained late recognition in his lifetime, eventually coming to influence other philosophers, but especially artists, with whom his fame was great—Wagner, Turgenev, Proust, Lawrence, and Mann all read and admired him.[56]

Following Schopenhauer, the nineteenth century witnessed an explosion of anti-natalist sentiments, provoked by concerns with both human suffering and human evil.[57] Soon, however, another argument appeared on the scene, one that should sound especially familiar to readers today. This new line of reasoning centered not on the qualities of human existence—human beings' moral state or their share in happiness—but on a longing for a different world. It called for a return to the Edenic—pristine, lush, and thriving—natural world that once was and could once again be, if only the planet were rid of humankind. Amid the welter of the industrial revolution, artists, freethinkers, and other malcontents dissented against faith in progress, the redemptive power of science, and humanity's unlimited right to remake and ransack nature according to its whims. Whether with the best or the worst of intentions, humans were laying waste to the earth— that much was obvious. Without them, maybe nature might one day be restored to its former glory. Here we find the first articulations of the kind of rhetoric that later would be adopted and popularized in the environmentalist literature of our lifetime. Human beings have gone too far, our relentless exertions have caused too much damage, reform is a lost cause.

In *Memoirs of a Madman,* Gustave Flaubert's 1838 semiautobiographical coming-of-age narrative, the narrator launches into an eschatological reverie about the "death of this mendacious and hypocritical vampire we call civilisation." The human race "was cursed from its infancy." Once extinct, a seventeen-year-old Flaubert mused, "rivers will flow in flower-studded fields," and "nature will be free." When "the orgy" of human existence ends, the earth will prosper once more: "Then the sea without walls will peacefully beat upon the shores and bathe the smouldering embers of cities with its waves. Trees will grow and blossom without any hand to break or destroy them."[58] Flaubert, for his part, never had children. "The idea of bringing someone into this world fills me with *horror,*" he wrote in his letters. "May my flesh perish utterly! May I never transmit to anyone the boredom and the ignominies of existence!"[59] The apocalyptic imagery Flaubert evokes would be taken up by later writers—Woolf, T. S. Eliot, and D. H. Lawrence among them—who captured the stifling and necrotizing effects of modernity. "Man is a mistake, he must go," Rupert Birkin, the author's stand-in, pronounces in Lawrence's 1920 novel *Women in Love:* "I would die like a shot, to know that the earth would really be cleaned of all the people. It is the most beautiful and freeing thought."[60]

Despite their grim prognoses for Western civilization, the modernists, for the most part, yearned for regeneration. Even if much of modern life was barbaric and dull, they persevered in the hope that, once the old values had been washed away, new ones might one day take hold. But by the mid-twentieth century, after the horrors of the Holocaust, Hiroshima, and Stalin's purges, such hope had come to seem laughable. The bitterly nihilistic view of human life formulated by Schopenhauer reached its apotheosis in the postmodern pessimism of writers like Emil Cioran, Thomas Bernhard, and, later, Michel Houellebecq, for whom human existence was alienation, pain, and decay all the way down. Amid Cold War fears of nuclear cataclysm and the neo-Malthusian rumblings about overpopulation in the sixties and seventies, antinatalist concerns had begun to occupy the popular imagination.[61] The essence of this outlook was conveyed with acid deadpan in Philip Larkin's 1971 poem "This Be the Verse":

> Man hands on misery to man.
> It deepens like a coastal shelf.
> Get out as early as you can,
> And don't have any kids yourself.[62]

Larkin's poem is best known for its opening lines—"They fuck you up, your mum and dad. / They may not mean to, but they do." But its conclusion goes beyond blame, exhorting the reader to avoid doing the same to others in turn.

In recent years, some avowed anti-natalists, most prominently the South African philosopher David Benatar, have sought to defend this comfortless view of human existence within mainstream Anglophone philosophy. In his *Better Never to Have Been*—the clearest articulation of the philosophical underpinnings of contemporary anti-natalism—Benatar argues that "coming into existence, far from ever constituting a net benefit, always constitutes a net harm."[63] Life inevitably causes human beings to suffer. If you are never born, Benatar reasons, you cannot be hurt, cannot be deprived, cannot have your dignity violated, cannot experience the terror and pain of death. Sure, humans may experience pleasures and satisfactions in their lives. But these potential pleasures are not likely to outweigh the misery. More importantly, allowing a human being to suffer is harmful, while no harm is done when you prevent positive experiences from taking place by refraining from procreation (for there simply isn't a person there to be deprived of any such benefits). And as if producing one life wasn't bad enough, Benatar notes, the act of procreation sets off a compounding and potentially infinite sequence of suffering, wherein all your descendants are condemned to endure the pains of life. Creating more people, Benatar concludes, is therefore an unequivocal moral wrong.

Benatar's book is only the latest iteration of an ancient refrain. Still, one senses things might be different this time around. No longer just the concern of philosophers, poets, and alarmist political scientists, voluntary childlessness is growing in popular appeal. Not having kids is now a theme of charismatic politicians' messaging, mainstream art, and widely disseminated essays. While few are willing to go as far as Benatar in affirming that having children is strictly immoral, for the first time in history, it has become common for ordinary people to find themselves face-to-face with the question of the legitimacy of bringing more human life into the world.

THE FACT THAT these arguments have a long history does not imply that the current fears about having children in light of climate change are naïve or trivial. On the contrary, acknowledging this lineage helps us see these worries for what they are: deep philosophical concerns, whose endurance reflects just how fundamental they are to the human search for self-knowledge and ethical clarity. What's more, only with this long line of predecessors in mind can we recognize what is unique and significant about the forms this question takes today.

When one considers its longevity and persistence, it is remarkably just how rarely the pessimistic attitude toward human life has been challenged, much less refuted. As we've just seen, for the ancient Greeks, it was a familiar, though for the most part practically inert, adage; for the Christians, a perennial threat, but one in whose shadow life continued more or less as usual; for Schopenhauer, a metaphysical truth. It was not until the twentieth century that the question of the legitimacy of having children was thematized as a significant ethical question. This inquiry took place largely within the confines of feminist debates about the meaning of women's reproductive roles and liberation. Only in the past couple of decades has the question of the "ethics of procreation," as it is known today, emerged as an explicit topic of public interest and mainstream philosophical debate. These concerns are no longer raised just in the abstract; the questions are being posed in such a way that demands answers.

So far, the preliminary attempts to meet this challenge have mostly testified to its intractability. Late in his meditation on climate change and having a child in the face of environmental decline, Daniel Sherrell recalls a time in college when he found himself tempted to embrace the pessimistic conclusion, "to center death and treat life as the afterthought."[64] The main inspiration for Sherrell's fatalism was "Learning to Die in the Anthropocene," a 2013 *New York Times* essay by the Iraq war veteran Roy Scranton, which he adapted into a book by the same name two years later. Drawing on his coping strategies in the field, Scranton claimed that the only appropriate response to the certainty of death in the future is to resign ourselves to death in the present. What enabled him to push through the fear of death in Iraq, Scranton wrote, was not casting it away from his mind but embracing its certainty: "I didn't need to worry, because I was already dead." According to Scranton, our own condition, considered as a species, is no different: "This civilization is *already dead* . . . there's nothing we can do to save ourselves."[65] Forget moral reorientation, political activism, and technological breakthroughs; the only thing left to do is to mourn.

This is the thought Sherrell returns to as he flirts with anti-natalism and suicide: "Being dead lowered the stakes on everything, softened out all the edges."[66] But Sherrell soon realizes he cannot abide by Scranton's doctrine. He still believes, he writes, in Scranton's assessment of the problem, but he no longer wants to surrender to it. It is "too resigned," he says, "too bereft of agency."[67] But how can one defend such a rejection of the pessimistic posture? On what grounds may we justify a future for humankind? Sherrell's answer is speculative, brief, and cryptic:

Of course the end would come—in some form, at some time—but wasn't the whole point to postpone it? Wasn't there something essential, some foundational spark of the human experience that sprang from exactly this friction, between the fact of death and the will to live?[68]

It is noteworthy that Sherrell formulates what is perhaps the most important claim underlying both his literary and practical endeavors as a series of rhetorical questions. Consider putting the basic idea in the form of a proposition instead: Why not resign oneself to death now? Because death "would come," but "the whole point is to postpone it." Cast in this form, it is easy to see that the argument is question begging: it assumes what we are hoping to establish. Sherrell is right that humans, as a matter of fact, have a "will to live"—in their own person, most still do—and it seems true enough that life and death and their "friction" are "foundational" to the human experience. But the question is, as it has been for hundreds and thousands of years, how to *justify* human existence in the face of the grave possibility that Sherrell himself captures so well when he bemoans the "weight of human frailty" or ponders whether something in our very "nature" has made the Problem necessary. It isn't just a matter of whether humans want life; it's whether they *deserve* it, and whether it's defensible to subject them to it. The real question that his book raises—one he can't quite manage to answer—is not whether human beings are bent on postponing their end but whether we are still justified in making more and more beginnings.

There is, however, one more current coursing through Sherrell's work that suggests a different strategy for justifying a future for humankind. Reflecting on his first encounter with Scranton's essay, Sherrell writes that the "raw pessimism felt scandalous, like Scranton was saying the unsayable, like he'd cracked open a Pandora's box."[69] Confronting the swarm of unleashed afflictions, Sherrell, like Pandora, realizes that the box is not yet empty: trapped inside remains hope. And so, despite his rejection of Pollyannaish optimism, Sherrell ends his book with a refusal to accept what many around him estimate is the like-

liest outcome of climate change: disaster. Addressing his hypothetical future child, Sherrell writes:

> In case it's of use, then, here is one piece of advice: Do not
> accept the vision of our future as a single road leading to a
> burning city. Compromised as it is, it still seems to me more
> like a fan, stretching out in front of us in a swath of possible
> outcomes—most of them scary, maybe, but none of them en-
> tirely predictable. In this indeterminacy, there is potential,
> which means there is still room for movement. Do not feel
> compelled to suffer Scranton's passivity on this point. How-
> ever grave the dangers become, however dire the warnings,
> they will never collapse your future into something as nar-
> row as a fate.[70]

These are meant to be rousing words. The future is not a single
road—different outcomes are possible; the indeterminacy of the
moment contains "potential" and "room for movement." But can
hope based merely on the openness of the future suffice?

Hope is the central theme of several recent reflections on the
permissibility of having children in the face of climate catastrophe. In "Is It OK to Have a Child?"—an essay in the *London Review of Books* that is being developed into a full-length book—the
writer Meehan Crist affirms, echoing Sherrell, "Pessimism may
be warranted; fatalism is not. The future is not written."[71] What
would it take to write a different future than the one that seems
most likely to come? Like Sherrell, Crist is suspicious of calls
to reconfigure personal consumer choices: much of her critical work is dedicated to dismantling the logic of the so-called
individual carbon footprint. This, she argues, is a futile and
morally dubious ploy to saddle individuals with responsibility

that should be lodged instead with the fossil-fuel industry—incidentally, the ones who actively promoted the idea of the carbon footprint in the first place, in order to deflect attention from their own practices. We should cast a skeptical eye on those who try to link the choice to have children to the climate crisis: "The real choice we face," she writes, "is not whether to eat meat or how many children to have, but how to make profound and rapid structural changes, without which no personal choices will matter." Recalling her conversations with her partner about whether they should have a child, Crist writes, "In the end, not having a child didn't seem, for us, like a powerful or particularly meaningful response to the realities of a changing climate, but a way of allowing the toxic logic of the carbon footprint to shape our sense of what was possible."

This is a compelling rejoinder to a certain kind of argument against having children that conceives of them crudely in terms of the harm that they would likely cause. But while Crist is persuasive on the sophistries underlying the logic of the carbon footprint, a deep and no less troubling set of questions is still mostly untouched. One's individual carbon footprint might not be a good reason not to have a child, but what about the suffering that they will face? And what about the economic and political systems that are responsible for trashing our planet and causing the immiseration of billions of people? Individuals might not be *directly* culpable for those actions, but these systems are man-made. They implicate all of us. It is hard to resist asking whether humankind itself is not reaching a decisive dead end.

Here, Crist, like Sherrell, places the weight of her argument on the indeterminacy of the future. Dire as the climate predictions are, she assures her readers that they do not foreclose the fate of humankind: "Even the most optimistic scenarios are fraught with uncertainty and potential catastrophe, but also the possibility of a renewed sense of futurity." She goes on:

> The future will always be more terrible and wonderful than any of us can possibly imagine. What will the climate crisis look like in ten years, twenty years, fifty years? We don't know. How fast can we achieve global decarbonisation? We don't know. This uncertainty both inspires dread and allows for the possibility of hope.[72]

In this way, Crist, like Sherrell, ends up affirming hope on the strength of little more than the unknown. And even they don't seem to find that fully satisfying. Sherrell maintains that Scranton's fatalism is still basically correct; Crist sympathetically quotes a scientist who counsels, "Fuck hope."

In his 2021 book, *Infinitely Full of Hope: Fatherhood and the Future in an Age of Crisis and Disaster,* philosopher Tom Whyman tries to reclaim the legitimacy and dignity of hope as a stance toward the future.[73] Drawing on Hannah Arendt's concept of "natality," which she traces to Augustine's remarks on creation, Whyman suggests that we follow Arendt in thinking of human beings not simply as "mortals"—beings defined by the fact of their necessary deaths—but rather as "natals"—beings who are, essentially, born. Birth, Arendt writes, is "the miracle that saves the world . . . from its normal, 'natural' ruin." The capacity for birth continues to define us, individually and collectively, throughout our lives: We are never simply determined by our pasts—by our history or circumstances or habits—we can always reverse course and start anew. We have the capacity "to undo what we have done" and are therefore never simply "the victims of an automatic necessity."[74] In short, the birth of a human being is always a "new beginning," and it is always in the power of human beings to make new beginnings themselves.[75]

Whyman suggests that it is this perennial possibility of renewal that justifies the belief in the possibility of progress: "If we dare to do something, anything, differently, in some way that might allow us to hit upon the right path . . . then things really could, conceivably, get better." While for Sherrell and Crist hope is the only thing that can justify the decision to have children today, Whyman proposes that "redemption is found in the fact of our children." Despair is unwarranted: "so long as there exist other human beings, new generations to come, there is hope for us together."[76]

There is something intuitive about Whyman's thesis. Surely the possibility of a better human future does not merely justify having children, it also depends on it. But Whyman's argument brings several difficult questions into focus. If the ultimate measure of what we do is whether or not it will lead to things "getting better," why think that birthing and raising a child would be the most effective way of accomplishing that goal? Perhaps our children will try to bring about a different future; perhaps they won't. Wouldn't it be better to direct all our available resources to trying to do so ourselves? Accepting that future generations might do better in theory is one thing; expecting them to actually do so is quite another. This difficulty is heightened, not resolved, by the fact that for all three contemporary writers—Sherrell, Crist, and Whyman—the problem is structural. Skeptical of attempts to place the burden of responsibility on the shoulders of individual agents, they call for deep, systemic change that requires nothing short of undoing the capitalist world order. Of course, they might be right about what it would take to change the course of climate change. But all of their arguments still leave the central question unanswered: Why would our children be any more up to the task, when we've failed at it so miserably ourselves? Sherrell, recall, wonders whether climate change might be a punishment for our collective sins; Whyman maintains that we live in "a very bad world" and adds that "given all the various horrors in the shadow of which we presently toil," the only "realistic conclusion one can possibly draw" is that life is "hopeless."[77] The performance of despair might seem like the only honest, or only responsible, position to take today. Yet at the same time it can strain the credibility of the effort to avert disaster. For something to *warrant* repair—to deserve it and be capable of it—we must be able to recognize some goodness in it. Utterly bad things— buildings rotten at the foundations, uninspired art, very bad relationships—can't always be improved upon; sometimes they need to be done away with altogether. A better future might require a radical break from our present condition, but it can't be a complete rupture. Not only because this does not seem very likely but because, if that is the case, what we ought to hope for is not a better world but an entirely different one.

HOPING FOR IMPROVEMENT solely on the basis of the hypothetical possibility of change is not just quixotic, it is nonsensical. If the only good thing we are able to say about our existence is that there's hope for things to turn out differently one day—not on any determinate grounds but because, well, anything could happen!—we shouldn't be too surprised if it starts to seem like keeping it going isn't worth the risk and trouble.

Among contemporary thinkers, the philosopher Samuel Scheffler stands out as one of the few to try to conceive of the importance of perpetuating humanity not in terms of the value of a possible future world but in terms of the value of the lives we lead at present. Scheffler's starting point is P. D. James's 1992

novel *Children of Men* (adapted into a successful film in 2006 by
the director Alfonso Cuarón). The novel depicts a near future in
which human society has been devastated by infertility. Facing
the prospect of no new births and the imminent extinction of
humankind, the world is thrust into chaos. Political institutions
fail, social bonds disintegrate, and the basic norms and practices
by which individuals conduct their private lives are lost or rendered meaningless. The sole glimmer of salvation takes the form
of a young woman, who against all odds gives birth to a healthy
human child. Scheffler credits *Children of Men* with an important insight:

> To the extent that we would indeed perceive this fact—the
> fact that no new people were going to be born—as a *catastro-
> phe,* this teaches us something important and perhaps sur-
> prising about ourselves. It indicates that . . . in addition to
> our attachments to particular individuals and communities,
> many of us have a concern for the survival of humanity as
> such.[78]

The grief and spiritual dissolution that extinction conjures,
Scheffler argues, surpasses in its intensity even the recognition
of our own personal deaths, compromising our very ability to
"lead fulfilling lives."[79] Trying to answer why it is that we so want
humanity to continue well after the end of our own and our
loved ones' lifetimes, Scheffler notices something interesting:
many of the activities and practices that give meaning to our
lives in the present are intimately connected with and sustained
by our belief in humankind's continued survival.

Remove the possibility of a future, and much of what we routinely do stops making sense; our very lives seem to lose their
point. But why is that? According to Scheffler, to see the depth of

our dependence on the future, we must attend to a particular set of activities of a few interrelated kinds. The most straightforward of these are collective activities with a long-term, goal-oriented structure, like meliorative research—whether medical, technological, or social—or activism aimed at durable social or political reform.[80] But they may also include tasks that belong to ongoing processes or practices that are "larger than oneself," which not only outstrip one's individual capacities and require the collaboration of others but transcend the temporal boundaries of one's life, like the life of a language, or philosophical thinking.[81] And, finally, there are those projects, such as the study of sociology or anthropology, that are meant to help us "make sense of our social world and its future possibilities," or those activities that are intended to sustain valuable forms of cultural or intellectual heritage. "History," as James writes in *Children of Men,* "which interprets the past to understand the present and confront the future, is the least rewarding discipline for a dying species."[82]

In taking part in such activities, one understands that their aims cannot be achieved in the span of just one lifetime. They involve people collaborating over large periods of time, and their provision of benefits extends far into the future. This is why, Scheffler notes, human extinction would render participating in such activities meaningless and without value.

The answer to the question Scheffler raises in the title of his book *Why Worry About Future Generations?*, this observation suggests, is that we should worry about future generations because without them, our present activities would become pointless. According to this line of thought, the import of human life in the future depends on the import of the various future-facing activities human beings engage in right now, in the present.

All this is true enough as a description of the ways our present activities depend on the presumption of continuity for their intelligibility. But as an answer to the further question of why we *ought to care* about the existence of future generations, the truth it articulates is only a conditional: one should care about, or value, future generations insofar as one should care about, or value, one's own. This account can tell us what would happen to many of our practical commitments if humanity were to reach its end, but it does not tell us whether those commitments—or humanity itself—are genuinely worthwhile. It is true that devoting yourself to preserving some aspect of human heritage would likely appear futile if you knew you were part of the last generation on earth; but for something to lose value, it needs to *have* value. Acknowledging the fact that our present activities depend on the future cannot settle the question of whether they were ever worth pursuing to begin with.[83]

Consider a simple example: planning a wedding. Planning a wedding involves many goal-oriented activities that would be pointless and futile to continue performing if it got called off. But whether the cancellation of the wedding is something to regret or celebrate would not be decided by the fact that there was no longer any need to perform the tasks leading up to it. After all, one does not decide to have a wedding in order to engage in all the necessary preparations. Whether the canceled wedding is to be lamented depends on answering questions like: "Is marriage an institution I should participate in?" "Am I marrying the right person?" "Should marriage be celebrated with a wedding?" "Why did it get canceled?" Returning to Scheffler's cross-generational projects, the value of engaging in a long-term goal-oriented activity cannot give us objective reasons to worry about, let alone work to ensure, the survival of humanity; it merely presupposes it.[84] Medical research is important if human life is important; the preservation of heritage, or culture, or history is valuable if those aspects of human existence are valuable.

While Scheffler teaches us to see how the value of future generations depends on the value of the activities we partake in in
the here and now, we want to know not only why we *do* care
about future generations but why we *should*. Insofar as nearly
all these activities—medical research, political reform, cultural
preservation—presuppose the value of human existence, what's
missing is an affirmation that these human activities are genuinely worthwhile, which is to say that the human form of life
is itself good. In other words, if we wish to justify life in the
future, we must first and foremost justify our own existence in
the present.

Grappling with Scheffler's arguments about the role of future
generations in sustaining the value of our present enterprises
leaves us with the same question as the arguments from hope:
Are any of our present activities worth preserving? Are we, for
all our faults, good? It is no coincidence that two of the most
prominent contemporary lines of thought about the future of
humanity end up bottoming out in the same question, the question of the goodness of human life. It is also no coincidence that
all these attempts shy away from answering it. Justifying our
present form of life can seem downright impossible.

WOULD THE WORLD not be better off without humans in it? Who
would miss us? These questions have become the driving themes
of a recent crop of novels that envision a not-too-distant future
in which human life is coming to its logical, self-imposed end.
Part of a growing genre known as "climate fiction"[85] or "eco literature," these works recall an older mode of dystopian disaster writing. Apocalyptic and postapocalyptic fiction has always been a
theater for exploring human nature and the value of human life:
In impossible circumstances, after disaster strikes, would we

choose to band together, help one another, try to repair our corner of the world, or would our worst impulses tear us apart? In classic dystopian fiction about the final days of humanity—Mary Shelley's *The Last Man* or, more recently, P. D. James's *Children of Men* and Cormac McCarthy's *The Road*—the drama is ultimately one of survival. The disaster sets the stage for a struggle to sustain, or a longing to restart, human life. In these novels, the end of the world raises questions like: What would it take to recover a dignified form of human existence once again? What would be lost if humans were no more? Though their answers vary, each of these more classic dystopian novels ends on some sort of affirmation, however ambiguous or provisional, that we should not give up, not yet—that, even amid societal and environmental collapse, humankind retains some share of goodness, something worth fighting, dying, and, crucially, living for.

The ecological novels of recent years provoke an altogether different sort of reflection: What if catastrophe was what we deserved? Though by no means the first works of fiction to point out the defects of our kind—a theme of literature stretching from Shakespeare to Aldous Huxley and Ursula K. Le Guin—they distinguish themselves from their literary predecessors not only by taking anthropogenic climate change as their subject but also by their totalizing anti-humanist sensibility. Eco-fiction is a relatively young and heterogenous genre, displaying various narrative conceits—romance, adventure, mystery, the detective story—but its novels share a thesis in common: the outlook for humankind is bleak, and we have no one to blame but ourselves.

Contemporary climate fiction got its start in earnest at the turn of the twenty-first century, with the publication of novels like T. C. Boyle's *A Friend of the Earth* (2000) and Margaret Atwood's *Oryx and Crake* (2003) and *The Year of the Flood* (2009). Then came Barbara Kingsolver's critically acclaimed Appalachian allegory *Flight Behavior* (2012) and Edan Lepucki's best-selling (and Stephen Colbert–endorsed) novel *California* (2014), which narrates the grim odyssey of a couple searching for a safe haven for their unborn child amid widespread ecological devastation and social collapse. By the mid-2010s, some had begun to wonder whether the literary potential of the genre hadn't started to exhaust itself, though you certainly wouldn't have known it by looking at the market. "Some literary critics have started to grumble about post-apocalyptic-fiction fatigue," wrote a publishing industry beat reporter for the *New York Times* in 2014, but "publishers, agents and authors are betting that readers' appetite for cataclysm is nowhere near sated."[86] The prediction has been vindicated by the public's craving for eco-dystopian page-turners, whose titles have become critical darlings and popular subway reads, regularly gracing end-of-year fiction roundups and bestseller lists.

An incomplete register of some of the category's most notable examples: Claire Vaye Watkins's *Gold Fame Citrus* (2015), a bad trip through a desertified American West populated by cultists, wastoids, and vandals; Richard Powers's Pulitzer Prize–winning sylvan epic *The Overstory* (2018) and his less-celebrated follow-up, the dad-jeans neuronovel *Bewilderment* (2021); Elvia Wilk's corporate-sustainability nightmare *Oval* (2019); Diane Cook's survivalist drama *The New Wilderness* (2020), shortlisted for the Booker Prize; Lydia Millet's dystopian kids' adventure novel and National Book Award finalist, *A Children's Bible* (2020); Jenny Offill's lauded character study of a doom-pilled librarian, *Weather* (2020); Michael Christie's apocalyptic time-travel narrative *Greenwood* (2020); Andrew Krivak's posthuman arcadia *The Bear* (2020); Joy Williams's absurdist parable *Harrow* (2021); and Alexandra Kleeman's dread-spiked California satire *Something New Under the Sun* (2021). Some are overtly political and dead earnest, like the terminally Obama-era novels of Richard Powers; others, like *Harrow, Oval,* and *Something New Under the Sun,* retain a cool and artful poise. But whatever their differences, the novels are united in their commitment to addressing what Amitav Ghosh has called the "crisis of culture, and thus of the imagination" provoked by climate change.[87]

Brimming with eschatological visions of fires, droughts, and great floods, the eco-disaster novel begins from the assumption that humankind has blithely laid total or near-total waste to the earth. We are not just afflicted; we are the affliction. Though the extent of the disaster is hardly in doubt, human beings are as a rule listless, passive, and apathetic. Readers are thrust into a distorted, diminished, and noxious reality that has become, for its inhabitants, utterly normal. In *Something New Under the Sun,* the once-lush SoCal landscape is burning; Malibu's tony hills are on fire, and the state's freshwater reserves have dried up, replaced with an eerily synthetic product marketed under the brand name WAT-R. Young and old are stricken with a mysterious new form of dementia and carted off to for-profit care homes. It's "terrible, definitely," thinks the clueless protagonist when reflecting on the present state of crisis, "but it's not really an emergency . . . if you can drive around it."[88] Many people don't even seem to realize anything has gone awry. In Williams's *Harrow,* an offscreen catastrophe takes place early in the timeline of the novel, but it is clear that the present is eerily continuous with whatever came before it. Now, *Harrow's* narrator reports, hardly anything grows; birdsong has been eradicated; the acid rain leaves "nasty bubbles in the puddled dirt"; dying, poisonous trees routinely fall on people ("They didn't used to be so nasty when there were more of them," notes one observer).

There is more devastation to come, but the general attitude is one of indifference: "Denial is now an art, a social grace, a

survival tool, as is apathy which has become a sign of refine-
ment."[89] Characters cling to objects that remind them of the
lives they led before the devastation overtook them. While eking
out a bare existence in an abandoned shed, *California*'s heroine
keeps a few treasured "artifacts": a turkey baster, a matchbook,
her mother's shower cap, "the dead Device."[90] *Gold Fame Citrus* begins in a water crisis, with two California holdouts sur-
rounded by Birkin bags and Hermès scarves, playing dress-up in
an empty Hollywood starlet's mansion.[91] Before disaster struck,
the protagonist of *California* admits that she didn't even read the
news; after the disaster, there is no news to read.[92]

The pervasive mood is exhaustion; characters in these novels
greet even their own impending ruin with ignorance or boredom or ironic disbelief, rather than the seriousness and terror
it demands. In *The Overstory*, a retelling of modern American
history from the standpoint of the trees, a silent environmental
holocaust is occurring right under our noses, but no one seems
to notice—or care. "Nothing I can say will wake the sleepwalk
or make this suicide seem real," Powers's scientist-protagonist
laments.[93] In *A Children's Bible* the adults ignore all warnings as
a hurricane approaches. "The parents insisted on denial as a tac-
tic," the protagonist explains. "Not science denial exactly—they
were liberals. It was more a denial of reality." Instead of preparing for the calamity, or trying to forestall it, they get "shit-faced"
before the coming storm: "We still didn't have the windows done
when the rain got harder. The fathers gave up, clearing throats,
shaking heads, retreating to mix their drinks."[94]

More troubling than people's willful obliviousness is their attitude when forced to acknowledge the damage. Not remorse,
or guilt, or shame but blank resignation: "The incomprehensi-
ble beauty of nature was no more, but most had accepted the
destitution done in their name," Williams's narrator intones in

*Harrow.* But soon the complacency turns to indignation, and then hate: "People think the planet is attempting to make threats—the withdrawal of spring—and nonnegotiable demands, and it pisses them off. . . . Let this fucking land of ours that has turned against us burn, is the prevailing sentiment." Indeed, callousness in the world of *Harrow* is cultivated like a virtue: "The more a person doesn't care the freer he becomes"; "Fuck the earth. The earth is worthless. . . . Long live the earth who has freed us from the obligation to save her!"[95]

Humankind has, in the words of *A Children's Bible,* "hung out way past its expiration date," only to become "litter, a scourge, a blight, a scab."[96] This cynicism finds expression overtly, through dialogue and narration, but also formally, in the novels' remarkable incuriosity about the people they depict. The narratives tend to eschew character development for mood setting and scenery. Back stories are fragmentary; the protagonists' memories are shattered, or too uncomfortable for them to revisit, or frankly beside the point in the aftermath of the disaster. Most of the supporting characters—and often the protagonists, too—are shallow, their inner lives flimsy and insubstantial. They are cardboard-cutout archetypes—hucksters, cultists, upper-middle-class phonies, bugged-out hippies, D-list celebrities, Burning Man burnouts. The real drama always occurs one or two clicks beyond their capacity for comprehension. Kleeman's *Something New Under the Sun* is full of plastic Hollywood operators; its protagonists are a self-absorbed novelist of middling talent and a scandal-ridden former child star modeled after Lindsay Lohan. *Gold Fame Citrus* centers on an erstwhile poster child, "Baby Dunn," who spent her childhood doing photo ops in a fruitless effort by a government agency to make people care about the water crisis. All the "slack-faced, listless" adults in *A Children's Bible* are decadent, indolent fools, whose own children think of them as "garbage-like figures," "lumpen bodies," who are, "for practical purposes, deceased."[97] They are OK boomer memes incarnate: the kind of people who might donate to NPR fundraising drives and shop at Whole Foods as the world burns. The characters end up feeling so inconsequential that it is hard for a reader to get invested in their fates, let alone root for their survival.

Novels like these seek to cut our self-regard down to size, to exile ourselves from the center of the cosmic order. They attempt to pan out from the petty theatrics of daily human existence in order to uncover a larger, more urgent drama. And, like a *vanitas* painting, they remind the reader that we, too, shall pass. This is what Powers seems to be getting at in *The Overstory* when he writes, "To be human is to confuse a satisfying story with a meaningful one, and to mistake life for something huge with two legs. No: life is mobilized on a vastly larger scale."[98] Or what Millet might have meant when, in an interview in *Bookforum*, she deplored the infiltration of the "assumptions of neoliberalism" into contemporary fiction: "That only the personal is a viable subject—the novel's consecrated form. That novels have to be exclusively about the personal." The claim that it is appropriate for the stories we tell to be about us, Millet warns, is "a specious idea, a self-inflicted wound. A Stockholm syndrome gesture."[99] As if to underscore the point, many of these novels end with a vision of life without any humans in it: the blissful quiet of a world without blaring car horns or factories, the seas brimming with new life, new species adapted to the denuded earth coming into being. In Krivak's *The Bear*, a dreamy reverie for humanity at its very end, animals such as bears and pumas and eagles are granted a noble interiority as they inherit the earth. Losing the human plot is not to be grieved. When we're gone, life will go on without us, and better things will come.

While there are no effective moral heroes to be found, there are faint glimmers of moral consciousness and virtue—characters who, unlike the clueless masses, are neither self-deceived nor self-justifying about their dire circumstances or the role humans have played in it. In *Something New Under the Sun,* the rare adults who do not ignore the problem cordon themselves off in a retreat center in upstate New York, where they make a religion of their climate grief: "Every day here we acknowledge that the planet is dying, that the life to come, the life our children will lead, is only a shadow of the life we enjoyed ourselves."[100] There are also the ecoterrorists and performative suicides of *Harrow, The Overstory,* and *California*—as unable to open the eyes of others in their deaths as they were in their lives. Their acts are desperate and without effect; perhaps, the novels suggest, this is the only option left for those adults who can't abide the destruction. But none of it ever amounts to meaningful resistance.

The real moral centers of the novels are plants, animals, and, most conspicuously, children. The children are precocious and possess otherworldly wisdom, which they dispense to the grown-ups, Greta-like, with surly righteousness. "The voices of oracles were said to be always those of children," Williams writes in *Harrow,* "possibly because a child can see everything in nothing whereas an adult has just the opposite inclination."[101] The figure of the last judge in *Harrow* is duly occupied by a know-it-all ten-year-old. In novels like *Bewilderment, A Children's Bible,* and *A New Wilderness,* children are endowed with messianic vision and a special empathic connection to nature. In *Bewilderment,* a nine-year-old who is variably diagnosed with Asperger's syndrome, ADHD, and OCD is uniquely attuned to the plight of endangered animals: "They used to be everywhere," he says angrily. "Before we got to them. We took over everything! We deserve to be alone."[102] In their wisdom, the children instinctively know to fear the adulthood that will rob them of their innocence and grace. When the kids in *A Children's Bible* discuss how dragonflies die at the height of their beauty, one of them wryly pronounces: "The opposite of humans . . . we turn ugly before we drop dead."[103]

Missouri Williams's debut novel *The Doloriad* takes the anti-humanist assumptions of the genre to their logical conclusion: A mysterious wave of ecological disasters killed off almost everyone on earth, leaving only four survivors; humanity has been reduced to a single encampment of grotesque, incestuous human beings. Their society, if you can call it that, is a maternal dictatorship where a single omnipotent Matriarch lords over an uncountable collective of progeny—most of whom are dumb, mean-spirited, feral, and uneducable. After the disaster, the Matriarch's life is consumed by the single-minded mission that she might reproduce and repopulate the earth from her own loins—though, unlike Lot's daughters, for whom incest was a last resort, the Matriarch might just be dressing up her taboo desire to sleep with her brother in the blameless language of survival. The hope to perpetuate human existence is revealed as a monstrous obsession, rooted in a woman's perverse and voracious sexual desire.[104] It is also completely futile—a civilized future for humankind is entirely foreclosed. And yet life in the camp continues to drag on, senselessly: "The leftovers of life. No flood, no sweeping-away, nothing but a slow and gradual decline."[105]

From the standpoint of the novel, this is no cause for despair. It is a fitting outcome, the natural course for the human species. For Williams, the Matriarch's fatal mistake is believing that life ought to be perpetuated. "The emphasis she places on the survival of the species is a reflection of her blindness and arrogance," Williams said in an interview. Redemption is out of the question. "The emptiness of the world around them," Williams explained, "is also the absence of the possibility for change."[106]

LIKE PULP GENRE fiction, eco-lit often prioritizes a narrow set of narrative tropes and moods over artistic innovation and voice. Even in its more ambitious iterations, the works repeat the same foregone conclusion like a mantra: the planet is lost, there remains no dignified human life to lead. No one is up to the task of meaningful resistance. If something good is yet to come, we will not be a part of it. Progress, if imaginable at all, is not continuous with our present. If there is hope, it is not for us.

What propels authors to so thoroughly subordinate originality to the message? Many of the writers are often eager to answer that they are not writing merely in the capacity of disinterested artists; they are consciously agitating for change. Some, like Lydia Millet, are actual activists. When she's not writing novels, Millet works in communications at an ecological-diversity advocacy group.[107] In an interview, she explained that the attitude of her adolescent characters is meant to convey a legitimate sense of outrage at our continued climate inaction: "My generation stubbornly refused to panic, when, for decades now, panic has been the only truly rational response." Now that there's "real fury" among the young, she said, "I'm grateful for the rage. It's overdue."[108] Richard Powers, who has been vocal about his choice not to have children out of concern for the environment, has said that he wrote *The Overstory* in order to encourage others to recant their anthropocentricism and accept that the earth is not their own: "'Environmentalism' is still under the umbrella of a kind of humanism: we say we should manage our resources better. What I was taking seriously for the first time in this book was: they're not our resources; and we won't be well until we realise that."[109] In the lead essay of her collection *Ill Nature*, Joy Williams was equally sharp in her opprobrium: "You want to find wholeness and happiness in a land increasingly damaged and betrayed and you never will. More than material matters. You must change your ways."[110] Elsewhere in the collection, in an essay titled "The Case Against Babies," Williams, herself a mother of one, rails against humanity's insistence on reproducing amid the unfolding environmental crisis: it's as if, she writes, "having glimpsed the imminent, we all, in denial of this unwelcome vision, decided to slam the door and retreat to our toys and make babies—those heirs, those hopes, those products of our species' selfishness, sentimentality and global death wish."[111] As Williams told *The Paris Review* in an interview in 2014, in what could double as a mission statement for the genre, "Real avant-garde writing today would frame and reflect our misuse of the world, our destruction of its beauties and wonders." Perhaps if it succeeded, she dared to hope, "the novel will die and even the short story because we'll become so damn sick of talking about ourselves."[112]

From the perspective of the writer-activist, the steady repetition of a message is exactly what is required to make sure it penetrates into the public consciousness. But why are people so eager to read about the apocalypse, and their own implication in it, over and over again? Back in 2014, when Alexandra Alter inquired after the unexpected hunger for climate fiction in the *New York Times*, the answer seemed self-evident to many of her sources. "It's in the air, isn't it?" said David Mitchell, whose 2014 fantasy novel *The Bone Clocks* culminates in a climate-induced dystopia.[113] "In a way, how can you be a sane and compassionate human being and not be increasingly alarmed by what's happening to the planet, when it's potentially civilization-ending?"[114]

Alarm is a sign of sanity and compassion, Mitchell claimed. But we might still wonder: Why does this alarm—as sane and compassionate as it might be—so frequently take the form of imaginative enactments of the most utter despair? Emily St. John Mandel, author of the disaster novel *Station Eleven,* which was later adapted into an acclaimed HBO television series, hazarded an answer: "It's a somewhat anxious time, and post-apocalyptic fiction is a way to channel our anxieties."[115] Channel where? One can channel anxiety *away*—as we do, say, with exercise—or channel it into productive efforts, or divert it elsewhere without addressing its source. It is not obvious which sort of channeling these novels perform. As the philosopher Jonathan Lear writes in his recent book *Imagining the End,* "There is cultural pressure to feel anxious about the future. Does this anxiety help us, perhaps by alerting us to the challenges we face? Or might it distract us or otherwise get in the way?"[116]

Contemporary eco-fiction shares a common intuition with the recent spate of anti-humanist and anti-natalist critiques: humanity's inability to face the challenge of climate change is a decisive indictment against our form of life. From this standpoint, we do not need to be provided with more information, but to grapple with our own blithe indifference to the certainty of disaster. The shape this reckoning must take is a hard—very hard—look in the proverbial mirror. That's why the reflection these works present us with is so horrifying: a monstrous amalgam of stupidity, callousness, and cruelty. The idea that humans' implication in their own demise might be unwitting, or unwilling, is dismissed as self-deception. When the novels do acknowledge that even those with their eyes open to their deteriorating reality are often helpless to do anything about it, this is presented less as tragedy and more as farce.

As a strategy, the rationale is clear enough: humans' hearts are hard, other means are failing, and we are running out of time. But the self-disgust and self-mockery these texts engender is at least as likely to produce numb resignation as to encourage action. Determined to disabuse their readers of faith in the worth of their lives and their capacities, they rid them of the grounds for belief in the possibility of the sort of radical reform they declare necessary.[117]

That the perspective of these novels is strategically self-defeating does not prove that it's false. If the misanthropic novel captures the true essence of human existence, perhaps depressive renunciation is the fitting attitude. But these narratives distort the truth in at least one obvious way: their effectiveness—whether as novels or as environmentalist tracts—depends on a capacity for recognition that is denied to practically all of the characters who appear in their pages. It follows that insofar as they purport to show their readers their own reflection, these works are self-undermining. Our world is not exclusively populated by blithe, selfish, self-deluded morons. The works themselves testify to the exceptions: surely at least their authors and audiences are capable of more. Denying this can constitute its own form of narcissistic indulgence.

In *Imagining the End*, Lear reflects on the pleasure we seem to take in fantasizing about our own extinction. We live, he writes, in a time that fosters anti-humanistic despair:

> In the name of drawing attention to the problems we face, there is a form of discourse that discourages creativity and hope in addressing them. Despair thrives when it is not fully conscious of what it is. It portrays itself as truthfulness—as the courage to face grim reality straight on, without the wishful illusions that keep us so complacent. It does not understand its own motivated fantasy structure.[118]

The novels, to use Lear's words, stage an "imagined punishment for our misdeeds." In doing so, they grant us a uniquely gratifying perspective on the spectacle, allowing us to indict humanity while remaining above the fray. There is "the *we* who are the official subject of the judgment, the *we* who are about to get what we deserve." But at the same time, there is a "*we who render the judgment.*" Here is where the potential for satisfaction lies: "There is pleasure to be had in imagining justice done, due punishment meted out to humankind—at no real cost to one's split off self." For Lear, enacting and reenacting the fantasy of our deserved demise isn't a sign of sanity or compassion, as Mitchell suggested, but a defensive gesture that spares us from having to face the possibility of genuine, profound loss. This is the loss of "all that is marvelous and good about us: our capacity for generosity and kindness, for stunning acts of creativity, for achievements of discovery and knowledge, for art and love, for our capacity to understand and appreciate self-consciously the world in which we live."[119] Forced to consider the terrifying possibility of extinction, it is easier—safer and more comforting—to think that it is all for the best, anyway. There is an advantage to doomerism: if any attempt at finding a solution is futile, we are exempt from trying.

To look into our own hearts and history for the grounds of self-respect does not mean ignoring our failures: discrimination, exploitation, and abuse across every possible line of difference within humankind—gender, race, ethnicity, culture, nation, class, sexual preference; tyranny; the degradation of the natural world; the infinitely many personal failures that each and every one of us exhibits every day. But these novels do more than confront us with our failings; they declare it foolish to expect any more of ourselves. The transformation the climate writers ostensibly wish to see in their readers seems to be incompatible with the image of humankind they propagate. Excessive self-regard can no doubt lead to arrogance, but we should not be surprised when those who have been denied all dignity fail to display moral courage. Self-respect might be as much a condition for the self-improvement of humanity as it is for the individual.

At the heart of the contemporary crisis of "literary imagination,"[120] as Amitav Ghosh calls it, is not just the imperviousness of climate events to figurative representation. The challenges we are facing are too difficult and demand too much sacrifice to expect effective deliberation and action to take place by those who have been deprived of an understanding of themselves as worthy of saving. Those who wish to encourage their fellow human beings to change must also remind them of their moral capacity, their strength, and their goodness. No less than the communication of the urgent need for action, what is needed is establishing once again our desert and our power.

WE'RE NOW FINALLY ready to address the substance of the antinatalist challenge, starting with the argument from evil. At last, we can ask: Do the pessimistic appraisals of humankind capture the truth about us? How could we begin to answer this question? Turning to the past, the evidence is mixed at best. Turning to the future, as the climate fiction novels do, we could try to imagine ourselves confronted with our end, waiting for our essence to emerge as we face our extinction head-on. But we do not have a way of knowing what would really happen as the end approaches. Would we stop at nothing to perpetuate a monstrous existence as the mean blobs of Williams's *Doloriad* do, or would we find the strength to play music and care for one another like Shelley's band of survivors in *The Last Man*? Who can say? It's an impossible question to answer—and not just because we are not omniscient. To think of humans as responsible beings—as we do when we hold ourselves accountable for the ecological degradation of the planet and insist, with Joy Williams, that we should "change our ways"—is to think of ourselves as capable of determining the course of our lives not arbitrarily or according to our whims but in light of a concern for what is the right thing to do. In other words, it is to think of ourselves as free. The fact of our freedom means we can never rule out the possibility of goodness, nor that of evil.

But we can say more on behalf of humanity than simply that our actions and their moral worth are up to us. It is not just the possibility of goodness but its *actuality* that fuels our deepest longing to ensure a human future. In starting with the global-infertility scenario dramatized in *Children of Men*, Scheffler focused on the anxiety provoked by the prospect of human extinction and the activities in our lives that would be rendered futile if it were to come to pass. But there is an even more fundamental concern the end of humankind raises—and it has to do not just with the fact that some of our projects happen to exceed our lifetimes but with those activities that make it genuinely worthwhile to live a human life.

Recall how Scheffler drew our attention to the way so many of the activities and practices we engage in at present—pursuits as diverse as cancer research, city planning, or long-term educational reform—are staked on the existence of human beings whose lives will outlast our own. The very meaning and value of these activities, activities with long-term ends, depend on other people continuing where we left off. The certainty of imminent extinction would leave a cancer researcher, a city planner, or an educational reformer at a real loss: How should they spend their remaining days? Insofar as their work gave them a sense that they were contributing to something that really mattered, that their lives were not for nothing, they would face a legitimate crisis. But, for all that, this does not justify their, or our, concern for the survival of humanity. The value of cancer research does of course depend on there being future people to benefit from such efforts, but as we've seen, cancer research is genuinely valuable only if human life—and its extension or the minimization of suffering within it—is valuable. If all there was to our extinction anxiety was the fear of a personal crisis of purpose, it would not constitute a genuine, objectively justified concern with humanity and its future. In the worlds of *Harrow* and *The Doloriad*, cancer research would be just as pointless—and just as harmful—as the humans whose lives it would aim to prolong.

But these kinds of reasons to worry about future generations do not exhaust the way in which our present-day activities bind us to the long-term fate of humanity. Scheffler is right that it is from the standpoint of our active commitments that we can evaluate our investment in the fate of humankind. We are dependent on other people to complete our projects. But we are also committed to the pursuit of activities that make human life, as such, worth living, the sort of activities that objectively justify the continued existence of humankind.

To see this clearly, we need to examine the structure of our actions more closely. In our day-to-day lives, we are constantly acting toward goals—or ends—that lie in the future. By an activity's "end," we mean that which it aims to accomplish and which gives it its character and standard of success. Suppose, to take a quotidian example, that you're making pancakes for breakfast. The end of your activity is to produce some pancakes you'll enjoy, and this is the point of everything you do in the service of that end: you shop for ingredients, measure them out, mix the batter, heat the griddle, etc. Your end—tasty, fluffy pancakes—determines the steps you will take in order to realize it. And it is with reference to that end that you can determine whether your activity was ultimately successful. Most of our ordinary activities aim at goals just like this: with an end in view, we act—we shop, measure, mix, preheat, fry, flip—until the job is done. Then, we're finished. The end is now complete, and there's nothing left to do (except cleaning up). In aiming at ends in this way, such activities are, in the words of philosopher Kieran Setiya, "self-destructive": once our goal is reached, the reason to act evaporates. Engaging in activities of this kind—activities with finite ends—is absolutely inevitable, but if everything we did had this structure, if we only derived meaning and value from such activities, our lives would be one long to-do list. "Your days," Setiya writes, would be "devoted to ending, one by one, the activities that give them meaning." This is a "structural absurdity," he warns: "In pursuing a goal, you are trying to exhaust your interaction with something good, as if you were to make friends for the sake of saying goodbye."[121] If that were all our lives consisted of, we would be in trouble.

There is, however, another way in which we go about things, a way of acting that avoids this kind of structural absurdity. Sometimes we act for an end that does not lie in the future but that we reach just by virtue of engaging in the activity. Such activities—activities with what we can call infinite ends—are therefore always complete and never self-destruct. Mundane examples include aimless pastimes like going for a stroll to nowhere in particular, or consistent habits like going swimming every weekend. An activity with an infinite end does not aim at a future target, like a destination or a fitness goal. A stroll will end at some point, you might one day break your swimming streak, but this won't be because that activity—strolling or swimming on weekends—has reached its intrinsic end. The end has already been reached by engaging in the activity in the first place. If we were to consider the stroll, or swimming habit, on its own, for all we know it could have gone on forever.

In the case of a stroll, that it contains its end at every moment and could go on forever merely expresses its aimlessness, the fact that you're not trying to get anywhere in particular; in the case of a swimming habit, the fact that it recurs might just mean that you think it's a good thing for you, personally, to do. But the special structure of activities like these—where the end is contained in them at every moment, and therefore they never reach exhaustion—also characterizes those activities we perform because we think they are unconditionally worth pursuing. These are the activities we perform not just to promote some goal or other, but for their own sake. Standard examples include friendship, appreciating the magnificence of nature or the beauty of art, and the commitment to justice. (Philosophers have been wont to claim that it is philosophy that has this quality most of all.) In being a friend, you are not aiming at some goal that lies in the future, which, once reached, will deem your attempt to be a friend successful and hence over and done with. In pursuing friendship, you might act for various finite ends—check in on a friend who's having a hard time, offer them help, take measures to celebrate their achievements—but none of these will exhaust what it means for you to be their friend. In being committed to justice, you do not think that there is a concrete goal to be achieved that will render your pursuit complete. The various particular pursuits that make up a commitment to justice—individual acts and political ones—all have their own concrete goals (returning a debt or a favor, protesting, voting). But in pursuing them one does not exhaust one's commitment to justice: one remains open and ready to express that commitment again on any future occasion that calls for it. Even if all injustices were remedied, justice would remain the light guiding your treatment of others. With friendship and justice, just as it is when you go strolling or keep up a regular weekend swimming habit, there is no natural endpoint to the pursuit. But in these special cases, the end is inexhaustible not because the action is aimless, like a stroll, or good for an individual, and possibly only them, like swimming on a regular basis. Ends like friendship and justice are *unconditionally* pursuit-worthy. These are the sorts of things that make it good to live a human life—not just for one person but for all human beings, and, crucially, not just here and now.

As concerns most of our ordinary goal-oriented activities, those aiming at finite ends, it would be merely an accident if they happened to continue indefinitely. Perhaps, hard as we try, humans never find a cure for cancer research, the grand unified theory of physics, or life on other planets. But as concerns those things that make it good to live a human life—the things that are worth pursuing unconditionally—it is no accident if they endure. Precisely because their ends do not exhaust themselves, there is no intrinsic reason for why they should give out at any point. We act to realize such ends until something forces us to stop. When it comes to the things that make life worth living, in the best-case scenario, the only thing that would put an end to their pursuit is one's death. But something else follows: since activities like friendship and justice contain their ends at every moment and are therefore always complete (unlike, say, cancer research or road construction), such activities would not be rendered meaningless or futile by our kind not lasting beyond our own lifetimes. Were you to learn that humanity would become extinct in the near future, *these* activities—your concern for your friends, your commitment to justice, your wonder at art—would not lose their meaning or their value. You would have as much reason to pursue them to the very end as you would were you to live forever.

The activities that make life worth living would be worth doing to the end of our natural lives. This is true whether or not others outlive us and follow in our footsteps. And yet it is they that ground our most profound concern for the future of humankind. This is because in pursuing an activity with an infinite end like justice, however tentatively and imperfectly, we recognize that it is worth pursuing not just by us, and not just here and now, but unconditionally: by others and indefinitely in time.

Scheffler begins from the assumption that knowledge of imminent extinction would render many of our future-oriented pursuits meaningless—that ethical, social, and political ties would falter, that people would sink into despair. But if our world is a world in which the knowledge of imminent extinction would render *all* pursuits meaningless, the implication would be that our world is one in which no one is pursuing the sorts of activities that make a human life worth living. In such a world, no one would be in a position to recognize the intrinsic goodness of a human future.

We could try to make the same point in yet another way. Let's recall the infertility scenario once more and consider the anxiety that the thought of our extinction provokes. Focus on the deep sense of loss that we are struck by in thinking about the demise of humanity. Think not just of the sense of deep practical disorientation—Does it still make sense to go to work? To go to college? To run in a 5K cancer fundraiser?—but of the grief, of the "black Melancholy" Mary Shelley conjures in *The Last Man* as the narrator recognizes "in every nerve, in every thought, that I remained alone of my race."[122] He is not just upset because it no longer makes sense to pursue the activities and projects he was committed to before the plague struck; he is in mourning.

Now, ask yourself: Are there not forms of future human existence that would cause no less distress? Suppose that the world is not coming to an end but that it continues indefinitely in a gravely diminished form. Would a world in which humanity survives solely in the form of cannibalistic bandits—like in Cormac McCarthy's *The Road*—provide us with any more comfort than extinction? Or consider the ethically and environmentally barren worlds of the climate novels: poisoned landscapes populated by selfish villains or ineffectual fools scavenging for scraps. Consider a world in which all human activities are reduced to mere atomized subsistence, in which no one recognizes the possibility of regarding any other human being as anything but a moving mechanism that either stands in one's way or might be usefully employed toward some end or other. Imagine a world in which humans do not concern themselves with the truth of things or with how they should conduct their lives. For many, these worlds would seem as bad as extinction—perhaps worse. The reason? They contain no trace of the activities that can make human life worth living. It is a commonplace that part of what it means to be human is to be able to recognize that there are fates worse than death. If this is true of the individual, perhaps it is also true of humankind. If you think that a world in which no human being is still capable of appreciating truth, goodness, and beauty is no worse than one in which humankind is no more, then what you worry about in worrying about the future of humanity is not the mere existence of human beings but the existence of human beings who are capable of recognizing and realizing the unconditional value of those things that make human life—your own as well as theirs—worth living.

In this way, the ability to recognize the goodness of human life in the future depends on our ability to recognize those things that render our life good at present: our capacity to pursue ends that do not merely gratify our interests, needs, and desires, but those that we recognize to be unconditionally pursuit-worthy. It is not inappropriate to hope for a better future. But hope cannot be based solely on an estimation of a future's mere open-endedness; it must rest also on the reality of our commitments at present. This does not require knowing everything that is practically necessary to solve climate change, or eradicate human ignorance, or secure world peace. No one person has a claim to this kind of knowledge. But what it does require is faith in our individual and collective capacity for moral courage and sacrifice, faith that is possible only on the basis of a recognition of the goodness in our own selves and our own lives. In other words, the legitimacy of human life does not depend on a remote possibility of a better world to come but is grounded in the objective goodness of at least some of our real commitments, here and now.

Crucially, this response to the argument from evil does not establish an independent conclusion, which everyone must or even can assent to, no matter what else they believe. Rather, it confronts every questioner with the task of determining what matters to them at present, and how. For some, it is going to be simply obvious that their lives contain, in whatever attenuated, imperfect, and partial form, the pursuit of the kinds of ends that make a human life worth living. Whether or not they decide to have children, whether or not they are able to, this argument will clarify what they already believe, which is that human life, however fraught, is not inhospitable to goodness, now or in the future.

For the rest, the argument will be a provocation: to examine their life, with its infinitely many assignments, appointments, and day-to-day hassles, and ask, What is it all for? Are these merely line items to check off, one by one, before starting the next—degree, job, promotion, house, retirement, death? Or do you manage to carve out room for those activities that make a human life worth living? Perhaps you are fortunate enough for these activities to make more than scant appearances in your life. Perhaps they also give it shape: you're not just trying to get a diploma, you're learning to think; you're not just clocking in and out, you're pursuing a vocation; you're not just building equity, you're trying to create a home; you do not just unwind in front of a screen or compile workout playlists, you let art move you; you don't just network, you let yourself care for others and, what is often even harder, let them care for you.

No one can determine for someone else whether or not their life is all shadow, or is illuminated, however faintly, by the good. But it is important to resist the pull of a certain kind of pressure to deny it. Today, to assert the goodness of one's own life is to risk coming across as privileged, or just hopelessly naïve. But to answer this question in the affirmative—to reject the argument from evil and to affirm the possibility of goodness in human life, now and in the future—is not to turn a blind eye to our human struggles and failings: the ways in which the competition and scarcity of our market economy threaten and too often foreclose genuine learning, or the possibility that one's career choices will be guided by anything like "a calling." It is not to deny that the unequal distribution of opportunities and resources can push the dream of a "home" out of reach. It is not to ignore that the institutions within which we find ourselves pursuing our destinies—our relationships, schools, places of work, societies, and nations—have not been and are not yet free of bigotry, violence, and exploitation. To say that your life contains goodness is not to say that it is simply good. It is not to ignore the tragic foreclosure of possibilities or overlook pain, harm, and loss. It is only to affirm that to some, perhaps small, degree, your life is not wholly determined by exigency and failure. It is to say no more and no less than that it is worth living.

Having addressed the argument from evil, we are ready to turn to the second anti-natalist challenge: the argument from suffering. Supposing humanity's intrinsic moral failures do not render procreation indefensible, one may still wonder how to justify bringing life into the world in light of the suffering that children born now could face in their lifetimes.

It is tempting to try to meet this challenge by contesting the particular underlying claims about the extent of the environmental devastation that will be actually caused by climate change. We might want to point out that while things are going to get bad, they won't get quite as bad as some of the worst, most alarmist predictions of the late 2010s might have led us to believe, and that, if recent research into displacement patterns is correct, however bad things get, it is doubtful they will result in the huge waves of mass migration we so often hear about.[123] We might find ourselves wanting to add that the worst of the effects are not going to be felt by those who are most likely to take the anti-natalist argument seriously. (The reality is that if you are reading this book, you and your potential children are not likely to be the ones who will go hungry when the crops fail.) At any rate, we might insist, having children has always been a gamble; our ancestors had children, intentionally or not, under far worse conditions than those we face today. Historically speaking, giving birth in the midst of a crisis may well be the norm, not the exception. But while all of this may be true, it will probably have little persuasive power, and for good reason.

Such rebuttals, one senses, are beside the point. The concerns expressed by those wondering whether it's right to bring children into a warming world can't be dispelled by fact-checking. That the argument from suffering has, after all, been raised for over two thousand years suggests the problem goes deeper than the historical exigencies of the present. And, as we've seen earlier in this chapter, though one hears echoes of both forms of the anti-natalist challenge—that is, of both the argument from evil and the argument from suffering—in the historical record, at least until the advent of Christianity, it was the argument from suffering that seemed to hold the greater sway. It's also the kind of anti-natalist concern that has been foregrounded by Anglophone philosophers who have debated whether or not it is possible to benefit and harm human beings by bringing them into existence and, if so, whether such harm can be morally justified. The most widely held combination of views among contemporary parties to the debate, who almost universally share a broadly conse-quentialist ethical framework, is that one *can* harm people by bringing them into existence, and one should refrain from doing so if the quality of their lives—understood as their level of well-being or welfare—will be sufficiently low. The clearest expression of this conviction is the so-called Procreation Asymmetry thesis, according to which there is a duty not to bring miserable people into existence, but no analogous duty to create people only be-cause they will be happy.[124] This, of course, hardly amounts to a wholesale moral prohibition on procreation. Though not a duty, it is perfectly permissible, according to this position, to bring people into the world as long as their lives will not be very bad. But the idea that a human life can be so bad that it might not be worth living, and that, moreover, it would be wrong to bring a person into existence who faced such a prospect, sets us on a course to more extreme anti-natalism. We may try one of several paths to get us all the way there.

One version of the argument from suffering starts with the following assumption: the moral permissibility of having children is correlated with the degree of suffering the child will experience. The appeal is intuitive: the more a child of yours will suffer, the more morally perilous it is to have children. Insofar as climate change means that environmental conditions for human life will worsen, it renders the choice to have children—children whose lives will be to that extent worse than before—less justified than it once was. But a troubling consequence follows. First, notice that because no one can know with any certainty how their children's lives will fare, from the standpoint of the individual navigating the choice, it seems reasonable that the moral permissibility of having children ought to be correlated not with actual but unknowable-in-advance outcomes but with the probable degree of misery the child is liable to experience. In this modified version of the claim, procreation becomes less permissible either the worse a child's life is likely to be or the more likely it is that a child will suffer a very miserable life. Now, if the choice whether or not to have children hinges on the expected welfare levels of those children, there's an obvious set of parameters you could use to try to predict how severely they will be affected by global warming: the socioeconomic circumstances of their parents. Extreme weather phenomena are no doubt dangerous to everyone, but they are most dangerous to those who are already materially and socially vulnerable. As was made direly evident in Haiti after Hurricane Matthew in 2016, or in New Orleans after Hurricane Katrina in 2005, poverty, subpar living conditions, and compromised governmental crisis responses all contribute to disproportionately high casualties in the event of natural disasters.[125] And of course material security can promote a child's well-being in many more ways than shielding them from massive storms or heat stroke; more mundane welfare determinants like the ability to ensure high-quality housing, nutrition, healthcare, and education all likewise depend on access to means, whether individually or socially.

The banal correlation of socioeconomic status with expected welfare, combined with the assumption that the moral permissibility of having children correlates with their expected well-being, yields a startling conclusion: having children can be justified in direct proportion to the social and financial security of their parents. According to this reasoning, a couple in Haiti will not only encounter greater material hurdles to providing their child with a good life than their counterparts in the United States; they are also less morally justified in having them in the first place.

But surely the choice to have children cannot be more ethically sound the higher your class status is. (And this is without taking into account the gross differentials in the contributions of the rich and poor to anthropogenic climate change.) Money can buy many things, but the ethical justification to have children ought not be one of them. To claim otherwise is perverse—and we may confidently reject an argument for leading us to such a conclusion. It is rather the other way around: in having a child, a human being assumes the responsibility to care for them, to the best of their abilities, whatever the challenges they will have to face. Parents who do so under circumstances of near-certain hardship, where that duty of care will likely exact more suffering and require more sacrifice, are not more morally blameworthy than their well-to-do peers; they might just be braver.

In order to avoid the perverse conclusion that the richer you are, the more morally justified you are in having children, we might try to argue for something altogether more extreme. Namely, that, given the inevitability of some suffering in *any* life, no matter how comfortable it might otherwise be, no one is justified in subjecting a future child to the risks and harms of existence. After all, we all get sick, we all endure loss and humiliation, we all die. This is the argument put forth by the most famous living anti-natalist philosopher, David Benatar. As we've seen, Benatar argues that we view sparing the unborn pain or harm as a good thing, but we view the opposite—not giving them pleasure or benefit—with neutrality; it is neither good nor bad. If that is right, in bringing a person into existence we may provide them with both benefits and harms, but if we refrain from procreation we do only good. This argument has been contested in the academic literature, but for our purposes, what is important is that on the face of it this absolutist version of the argument from suffering—according to which any suffering whatsoever renders procreation immoral—is not what most people seem to worry about. We don't usually think that the mere occurrence of some pain in a life will invalidate its worth, whether our own or others'. On the contrary, we acknowledge that certain difficulties and pains are necessary to attain the things we value most in life. All learning, for example, involves varying measures of discomfort: whether it be the learning of artistic skills like playing the piano and ballet dancing or virtues like courage and generosity. And, insofar as the argument from suffering has popular appeal, it is usually provoked by the possibility of some sort of exceptional suffering—like an environmental hellscape—not just any run-of-the-mill trial or tribulation. The claim that it is immoral to have children simply because their lives will contain some discomfort, loss, and disappointment is not what is underlying the intensifying ambivalence today.

Arguably, what troubles people most is not the thought that any measure of suffering will invalidate their choice to have children, nor is it the idea that the more challenging their child's life is likely to be the less justified they are in having them. It is, rather, the ineliminable anxiety in the face of overwhelming uncertainty and powerlessness. How can I, a prospective parent, bring a child into a world where I can never guarantee their basic safety and well-being, let alone happiness? Whatever the odds may be, the potential scope of human misfortune and tragedy can seem so great as to render any risk too high.[126]

To see the problem with this final version of the challenge—and with the arguments from suffering more generally—let us suppose, for a moment, that it is right. Suppose, that is, that since no one, no matter how favored by chance, can guarantee that their child will not suffer catastrophically, all procreation is unjustified and therefore impermissible. A curious result follows. If it is wrong for anyone to bring a child into the world in the present, it has been wrong for everyone to have brought a child into the world in the past. In other words, every single human being—you, everyone you know or know of, everyone who has ever lived or will live in the future—was born out of a grave moral failure. It means that anyone who has voluntarily attempted, or just voluntarily risked, procreation has committed a serious moral offense. This is a conclusion that a philosopher like Benatar would happily embrace. And the very idea that an argument implies that many or most human beings have significantly morally erred is of course no objection to it—Aristotle thought ethical virtue was the share of the few, not the many, and Kant was happy to concede that perhaps no human being had ever done a truly morally worthy deed in their lives. The problem is that this argument implies something far more drastic: that the very possibility of human life—and with it, the very possibility of human action, which is to say, the very possibility of good and evil—turns out to be always predicated on a grave moral transgression. For anything good to have ever taken place, someone had to first commit a serious moral wrong. But here, we appear to have gone off the deep end. Starting with an understandable worry about the impossibility of guaranteeing the safety and happiness of our children, we've ended up on the verge of affirming that all human life is premised on a moral calamity. Could the basic fact of human vulnerability to the unpredictability of the future really render the reproduction of human life immoral? Is the reproduction of human life unjustified simply because we are neither omniscient nor omnipotent, that is to say, because we are finite beings, not divine?

It makes sense to be anxious about the future of the children you may or may not have; to be frustrated about how helpless you are to ensure they will be spared illness, accidents, cruelty, and injustice, let alone that they will achieve satisfaction and joy; to fear the way in which every adversity that will affect them will affect you, too. When one focuses intently on all that could go wrong, the weight of the risk can seem so great that it's astounding anyone would ever willfully take it on. But the conclusion to draw is not that going ahead with it, under any circumstances, is morally irresponsible. On the contrary. To have children is to face a tremendous task, whose magnitude we can never ascertain in advance; it means assuming a great responsibility, not abnegating it.

Whether we act responsibly does not depend simply on whether we bring children into the world, but on how seriously we take our duties as parents and as human beings. This is why we have no more reason to fear that our children will demand an explanation for why we brought them into the world than we are in the habit of demanding such justifications from our parents. The question our children will be justified in asking us is not why we dared have them but why we didn't do more to care for them, and why we didn't do better by the only world they have to live in. The answer they will demand is not why we gave them life but why we didn't lead a better life ourselves.


BRINGING A CHILD into the world, to state the obvious, is not the only way to take a stance on the worthiness of human life. Throughout history, many men and women—whether or not they have had children—have taken other paths. They have pursued religious callings, art, philosophy, social reform, and the struggle for political progress. But having children might still be the most basic way to affirm our existence. This is not only because bringing forth and nurturing life is the most literal way of doing so. Nor is it simply because parenting is the greatest responsibility an individual human being can assume for another. Having children is the most basic way of affirming life, above all, because the fact of human life is the condition for all others.

In Plato's *Symposium,* Socrates claims that begetting ideas is nobler than begetting children.[127] But how would ideas endure without anyone to examine, share, and transmit them? Two millennia later, Sheila Heti's narrator in *Motherhood* similarly tries to weigh the benefits of children against those of art. Both, she says, are "viable" ways of having "your mind set on eternity."[128] In having children and in creating the sort of art that others will labor to maintain in living memory, one leaves something of oneself that will outlast one's natural life. But Heti puts a twist on this idea. Children are indeed "eternity forward," but art is "eternity backwards," she declares. "Art is written for one's ancestors." What does this mean? Even Heti admits that it is "hard to conceive of making art without an audience who will eventually see it." In a 2020 essay written after her father's death, Heti continued reckoning with the kind of transcendence art can and cannot afford: "A person who makes art wants to be trapped in the collective mind of humanity. Artists make earthbound things that live among living humans . . . no one is more afraid of leaving the earth than the artist who hopes his or her work will endure for centuries."[129] Socrates, who purportedly had three children, and Heti, who has none, are both tempted to consider philosophy and art in isolation, separately from the human beings who would be required to ensure their endurance. In these accounts, the real value of a human future remains indeterminate. At the same time, in her concern for that which can be pursued for its own sake—in this case, art—even Heti cannot but admit that caring for it means caring also about the possibility of perpetuating it into the distant future.

What are children for? There is no abstract justification, much less a list of benefits, that can exhaust the question. To affirm life requires more than acknowledging its merits and countering the charges of its detractors. In deciding to have children, one takes a practical stance on one of the most fundamental questions a person can ask: Is human life, despite all the suffering and uncertainty it entails, worth living? But while the problem of how to affirm life in the face of pain, sacrifice, and failure has the structure of a question, like the apparent questions of who we are and what we are here for, it is far from obvious that what we are meant to do with it is to search for an answer, let alone settle on one. There is no fixed solution to this problem, no set answer that can be discovered and established once and for all, case closed.

To affirm life is to live, and to do so in a certain way: finding room for the sorts of unconditionally good activities that make a human life worth living, committing to projects of value and relationships defined by love, accepting the burden of responsibility, allowing things to matter to you. And as hard as the question may be, we should also not forget that affirming life is something that we do every day, with every breath we take. However difficult the going gets, however much we complain and protest, most of us still treat our lives not only as valuable but as precious. In this way, the answer to the question whether life is good does not really await our decision to have children; we answer it already every day, with every genuine commitment that we make. It is because the decision to have children entails just such a commitment—as personally consequential as it is philosophically profound—that only you can determine whether it is the right one for you.

# Hello from the Other Side

## —*Anastasia*

Soon after I gave birth—masks mandatory, partners allowed—
questions about my well-being started to take a new, unexpected form. Interest seemed to shift away from my physical
state—how was I feeling, how much sleep were we getting—
toward something else. "So, how's *motherhood*?" "How is *being
a mother*?" I had no idea what they were talking about. There
were many obvious changes: new tasks, new research assignments, new things—soft things, plastic things—that I could
not fit anywhere in the cupboards and closets. But when asked
about "motherhood," I didn't know where to look. Which bit
was *that*? There was the baby—who really was never "the baby"
at all but was always herself, with her name and many nick-
names, her little belly and cheeks. She had as many appointments as a midlevel executive and was steadily achieving all
sorts of rather opaque developmental milestones, like learning "to detect contrast," which we pretended to understand
and tried hard not to impose on other people. But they weren't

asking about her. Something more fundamental was supposed to have happened—to me.

To have a child, it is often said, is to transform one's identity. What this might have meant in the past is more or less obvious: with few exceptions, for the better part of history, to have a child meant it was time for a woman to say her final farewells to whatever public existence she managed to forge up to that point and, henceforth, dedicate herself to the well-being of her children and maintenance of their household. But now there is another, more mysterious change that becoming a mother is understood to imply. Because it is more basic than the historical conditions of oppression, the threat of this metamorphosis continues to loom even as the material, social, economic, and political circumstances of women's lives have been radically improved. This change is supposed to reconfigure the deepest core of one's being. When the contemporary analytic philosopher L. A. Paul wanted to introduce the idea of a fundamentally transformative experience, one of her central examples was having a child. For women, especially, becoming a parent is frequently described as a total revolution of the self. "Giving birth to a baby is, literally, splitting in two, and it is not always clear which one your 'I' goes with," philosopher Agnes Callard wrote in a reflection on the relief she felt after losing an unplanned pregnancy. "Actually, it is clear," she added. "It is clearly not *you*."[1] The writer and artist Darja Filippova, musing with fascinated horror about her own postpartum metamorphosis, wrote similarly: "Something has made it out, but I am not sure it is me."[2]

This is what concerned onlookers wanted to know when they asked me about *being a mother*. They were asking about the status of this new thing that was supposed to have emerged, split itself off from me, and usurped my place. They weren't asking about me at all, they were checking in on my successor. I looked around. The baby was still there—mastering spit bubbles—but no one else. Did I do it wrong? Was I already gone?

Filippova likens the physical battering involved in labor—her body lashed, hollowed out, and subsequently made to shed, crack, and ooze—to the ecstatic visions of medieval female mystics, who longed for a divine encounter so powerful that it would shatter them to pieces, dissolve them into unity with the All. But, she insisted, the postpartum devastation of the physical body is only the appearance of the real, mental, drama. New mothers aren't just torn asunder, they are delivered out of their minds. After birth, Filippova scours "What to Expect" web forums for women wondering whether they are going crazy. One post reads:

> I forgot my name. I was at the register making a return at Buy-BuyBaby, the guy asked for my name, and I totally blanked. Had to text my husband. Thankfully it happened at a baby store—he said it happens all the time! Haha ma liiiiife.[3]

In Filippova's telling, the postpartum annihilation—the corporeal dissolution, the self-forgetting—was as much something to long for as to dread. But inching my way toward birth, I felt neither fear nor yearning. The whole thing seemed too fantastical, too absolutely wild, to merit expectations.

In *A Life's Work,* Rachel Cusk writes that ever since she had first found out what childbirth entails, she worried about the violence of it, the agony, and tried to find in her ordinary, daily run-ins with pain the prefiguration of the One to Come. But I did not understand what it would mean to consider, in advance, the absolute limits of pain. The dopey instructor of my prenatal "hypnobirthing" course tried to assure us that you can handle the pain if you prepare for it. She introduced techniques that we were meant to draw on during labor—how to breathe (deeply), how to make figure eights with your pelvis (whichever way you like), where your partner should apply pressure (the back)—but it was clear to me birth would not be a good time to test how much attention I had paid in class. And, besides, I didn't believe her. A woman I had met at a prenatal clinic who was about to give birth to her third child told me the pain of the contractions was like this: "You go up, give God a high five, and come back down." I hadn't given birth yet but I instinctively knew that this one was telling the truth. What visualization exercises could prepare someone to face her creator?

The medicalization of birth has rendered women more passive and more vulnerable during pregnancy and labor, but even under the best, most enlightened circumstances, birth is not simply something you do; you do not breathe out a baby or wiggle it out with a twist of your hips. The body produces contractions strong enough to force a human infant out of itself. You can stand and crouch and squat and do whatever you please with your pelvis, but this will still be something you *undergo*. I underwent it without an epidural, which, if given the opportunity, I would probably try to do again, and would recommend to absolutely no one. Even saying that you "undergo" it is a bit of an overstatement. It is not exactly an experience. Some events are so unlike anything else that we lack the means to fully process and integrate them into our self-understanding. They tear a hole in the fabric of our existence. That our humanity is compatible with being ripped apart, that pain can be so great as to make you plead for mercy, that other people can witness such things again and again in the course of a day's work and continue on their merry way—these, I maintain, are not things that a Rainbow Meditation audio file can help you take on with any more equanimity, no matter how often you play it. And because such events cannot be well integrated into one's self-understanding, they do not leave marks like ordinary experiences do. Find a woman who's given birth and tell her about an encounter you've had with pain: a broken ankle, a burn, a killer migraine. Invite her to relate to your experience: try saying, *Do you know what I mean?* Or, *Have you ever had anything like that happen to you?* Whatever she may offer in response, she's not likely to mention her labor. Some things burrow so deep inside you they barely leave a trace on the surface.

Birth's resistance to integration manifested in my case in the curious sense that nothing really happened. Wheeled to the maternity ward with our baby in my arms (a matter of policy, I had offered to walk), there it was: everything just as we had left it the day before. A friend warned I would not be able to think for months after the birth; but I replied to work emails from the hospital bed. They didn't make less sense, they didn't seem any less important. The only thing standing in my way was the restricted use of my arms. Strange—all the same things continued to matter to me: the same philosophical questions, the same friends and their same problems, the same politics, the same petty gossip. Imagine surviving a car crash, crawling out, hesitantly fumbling over the surfaces of your body to assess the damage and realizing you have emerged unscathed. There you are: not dead, not reborn, just lost, wondering how you are supposed to get to your final destination without a means of transportation. And so it was from that day on: my world did not become narrower, it continued to expand at its steady pace—I just had to work much harder to keep up with all those cars racing past me.

Parents, mothers especially, like to claim they have become better people subsequent to the birth of their children. I am not here to call anyone's bluff or forswear the possibility of my own personal growth in the future, but as a description of my condition, the thought evokes a haughty smile on a good day and an eye roll on a worse one. No doubt, I learned new tricks. How to keep milk cold on the go,[4] how to never ask a small child *whether* they wanted to do something but *which* of two options they preferred. But I did not unearth new practical or ethical or emotional resources. You could say I have become better at managing time. But all that really happened was that the days, which still only had twenty-four hours each, became much fuller and more unpredictable, forcing me to adapt. The workday narrowed to a block that I could pretend was eight hours long, but in effect was almost always shorter, so I had to work faster, and after the baby's bedtime. At the same time, our mornings started so early that very late nights were out of the question. For the first time, weekends assumed a markedly different character than weekdays, not because I had learned to "unplug" but because I didn't have childcare. I finished the weekend, like most parents of small children do, feeling more, not less, tired.

I am, it is true, far more patient with my daughter than I would be with anyone else exhibiting comparably high levels of incompetence, need, or obstinance. But this tolerance does not extend to anyone else. There is less of it to go around. Nor am I more compassionate. As the birth approached and in the weeks after, I was noticeably more sensitive to helpless suffering. When I was nine months pregnant, I tried to rescue a blind, sickly kitten that had gotten lost in the rain under our building. We drove it to the vet; there was nothing to be done but to put it down. But if my heart has genuinely, permanently expanded, it is by the measure of my love for my daughter, not much more.

But what of this love? Is it not unlike anything I've ever known? Is there not *so much* of it? Have I not been unmade and remade by its force? The rumor of this love drives much of the fear of missing out among those debating whether or not to have children. One hears: I am afraid that if I don't have a child, I will never know what that love is like. But while the relationship between a parent and child is doubtless unique, what if I told you that, phenomenologically speaking, it is not really grand and tremendous? That it's not even particularly extraordinary? When I try to focus on it—which feels a little like trying to focus on the transparency of the air—it shows up as something rather basic. Integrating parenting with everything else I happen to care about is a hard, complicated struggle, full of misgivings. But loving my daughter is the easiest thing I've ever had to do. It is easy not because this love is unadulterated by other emotions—frustration, resentment, fear—but because to the extent that *it* is not pure, no love is. Because whatever contradictions my love for her contains, and however much hesitation attends the unending stream of decisions that raising her requires, I cannot doubt it any more than I can doubt my own existence.

Groping for language with which to explain this love, I think of the words we use to describe children when we want to capture what they evoke in us, how they make us feel—words like *cute* and *sweet* and *adorable* and *wonder* and *responsibility* and *protectiveness* and *sacrifice* and, yes, *love* itself—and I wonder if we would have come up with such notions if not for the encounter of a parent, maybe a mother, with her child. I wonder whether the other ways we use these terms, in other contexts, aren't all derivative of the one original application. Whether or not this is because all other love really is made in the image of this one, this means that to love your child isn't like nothing you've ever known. It isn't unimaginable. If you have known love, you have also known it, or something like it. If you have known love, your love for your child will be very like what you think it will be. What is so special about this love isn't how exotic, mysterious, or astounding it is, but just how simple and familiar.

You are no longer the center of your world, they say, as if parenting effects a Copernican revolution: now, your child is the sun, and you are running circles around it. When oil started crackling in the pan while I was making pancakes with my daughter the other day, I witnessed myself instinctively walk into the line of fire instead of out of it, so as to shield her. *Would you look at that,* I thought. *Never moved* toward *hot oil before.* If she really needed me, it is hard to imagine there is much I would not sacrifice for her. But a lot is covered over by the idea of "really needing me." My interpretation of it is certainly not coextensive with how much she asks for me; and I cannot pretend that I subject her to my departures and absences strictly for her sake. Under normal circumstances I often choose "myself," which means something else I care about, and I prefer not to tell a complicated story about the benefits accrued to her on account of me doing so.

Indeed, today one often hears that the pursuit of independent interests will in turn render a woman a better mother. In a viral commencement speech, delivered at Dartmouth in 2014, the TV writer and producer Shonda Rhimes (of *Grey's Anatomy* and *Scandal* fame), a single mother of three, volunteered an answer to a question she gets all the time: How does she do it all?[5] Echoing Anne-Marie Slaughter, she confessed that she doesn't, it's not possible. Whenever you see her succeeding in one area in her life, she said, it almost certainly means she is failing in another. (If she is "killing it" on a script, she is missing bedtime; if she's sewing her kid's Halloween costume, she's blowing off a rewrite.) For a successful career woman and single parent, every choice to fulfill one commitment means sacrificing another, and getting help can only get you so far. Coming from Rhimes, a woman whose work appears to be a true labor of love, the admission hints at the ways in which the conflict between vocation

and family runs deeper than the inequities of current work practices and culture. No doubt, there is much more that we can do
to support parents: I do not appreciate when my colleagues suggest scheduling departmental meetings outside of work hours,
or when it doesn't occur even to the organizers of a women-only
academic conference to help participants secure childcare. But
to the extent that parenthood and one's professional, intellectual,
and artistic ambitions are *all* potentially infinite pursuits, the
conflict between them can never be fully eliminated. The reason
I stay up writing this book at night is also because I want to.

Rhimes goes on to suggest that the necessary trade-offs aren't
ultimately as harmful to her kids as one might initially suppose.
Though work takes her away from her children, she is confident
she is "a better mother for it"—"happy," "fulfilled," "whole." Like
Rhimes, I, too, spend my days thinking and writing, but I am
not as confident as she is that doing so intrinsically and necessarily improves my parenting. The intuitive appeal of her argument is transparent: children benefit from having their mothers
model the cultivation of independent interests, an inner world,
ambition. It is a nice thought: that my daughter will consider
herself lucky to have a mother who asked difficult questions
and showed some aptitude in answering them, a mother who
applied herself for the sake of things that she thought mattered.
It is pleasant to suppose my daughter will feel confident to forge
a path for herself because she's seen me try to do that before her.
I hope she will. But if our work makes us better mothers, where
does this leave those women who were not or are not able to
spend their days reading and writing, to find fulfillment, to be
"whole"—whether because they were prevented from doing so
or chose not to? Are they also worse mothers for it? I wish on
every woman my or, better yet, Rhimes's freedoms, but I draw the
line at adding to the conditions of good mothering the aspiration

to artistic, intellectual, and professional distinction, much less its achievement.

Some ambitious, successful women who pursue their passions are better mothers for it, but this is obviously not the case for all. Intellectual, artistic, and professional ambition has pulled men and women away from their homes, and sometimes not only temporarily. Reflecting on having left her first two children in infancy, the novelist and 2007 Nobel Prize winner Doris Lessing famously said, "There is nothing more boring for an intelligent woman than to spend endless amounts of time with small children." She suggested that not dedicating herself to writing would have made her into a worse person: "I would have ended up an alcoholic or a frustrated intellectual like my mother."[6]

And yet—did motherhood not shape her writing? Has it not shaped mine? While becoming a mother did not temper Lessing's intellectual ambitions, motherhood and its difficulties emerged as a major theme of her work. Likewise, the transfiguration of the personal experience of motherhood—centered on the conflict between raising children and creative work—has arguably helped the motherhood ambivalence writers of recent years to discover their literary calling (not to mention critical and commercial success). Motherhood may not enable the intellectual, creative woman to do *more* work, but might it not make that work better, richer? Perhaps; perhaps not. Writing about Sylvia Plath, Elizabeth Hardwick concluded that "it is sentimental to keep insisting that the birth of her children unlocked her poetic powers."[7] Hardwick reached the judgment on "the evidence of her work" but also on principle: the assumption that motherhood should improve the writing is based on fantasy. "Why should that be?" Hardwick insisted. "The birth of children opens up the energy for taking care of them and for loving them," no less and no more. Plath did not become either nicer or wiser; neither did I.

THE ASSUMPTION THAT motherhood is transformative is related to the idea that "motherhood" is its own freestanding identity category. Today, it is not uncommon for successful, ambitious women—journalists, politicians—to include "mom" in their Twitter and professional bios, while eager psychologists recommend adding a new "reproductive identity" category: "Like gender and sexuality, reproduction is a healthy aspect of human expression to be openly explored, destigmatized, and self-authored."[8] For new mothers especially, the temptation to conceive of "motherhood" as an identity is intense. Enterprising middle-class mothers are organizing self-help communities online to help women deal with "matrescence": a "groundbreaking new science that captures the physical, psychological, social and emotional changes women go through during the monumental transformation that motherhood evokes."[9] Mommy influencers pop up on Instagram feeds with no apparent interests besides ranking baby nests and breast pumps. Mom-advice forums feature more shibboleths and obscure acronyms than an incel subreddit.

In a representative 2020 *New York Times* piece titled "When Your Name Becomes 'Mom,' Do Your Other Identities Matter?" the writer Rachel Bertsche confessed to finding herself "mourning the person I was before parenthood." She explained, "I get nostalgic for the woman who took vacations to exotic countries or went out to dinner with friends at a moment's notice."[10] Although she had longed for the "mom" title, it now diluted all the others:

I wasn't working out like I used to, and I couldn't find the time to string a sentence together on a page, let alone write—or even read—a book. I didn't have time (or didn't make time) for friends, and as for pop culture, well, I didn't stop watching TV—what else is there to do when you're pumping incessantly?—but I wasn't a wealth of useless entertainment knowledge anymore, either.[11]

I know what Bertsche means. For years, I used to go to the cinema on a weekly basis. I believe we are meant to watch films just like that, together, in a collective dream. I love watching trailers, eating popcorn, drinking soda watered down by melting ice; I love a huge screen and immersive sound. Since my daughter was born, I've been to the movies twice. But I also find myself wanting to insist that how you watch films—just like how much you work out, how exotic your vacations are, or how freely you can schedule impromptu dinner dates—does not constitute an identity. I used to attend classes all day and dance on tables at night. Now, I teach classes on some days and dance at 6:00 P.M. with a child in the kitchen. College doesn't last forever: you're meant to graduate. No one has died, you've just grown up. Or rather, if someone has died, it's because growing up involves these kinds of deaths all along the way.

Treating motherhood—or its inverse, being "child-free"—as an identity category can help women make sense of their experience, broadcast its challenges effectively, and find the support they need to navigate it. But it comes at a cost to mothers and non-mothers alike. The assumption of obligatory identity change can imply that our myriad other identities will necessarily be flattened, or even lost. For prospective mothers, this can make the decision whether to have children that much more daunting. In such cases, the motherhood "identity" becomes not a liberatory category of self-understanding but yet another source of anxiety.

At the same time, for mothers, conceptualizing parenting as an identity can render the experience more, not less, fraught than it already is. "Identity" is a way of marking distinction, that is to say, difference. As an identity, motherhood distinguishes women with children as significantly and importantly different from people who do not have them. On top of all the practical require-ments that tether parents to the home, literally and figuratively, the expectation implied in the idea of "being a mother" can add to the pressure to withdraw and isolate. Sheila Heti laments in *Motherhood*, "When a person has a child, they are turned to-wards their child. The rest of us are left in the cold."[12] But treating motherhood as an identity not only encourages a mother to turn away from the world, it also encourages the world to turn away from her. Concerns arising from one's identity are best, we often assume, addressed "in-group." And then, when a woman is told to expect a momentous change in her sense of self and it fails to occur, she can come to feel like she is doing things wrong: not giving herself over sufficiently to the experience, lacking in com-mitment if not in feeling, selfish.

Goodness requires "unselfing," wrote the novelist and phi-losopher Iris Murdoch.[13] To be good requires transcending the things that make you a unique individual, for the sake of some-thing greater than yourself. She added that goodness "is perhaps most convincingly met with in simple people—inarticulate, unselfish mothers of large families."[14] The implication: for a woman to hold on to her identity, resist transformation, and fail to sufficiently "unself" herself is not to fail just as a mother but as a human being.

IF YOU ARE the sort of person for whom my tale of survival and perseverance appeals, if you are feeling yourself buoyed by the promise and legitimization of permanence, let me assure you: resisting transformation comes at a cost. Whatever success I may have enjoyed in my dogged efforts to hold myself together, it made the impossibility of carrying on as before all the more frustrating. Staying the same did not assuage the weight and burden of the responsibility of parenting—it increased it. My priorities might not have changed much, but they had to contend with unruly new company, a child who has been doing everything in her power to destroy her competition for my attention, time, and energy from the moment she was born. How much easier it would have been if I really did come to care less about anything else.

The first night we brought our baby back from the hospital, I saw a dark glimmer of what life would look like from then on, an inkling of the extent to which my hopes of carrying on as before—or better!—were absurd. "What have we done?" I heard myself weeping. "What have we done? Our life was good." Sitting across from me, my husband said, "It's a good thing that our life was good. It does not make more sense to have a baby when it isn't." He was right; but the more you have, the more you stand to lose. The more you like your life, the more often you might find yourself wondering what life would have looked like had you not had children. The older you are, the more confident and settled in your ways, the less you will appreciate having to change them.

When I try to convey what it has been like to raise our child, I hear an echo of David Wallace-Wells on the climate crisis: "It is, I promise, worse than you think."[15] Then I go blank. If it is difficult to express the purported joys of having children, it might be even harder to express the quotidian misery of it. I probably find this particularly hard because I used to believe that the inability to enjoy one's child, wholly and completely, was a sign of personal failure. I recall vividly—the vividness due mostly to the embarrassment I now feel thinking about it—a friend of mine, who had a child a few years before I did, complaining that spending time with kids is very boring. How sad, I thought, that he did not love his own child as much as I would one day love my own. Did he not know how fascinating kids are? How much fun one could have playing with them? How fortunate one was to be let into their worlds of imagination and whimsy? Mind you, I was speaking from experience. Prior to having my daughter, I would have wholeheartedly declared that I liked children very much and was "very good with kids." If there were children around, I would read them stories in different voices and with special effects, choreograph airborne gymnastic shows, crawl, climb, stand on my head. I enjoyed giving them my undivided attention, thrilled as I gained their confidence and affection. He, I concluded, lacked the capacity to appreciate the gifts children bestow upon us. To each his own! About a year into raising our daughter, I was ready to admit defeat. I do not think I suffer from a lack of feeling toward her. I am affectionate, admiring, adoring. My responses to her are not affected or insincere. But hardly a moment is simple, unadulterated. Everything feels like an imposition on my time. After an extended period without childcare, even grading can feel like a form of self-care. "Boredom" is as good a name as any for the distinct irritation that I experienced for much of the time I had to spend with her.

The sudden clarity had to be broadcast, confessed, and to whom but Rachel—my best friend, my intellectual accomplice, godmother of my child. She had just spent a little while playing with my daughter while I cooked, and she assured me she understood exactly what I meant. She said I shouldn't beat my-self up: "Of course it gets boring applying gel stickers on the win-dow all day long." She had understood nothing. If only this were how we spent most of our time together. What I wouldn't give to play with stickers all day, I thought then: a concrete activ-ity, focused and self-contained, that made a modicum of sense. The time spent with my young daughter was disordered, and yet I had to remain vigilant, the threat of accidents and stubborn-ness lurking behind every corner. Most of the time, my daughter comported herself as a cross between the queen of hearts and a slippery fish: Catch me!—my attention, my whims, what is up-setting me, what would comfort me, and sometimes just physi-cally, try to catch me, I dare you!—if you can.

Pajamas off! Pajamas on! New socks, night socks, no socks. Yes hat, no hat, always hat, not that hat. Slippers on, slippers off, slippers in bed, slippers in bath, slippers to daycare, papa takes to daycare, mama takes to daycare, papa *and* mama take to day-care, NO DAYCARE. Bread, no bread, cheese, no cheese, milk in bottle, coffee in bottle, now we drink the bath water. No wipe. No bath. No hair. No nappy. Hug, hug, hug! Which sounds sweet but must never be delivered while her feet are on the floor: Up! Up! Up!

Wait a second, not so fast. But what about . . . *books*? The to-temic emblem of literary parenting. Surely you like . . . the books? Yes, I do. But do yourself a favor and get your hands on a chil-dren's book; to make things interesting, make it a magical, mov-ing, poignant one, make it one with little messages just for you, the adult. Make it *The Tiger Who Came to Tea*, or *Runaway Bunny*, or *Where the Wild Things Are*. Make it your absolute fa-vorite. Read it through. Nice, isn't it? Do it again. Did you notice something you didn't notice before? They are very rich, books, aren't they? Now read it one more time. Look at all the little obscure details that begin to pop out of the page. Magic! Read it again. This text is infinite! But is it? Read it again. Read it again. Read it again. Perhaps you still enjoy it. But, perhaps, with all your love of books and illustrations and magic and your child, you don't, or not quite as much as you did the first thirty times.

Now, I am going to say something about sleep. It is almost as excruciatingly dull to listen to other people complain about how tired they are as it is to listen to them describe the technicalities and ethical quandaries surrounding sleep training. I will be mentioning neither and will keep it brief. Our daughter was and is an okay sleeper. It could be—as the forums, and blogs, and friends all assure me—much worse. She sleeps, we sleep, and that she sometimes wakes up too early for our comfort was not something we hadn't been warned about. But for long stretches of time, getting her to *fall* asleep was hard, and the naps were not long. This sounds minor and prosaic. It is, very. In a sense, this is the problem. Getting a baby to sleep is a very prosaic thing, no intellectual or physical feat at all, and you have to perform it thousands, *thousands,* of times. You have to do it all day, every day, and no one can tell you, going in, how long the next attempt will take. I think back on how I felt reassured by the fact that little babies take four naps a day (a living, breathing Pomodoro timer!) and I can't even muster a shrug. Imagine trying to get a teddy bear out with a metal claw four times a day, fifteen or twenty or thirty minutes at a time, suspecting the machine might be rigged, while the teddy was sobbing.

At one point, in our mercurial quest for "independent sleep" (place baby in bed, say goodnight, leave), we lost the ability to leave the room. For months, every evening we sat next to her, in the dark. A screen would have distracted her. So we just sat there, listening to her breathe. She demanded songs, but "not this one," she babbled, she cried for whoever was not in the room. She asked for stuffed animals she was already holding. Adding up the hours, I've spent whole days—my husband, weeks—staring into the dark for unspecified and unpredictable periods of time, emerging into the living room squinting, irritated. I don't know if I've ever felt simultaneously so overqualified and underqualified before. Once I sat for an hour watching her cry so hard she drooled and drooled and banged her head against the bars of her crib. (She was equally unhappy when I held her, and eventually fell asleep; she woke up, psychopath-like, perfectly content.)

Writing about the possible advantages of having children young, Elizabeth Bruenig assured those who still haven't had children that doing so is "not the end of freedom as you know it but the beginning of a kind of liberty you can't imagine."[16] I have a child and I still can't quite imagine it. I have spent my entire life tracking excellence like a hound dog. Finding what I could do best has become a habit for me as much by temperament as by circumstance—my family life was so unstable, and the financial resources available to me so limited, that it became clear very early on that whether I would attain any measure of success beyond mere survival depended on my ability to excel. Excelling opened access to the scholarships I relied on for my education, which was in turn the basis of nearly every relationship and opportunity I have enjoyed since. The problem wasn't that having a child kept me from excelling at my job. It didn't help, but the real issue was that for most of my time spent with her, I wasn't giving expression to any talent or ability whatsoever. I wasn't growing, I wasn't learning. So often I was barely doing anything at all.

This is the maddening paradox of parenting: it both had to be me and it absolutely didn't. It had to be me: I wanted to offer my daughter the benefits of having a loving mother stably present

in her life, there with her, attentively, day in and day out, dead-
lines permitting. But often it seemed like it really didn't have to
be *me* at all. Nothing about me—my ideas, my personality, my
judgment, my sense of humor—really mattered. She wants her
mother to sit next to her while she's on the potty, or in the bath,
or in bed, or in the car, but I'm at best just okay at sitting. She
wants her mother to follow her on the playground, but I have
no unique talent for the seesaw or pushing a child on a swing.
I've always considered myself to be rather whimsical, silly, play-
ful, and I assumed that drawing on these qualities would render
parenting a small child easy and pleasurable. I try to summon
them as often as I can, but I did not consider how much time
small children spend struggling to process discomfort, frustration, and disappointment; how much time I would have nothing
to do but stand there and absorb a baby's vociferous expressions
of displeasure. It needed to be me, but a me not so much transformed as reduced to very basic functions. This is not what I
think of when I think of freedom.

At some point, due to some combination of neglecting exercise and giving one too many piggyback rides to a baby the size
of a pig, an old spinal injury recurred. I fell down to the floor
and couldn't get back up for a week. The pain of standing up
was blinding; it took my breath away. I lay on the floor to do
my work. I rolled from room to room in our apartment. I show-
ered squatting. I rushed into doctors' offices, and witch doctors'
incense-laden practices, dropping to my knees the second I en-
tered through the door: Can you fix me? No one could tell me if
I would regain normal functioning. Surgery, I was told, was often ineffective. We were trying for a second baby, but this meant
I couldn't take any painkillers. After thirty-six hours, I had my
husband drive me to the pharmacy where, crouching, I asked

for a morning-after pill, only to discover that the anesthetics did nothing to help anyway. Then he had to travel out of the country for a conference, so I solo-parented for a few days, from the floor. I don't know how that worked or what I did. Eventually it got better. I can walk again. I try to work out, not in order to maintain my identity as a reluctant exerciser but to maintain basic core strength. "Mama horsey!" she demands. She is now the size of a horse. I pick her up.

Was this what they were asking about in asking me about motherhood? Were they asking not about a spontaneous transformation born of love and wonder but the necessary self-effacing that even a happy, funny, loving little girl mercilessly demanded her mother to perform in order to give her what she needed?

I imagine it will get easier, at least in some ways. She speaks in full sentences now, we've started playing games with rules and goals, I read her books I can't memorize on the first go. One day, when I explain that we do not have something, or it is physically impossible for such a thing to exist, or it would be fatal for a child to possess it, the explanation will do something to mitigate the insistent demand for it. But now I understand something I would have absolutely refused to accept before: that when that day comes, when we can play sophisticated games, read longer books, conduct elaborate two-way conversations, I might still wish, at that very moment, that I were doing something else.

LILA IS TWO years and two months old, and I take her to the museum. We like to visit the large sculpture garden, the kids' library, but, first, the coffee shop. For the first time this year, it is warm enough to sit outside, and I find us a table next to two old men. There are always old people at the museum, usually women. Out of courtesy, I move our table a little farther away from them, but we are still close enough to overhear the conversation. Our small table is littered with the many wholesome snacks I packed for us at home while Lila is eating a giant cookie I just bought her. This is when I realize that the conversation of the two old men is rather tantalizing. They are discussing the art world, or rather the art world as they knew it once, when they were at the very center of it. They are speaking German, exchanging glamorous, scandalous gossip as if trading war stories, too sensitive to be aired in public. I am speaking English to Lila and they assume I do not understand them. The one who does most of the talking is a painter. Back in the day, he exhibited his work all over Europe, all over the world. But I can't quite place him; I listen, riveted.

The painter explains what you used to do when trying to sell a painting to the royal family (I can't make out which). He walks his interlocutor through the process as though explaining how to change a tire, but when he tells the story of how he had to meet the queen in person, he adds, matter-of-factly, that as soon as he left her company, he threw up. He says it wasn't the drugs. If his friend—or is it his interviewer, I can't tell—is also an artist, he is keeping it to himself. He is mostly asking questions and sharing thirdhand information. Whenever I feel they need to be reassured that I can't understand them, I say something to Lila in English. I really should have been a spy, I think.

Having a child has made the reality of aging harder to ignore but no easier to accept. It is easier for me to imagine waking up a bug than being as old as they are. Suddenly, the topic changes and they move on to discuss their children. *I don't care about your children*, I think, preferring the shop talk. They do not know each other's families, that much is clear. "Our youngest boy has type one diabetes," the painter says. "The other day, we found out he went into hospital, but he didn't say anything to us. *He didn't want to worry us,"* he grumbles. "And he's fifty-five now, mind you." At this, the milder-mannered man lights up. The awkward form his eagerness to speak takes reveals just how reticent he usually is. But he knows *exactly* what the painter is talking about, and he cannot help himself: "Yes, yes, that awful phrase, *I didn't want to worry you!* I hear it all the time. I'm sick of it." And then he says something that catches me even more off guard than the royal deal: "What do I get up for in the morning," he demands, "what do I live for if not for these worries?" The other nods.

*What do I get up for in the morning?* I look at my daughter and think, he doesn't mean that his life has lacked in purpose. He has not lived vicariously through his children. At that moment, I understand why they moved from tales of their prime to their children. They were answering a question. It was: What now? At the very far end of life, when getting up in the morning was not as easy as it used to be, this man was saying that he did not need his children for support or company or care, though I was certain he got those, too. There are "reasons to have children" that are raised only to be dismissed as anachronistic or inappropriate. One of these is the idea of having children as a more or less literal retirement plan. Whether or not it is true that people ever had children solely so that there would be someone to support them in old age, it is now understood that this is no longer a particularly legitimate or reliable strategy. But what this man said was even stranger. He was not saying that his children were there to take care of him. He thought, *still,* that he was there to take care of them. Did that mean that they were there so that he could worry about them? Why would anyone choose to worry?

Parents stand to gain many things from parenting a child—some will enjoy ethical growth, others artistic inspiration and intellectual insights; some will find spiritual liberation or just the permission to really take time off of work; others will find the pleasures of play, pride, love. At the same time, children can take away from us as much or more, turning us haggard, bitter, and resentful. What one's children will give and take is not for anyone to know in advance. But to have children is to allow yourself to stand in a relationship whose essence is not determined by the benefits it confers or the prices it exacts. That's what it means for it to be not just another good among others. People say that having a child is a gift, but if that's true, it's not because it's like getting a gift. If having a child is a gift, it's because it's like giving one. And I don't just mean the gift of life.

Like many parents, I like to make my daughter laugh. To this effect I blow raspberries and swing her around and roll her on our bed by pulling the blanket from underneath her. Her laughter is so pure, so unambivalent that it's just almost unbearable. Thinking about it brings tears to my eyes every time, my throat clenches. When that happens, I know that I am already mourning the loss of the ability to laugh like that, the one she will incur in the future and the one I have incurred in the past. No adult can laugh like that. Not I, not you. We lose the capacity to laugh like that when we learn what great cruelty and cowardice can exist in the world, and that we are not immune to either. To raise my daughter means I will have to help her learn this lesson. That I will have to relive that loss of innocence as she encounters frailty, pain, loneliness, grief, shattering disappointment. It's one thing to know that evil knows no limits, it's another to watch a being in love with the moon, puddles, sticks, and blueberries discover it for herself.

Parenthood is many things to many people, but the hardest part for me is this custodianship. To become a parent is not to transpose the value of your life onto that of a child, as if you no longer matter except insofar as you can benefit them. That sometimes they will come first is not because you no longer matter, it's because they need help and it is up to you to give it to them. I imagine that is why it seemed so ridiculous to the man at the museum that his children would try to spare him worries. I imagine Lila telling me she didn't want to worry me. I have worried a lifetime on her behalf already, and I worry about nothing more than what her life, even if it is a decent one, even if it is good, will force her to learn and to try to understand.

To choose to be a parent is a strange thing: it is to choose to become inalienably vulnerable. People say children give you a kind of immortality because you live in the memories of those who love you, or maybe they carry something of you, something of the things that you cared about and loved, in their own practices and actions. But there is another, less comforting, kind of death-transcendence in parenting. When you have a child, you bind your fate, how well things fare for you, with that of another being as infinitely vulnerable as you. This means that when you die, even if all goes well, you die with your own fate still unsettled, up in the air. That, too, is a kind of immortality.

# ACKNOWLEDGMENTS

This book's seeds were sown in a short editorial letter we wrote for *The Point* magazine's twentieth issue, which featured a symposium on the question "What are children for?" The first thanks must therefore go to Jon Baskin, founder and longtime editor in chief of the magazine, a title he would never assume. Jon has served as a mentor to us both—we would not be the thinkers or writers we are today without him—and his unreserved enthusiasm for this project buoyed us in moments of uncertainty. His editorial notes on an early draft were as discerning as he always is. Perhaps most importantly, under his leadership the magazine has fostered a genuine intellectual community—equal parts supportive and agonistic—that has sustained us throughout. It is no coincidence that the next thanks go to two other colleagues of ours at the magazine. First, to Becca Rothfeld, who read the manuscript with the keen eye of a great writer and philosopher: every objection she raised made the final version better. And to Julia Aizuss, who went far beyond the ordinary duties of a fact-checker and pushed us to address some of the thorniest moral quandaries our analysis and claims raised.

We are grateful to Ann Davidman for generously connecting us with many of her former clients and allowing us to reference her work, and to all the women and men who spoke with us about what children are for, for them. Audiences at Rutgers University, the University of Chicago, Northwestern University, Bar Ilan University, the Hebrew University of Jerusalem, the Hebrew University's Centre for Moral and Political Philosophy's Summer Ethicists' retreat, and the Israeli Philosophy Association meeting at Ben Gurion University, as well as students in Anastasia's 2023 MA seminar on the Value of Human Life and PhD workshop on the same topic, all commented helpfully on versions of the arguments in the second and fourth chapters. We'd like to especially thank Agnes Callard, Arnold Brooks, Matthias Haase, and Sam Scheffler for their responses and suggestions, and Rory O'Connell, for his philosophical rigor and creativity, which made the fourth chapter immeasurably better. We are very grateful to our illustrious agent Alia Hanna Habib for her guidance, reading, and advice (but perhaps most for her savvy handling of the foibles of not one but two whole authors), as well as to our editor at St. Martin's Press, Anna deVries, for her faith in the project and for helping us responsibly navigate the tangled cultural terrain we set out to explore.

A shorter, earlier version of the second part of the first chapter appeared in "The Paradox of Slow Love" (*The Atlantic*); some of the material from the third chapter corresponds to "Motherhood and Taboo," on a film adaptation of Elena Ferrante's *The Lost Daughter* (*The Point*). The thoughts underlying two other pieces published in popular outlets are to be found throughout, but especially in the fourth chapter: "Now Is as Good a Time as Any to Start a Family" (*New York Times*) and "On Choosing Life" (*The Point*). We are grateful to our editors at these publications for helping us think through our questions and begin sharing them with others.

A big thanks to Penny Lamhut, Alan Wiseman, Sara Wiseman, and Catherine O'Connell for their steadfast support, and finally, to Rory and Phil, for their love, and a lot of patience. And to Lila: Mama and Rachel love you very much.

# NOTES

## INTRODUCTION

1. According to the CDC, the average age at which an American woman has her first child reached an all-time high of 27.3 in 2021. Michelle J. K. Osterman et al., "Births: Final Data for 2021," *National Vital Statistics Reports* 72, no. 1 (January 31, 2023). In 2000, it was 24.9; in 1980, it was 22.7. T. J. Mathews and Brady E. Hamilton, "Mean Age of Mother, 1970–2000," *National Vital Statistics Reports* 51, no. 1 (December 11, 2002). Women in the United States are now expected to have an average of 1.7 children in their lifetimes (the so-called replacement rate, the average number of children per couple required to maintain a stable population, is 2.1). See also: Lindsay Monte, "More Women in Early 30s Are Childless," U.S. Census Bureau, November 30, 2017, https://www.census.gov/library/stories/2017/11/women-early-thirties.html.

2. A 2020 Pew Research Center report on millennials' approach to family life found that millennial women (then twenty-two to thirty-seven years old) were less likely to have given birth at that stage of their life than their predecessors. Fifty-five percent of millennial women had had a child by that point, compared to 62 percent of Gen Xers in 2002 or 64 percent of boomers in 1986. Amanda Barroso, Kim Parker, and Jesse Bennett, "As Millennials Near 40, They're Approaching Family Life Differently Than Previous Generations," Pew Research Center, May 27, 2020, https://www.pewresearch.org/social-trends/2020/05/27/as-millennials-near-40-theyre-approaching-family-life-differently-than-previous-generations.

3. The national fertility rate in 2020 was 55.8 births per 1,000 women (ages fifteen to forty-four), down 4 percent from 2019, and "another record low." Brady E. Hamilton, Joyce A. Martin, Michelle J. K. Osterman. "Births: Provisional Data for 2020," *Vital Statistics Rapid Release*, no. 12. Hyattsville, MD: National Center for Health Statistics, May 2021. DOI: https:// doi.org/10.15620/cdc:104993. The first two months of the pandemic were responsible for a 7.1 percent drop in the United States' crude birth rate compared to the same period the year before. Arnstein Aassve, Nicolò Cavalli, Letizia Mencarini, et al., "Early Assessment of the Relationship Between the COVID-19 Pandemic and Births in High-Income Countries," *PNAS* 118, no. 36 (August 30, 2021): 1, https://doi .org/10.1073/pnas.2105709118.

4. According to a 2022 National Bureau of Economic Research report, the COVID-19 pandemic resulted in sixty-two thousand "missing births" between October 2020 and February 2021—or babies that would have been conceived between January and May 2020, which was followed by a rebound of fifty-one thousand conceptions later in 2020, leading to a small overall reduction in births for that year (roughly ten thousand fewer conceptions than anticipated, or a birth rate reduction of 4 percent), which was less severe than experts' worst-case projections. There was even evidence of a small "baby bump" in 2021, where there were roughly thirty thousand more births than were likely, based on pre-pandemic fertility trends. Melissa Schettini Kearney and Phillip B. Levine, "The U.S. Covid-19 Baby Bust and Rebound," *NBER Working Papers,* no. 30000 (April 2022).

5. Melissa S. Kearney and Phillip Levine, "U.S. Births Are Down Again, After the COVID Baby Bust and Rebound," the Brookings Institution blog, May 31, 2023, https://www.brookings.edu/2023/05/31/us-births -are-down-again-after-the-covid-baby-bust-and-rebound.

6. Childlessness among women past their reproductive years was around 20 percent in 2006, double what it was in 1976, with most recent data placing the current figure at around 15 percent. Tomaš Frejka, "Childlessness in the United States," in *Childlessness in Europe: Contexts, Causes, and Consequences,* ed. Michaela Kreyenfeld and Dirk Konitezka, Demographic Research Monographs (Cham: Springer 2017), 159–79.

7. Tayelor Valerio, Brian Knop, Rose M. Kreider, and Wan He, *Childless Older Americans: 2018,* U.S. Census Bureau, Current Population Reports, August 2021, 1.

8. Anna Brown, "Growing Share of Childless Adults in U.S. Don't Expect to Ever Have Children," Pew Research Center, November 19, 2021, https://www.pewresearch.org/short-reads/2021/11/19/growing-share-of-childless-adults-in-u-s-dont-expect-to-ever-have-children.

9. Caroline Sten Hartnett, "US Fertility Keeps Dropping—But That's Not a Reason to Panic," *The Conversation,* May 15, 2019, https://theconversation.com/us-fertility-keeps-dropping-but-thats-not-a-reason-to-panic-117242.

10. "After Roe Fell: Abortion Laws by State," Center for Reproductive Rights, accessed June 4, 2023, https://reproductiverights.org/maps/abortion-laws-by-state; Roni Caryn Rabin, "Pregnancy's Most Dangerous Time: After New Mothers Come Home," *New York Times,* May 28, 2023, https://www.nytimes.com/2023/05/28/health/pregnancy-childbirth-deaths.html; Claire Cain Miller, Sarah Kliff, and Larry Buchanan, "Childbirth Is Deadlier for Black Families, Even When They're Rich, Expansive Study Finds," *New York Times,* February 12, 2023.

11. Denise L. Carlini and Ann Davidman, *Motherhood—Is It for Me?: Your Step-by-Step Guide to Clarity* (York, PA: Transformation Books, 2016), 67.

12. Ibid., 188.

13. Ibid., 154.

14. Agnes Callard, "Acceptance Parenting," *The Point,* October 2, 2022, https://thepointmag.com/examined-life/acceptance-parenting.

15. Sylvia Plath, *The Bell Jar* (New York: Harper Perennial Classics, 1999), 77.

16. Adrienne Rich, "Dreams Before Waking," in *Your Native Land, Your Life* (New York: W. W. Norton, 1986), 46.

17. Andrea González-Ramírez, "Closing the Door on Motherhood," *The Cut,* July 3, 2023. https://www.thecut.com/2023/07/closing-the-door-on-motherhood-after-dobbs.html.

## CHAPTER 1: THE EXTERNALS

1. Carlini and Davidman, *Motherhood—Is It for Me?* 42. (Italics are Carlini and Davidman's.)

2. Ibid., 350.

3. Ibid., 351.

4. Alexandria Ocasio-Cortez, Twitter post, March 3, 2021, 2:42 P.M., https://twitter.com/AOC/status/1367213849963859968.

5. Moira Donegan, "The Decline in the US Birth Rate Is Not About Moral

Failure, It's About Economics," *The Guardian,* February 9, 2021, https://
www.theguardian.com/commentisfree/2021/feb/09/us-birth-rate
-decline-one-economics-coronavirus.

6. Heidi Shierholz and Lawrence Mishel, "The Worst Downturn Since the
   Great Depression," Economic Policy Institute, January 2, 2009, https://
   www.epi.org/publication/jobspict_200906_preview; Meta Brown, Andrew Haughwout, Donghoon Lee, Joelle Scally, and Wilbert van der
   Klaauw, "Measuring Student Debt and Its Performance," Federal Reserve Bank of New York Staff Reports 668 (April 2014), https://www
   .newyorkfed.org/medialibrary/media/research/staff_reports/sr668.pdf.

7. Center for American Progress, "When I Was Your Age: Millennials and
   the Wage Gap," report, March 3, 2016, https://www.americanprogress
   .org/article/when-i-was-your-age/; Kassandra Martinchek, "Young
   Millennials and Gen Zers Face Employment Insecurity and Hardship
   During the Pandemic," Urban Institute, December 18, 2020, https://
   www.urban.org/urban-wire/young-millennials-and-gen-zers-face
   -employment-insecurity-and-hardship-during-pandemic; Sharon Insler, "Do Millennials Have It Worse Than Generations Past?" Lending
   Tree, May 30, 2018, https://www.lendingtree.com/student/millennials
   -have-it-worse-study; Venessa Wong, "It's Not Just Millennials—Gen
   Z Is Dealing with a Lot of Debt Now Too," *Buzzfeed,* September 17,
   2019, https://www.buzzfeednews.com/article/venessawong/millennials
   -average-debt-2019; OECD, *Under Pressure: The Squeezed Middle Class*
   (Paris: OECD Publishing, 2019), https://doi.org/10.1787/689afed1-en;
   David Greene, "Millennials to Bear the Burden of Boomers' Social
   Safety Net," NPR, *Morning Edition,* March 4, 2014, https://www.npr
   .org/2014/03/04/285581006/millennials-to-bear-burden-of-boomer-s
   -social-safety-net.

8. Michael Hout, "State of the Union 2019: Social Mobility Report" (2019),
   https://inequality.stanford.edu/sites/default/files/Pathways_SOTU_2019
   _SocialMobility.pdf.

9. Federal Reserve, "Distribution of Household Wealth in the U.S. since
   1989," https://www.federalreserve.gov/releases/z1/dataviz/dfa/distribute
   /chart, accessed August 31, 2023.

10. Andrew Van Dam, "The Unluckiest Generation in U.S. History," *Wash-
    ington Post,* June 5, 2020, https://www.washingtonpost.com/business
    /2020/05/27/millennial-recession-covid.

11. YouGov, "The American Dream Survey" (New York: YouGov, 2023),

https://docs.cdn.yougov.com/wgu9xa8nwm/crosstabs_The%20American%20Dream.pdf.

12. Ana Hernández Kent and Lowell R. Ricketts, "The State of U.S. Wealth Inequality," Federal Reserve Bank of St. Louis, July 31, 2023, https://www.stlouisfed.org/institute-for-economic-equity/the-state-of-us-wealth-inequality; Jeremy Horpedahl, "The Wealth of Generations: Latest Update," *Economist Writing Everyday* (blog), December 21, 2022, https://economistwritingeveryday.com/2022/12/21/the-wealth-of-generations-latest-update.

13. Amelia Josephson, "The Average Salary of a Millennial," SmartAsset, December 1, 2022, https://smartasset.com/retirement/the-average-salary-of-a-millennial; Richard Fry, "Young Adult Households Are Earning More Than Most Older Americans Did at the Same Age," Pew Research Center, December 18, 2018, https://www.pewresearch.org/fact-tank/2018/12/11/young-adult-households-are-earning-more-than-most-older-americans-did-at-the-same-age.

14. Rob Warnock, "Apartment List's 2023 Millennial Homeownership Report," Apartment List, April 18, 2023, https://www.apartmentlist.com/research/millennial-homeownership-2023.

15. William R. Emmons, Ana Hernández Kent, and Lowell R. Ricketts, "The Demographics of Wealth: How Education, Race and Birth Year Shape Financial Outcomes," Center for Household Financial Stability, Federal Reserve Bank of St. Louis (2018), 5.

16. Ana Hernández Kent and Lowell R. Ricketts, "Millennials Are Catching Up in Terms of Generational Wealth," *On the Economy* (blog), Federal Reserve Bank of St. Louis, March 29, 2021, https://www.stlouisfed.org/on-the-economy/2021/march/millennials-catching-up-earlier-generational-wealth.

17. Alex Cook, "Millennials' Net Worth Has Doubled Since Start of Pandemic," *Magnify Money,* July 25, 2022, https://www.magnifymoney.com/news/net-worth-of-millennials.

18. According to the conservative estimates of the investment firm Accenture, millennials' parents and grandparents will bequeath them up to $30 trillion by 2030 and $75 trillion by 2060; see Zoë Berry, "The Rich Kids Who Want to Tear Down Capitalism," *New York Times,* November 27, 2020, https://www.nytimes.com/2020/11/27/style/trust-fund-activism-resouce-generation.html. The asset management firm Cerulli Associates has forecasted that as much as $68 trillion will be passed

down from boomers to millennials by 2030 (Cerulli Associates, "A Look at Wealth 2019," October 16, 2019, https://blog.coldwellbankerluxury .com/a-look-at-wealth-millennial-millionaires, 2) and $84 trillion by 2045 (Cerulli Associates, "Cerulli Anticipates $84 Trillion in Wealth Transfers Through 2045," January 20, 2022, https://www.cerulli.com /press-releases/cerulli-anticipates-84-trillion-in-wealth-transfers -through-2045).

19. Jean M. Twenge, "The Myth of the Broke Millennial," *The Atlantic*, April 17, 2023, https://www.theatlantic.com/magazine/archive/2023/05 /millennial-generation-financial-issues-income-homeowners/673485.

20. Millennials with college degrees have median annual earnings equivalent to those of college-educated Gen Xers at the same stage in life, but those without university diplomas have been doing significantly worse than their predecessors. In 2023, the family wealth of the typical millennial with a four-year degree was only 4 percent behind college graduates of previous generations. Millennials with only a high school education or some college, however, were on average 19 percent behind those without college degrees in previous generations. (Pew Research Center, "Millennial Life: How Young Adulthood Today Compares with Prior Generations," February 14, 2019, https://www.pewresearch.org/ social-trends/2019/02/14/millennial-life-how-young-adulthood-to-day-compares-with-prior-generations-2/). Wealth disparities within the millennial cohort likewise break down along race lines: white Americans have mostly caught up to their counterparts in other generations, lagging by only 5 percent; Black millennials, on the other hand, are 52 percent behind (Greg Rosalsky, "There Is Growing Segregation in Millennial Wealth," NPR, Planet Money newsletter, April 27, 2021, https://www.npr.org/sections/money/2021/04/27/990770599/there-is -growing-segregation-in-millennial-wealth). And of course, no matter your background, only those with wealth will one day be able to transfer it to their millennial children.

21. Morning Consult, "The State of Consumer Banking & Payments" (Q1 2022), https://pro.morningconsult.com/analyst-reports/state-of-consumer -banking-payments-h2-2022; T. Rowe Price, "How Do You Compare?" *T. Rowe Price Investor* (Spring 2019), 18.

22. Echelon Insights, *Opening the Door to Opportunity: Millennials and Gen Z Speak* (October 2020). In the 2019 Deloitte Global Millennial Survey, most respondents likewise expressed the belief that their ambitions are within reach: "Two-thirds who want to reach senior levels in their

careers believe it's attainable. Seven in 10 who want to see the world think it's possible. Three-quarters who want to buy homes are confident they'll be able to. And 83 percent of those desiring families don't believe barriers will prevent it." Deloitte, *The Deloitte Global Millennial Survey,* 2019, https://www2.deloitte.com/content/dam/Deloitte/global/Documents/About-Deloitte/deloitte-2019-millennial-survey.pdf. Charles Schwab, *Modern Wealth Survey 2023* (Westlake, TX: Charles Schwab, 2023), https://www.aboutschwab.com/schwab-modern-wealth-survey-2023.

23. See note 20.

24. U.S. Census Bureau, S1301 Fertility Data, "American Community Survey," September 2022, https://data.census.gov/table?q=S1301&tid=ACSST1Y2019.S1301.

25. "How Do Countries Fight Falling Birth Rates?" BBC News, January 15, 2020, https://www.bbc.com/news/world-europe-51118616.

26. "Fertility Rate, Total (Births per Woman)" (2021), World Bank, accessed September 1, 2023, https://data.worldbank.org/indicator/SP.DYN.TFRT.IN.

27. Tomáš Sobotka, Anna Matysiak, and Zuzanna Brzozowska, *Policy Responses to Low Fertility: How Effective Are They? Working Paper No. 1,* United Nations Population Fund, May 2019, 6.

28. Since 2010, the total fertility rate has been on the decline in all Nordic countries, though public support for families remains high. Chiara L. Comolli, Gerda Neyer, Gunnar Andersson, Lars Dommermuth, et al., "Beyond the Economic Gaze: Childbearing During and After Recessions in the Nordic Countries," *SocArXiv,* no. 37 (November 19, 2020): 473–520, DOI: 10.1007/s10680-020-09570-0. In response, some Scandinavian countries have released PR campaigns to encourage young people to procreate, like Denmark's cheeky "Do It for Mom" ads. Terrence McCoy, "'Do It for Denmark!' Campaign Wants Danes to Have More Sex. A Lot More Sex," *Washington Post,* March 27, 2014, https://www.washingtonpost.com/news/morning-mix/wp/2014/03/27/do-it-for-denmark-campaign-wants-danes-to-have-more-sex-a-lot-more-sex.

29. United Nations Regional Information Centre for Western Europe, "Family Day: Nordic Fertility Rates in Steady Decline," May 15, 2023, https://unric.org/en/family-day-nordic-fertility-rates-in-steady-decline.

30. "Summary of Population Statistics 1960–2022," Statistics Sweden, https://www.scb.se/en/finding-statistics/statistics-by-subject-area

/population/population-composition/population-statistics/pong/tables
-and-graphs/population-statistics---summary/summary-of-population
-statistics/, accessed September 1, 2023; "Total Fertility Rate (Ages
15–49) by Ancestry," Statistics Denmark, https: //www.statbank.dk
/FERT1, accessed September 1, 2023; "Fertility and Reproduction Rates
1853–2022," Statistics Iceland, https://px.hagstofa.is/pxen/pxweb/en
/Ibuar/Ibuar_Faeddirdanir_faeddir_faedingar/MAN05202.px, accessed
September 1, 2023; "Total Fertility Rate, 1776–2022," Statistics Finland,
https://statfin.stat.fi/PxWeb/pxweb/en/StatFin/StatFin_synt/statfin
_syntpxt12dt.px, accessed September 1, 2023.

31. "Total Fertility Rate, Women (C) 1968–2022," Statistics Norway, https://
www.ssb.no/en/statbank/table/04232/, accessed September 1, 2023.

32. Sobotka, Matysiak, and Brzozowska, "Policy Responses to Low Fertility," 77.

33. Anna Sussman, "The End of Babies," *New York Times*, November 16,
2019, https://www.nytimes.com/interactive/2019/11/16/opinion/sunday
/capitalism-children.html.

34. *Inconceivable: Reproduction in an Age of Uncertainty* is the title of Sussman's forthcoming book, expanding on the reporting and analysis of
the article.

35. Sussman, "The End of Babies."

36. Deloitte, *Deloitte Global Millennial Survey*, 2019. More recent data from
the Deloitte survey about young people's ranked ambitions is not available in later reports.

37. Claire Cain Miller, "Americans Are Having Fewer Babies. They Told
Us Why," *New York Times*, July 5, 2018, https://www.nytimes.com/2018
/07/05/upshot/americans-are-having-fewer-babies-they-told-us-why
.html.

38. Pew Research Center, "Raising Kids and Running a Household: How
Working Parents Share the Load" (November 2015), 3; Gina Schouten,
*Liberalism, Neutrality, and the Gendered Division of Labor* (Oxford: Ox-
ford University Press, 2019).

39. Anne-Marie Slaughter, "Why Women Still Can't Have It All," *The Atlantic* (July/August 2012), https://www.theatlantic.com/magazine/archive
/2012/07/why-women-still-cant-have-it-all/309020.

40. Judith Warner, Nora Ellmann, and Diana Boesch, "The Women's Leadership Gap: Women's Leadership by the Numbers," Center for American Progress, November 20, 2018.

41. Slaughter, "Why Women Still Can't Have It All."

42. Ibid.

43. For an interesting anecdotal social history of childlessness among women, see Peggy O'Donnell Heffington's *Without Children* (New York: Seal Press, 2023).

44. Kim Parker and Rachel Minkin, "Public Has Mixed Views on the Modern American Family," Pew Research Center (September 2023), 32.

45. Samuel H. Preston and Caroline Sten Hartnett, *The Future of American Fertility*, NBER Working Paper Series, 2008.

46. Élisabeth Badinter, *The Conflict*, trans. Adriana Hunter (New York: Henry Holt & Co., 2012), 13.

47. Ibid., 2.

48. Jennifer M. Silva, *Coming Up Short* (Oxford: Oxford University Press, 2013), 128, 21, 18, 21–22, 33.

49. Charles Schwab, *Retirement Reimagined* (Westlake, TX: Charles Schwab, 2022), https://content.schwab.com/web/retail/public/about -schwab/Retirement_Reimagined_Study_deck_0422-2S73.pdf.

50. Sabrina Tavernise, Claire Cain Miller, Quoctrung Bui, and Robert Gebeloff, "Why American Women Everywhere Are Delaying Motherhood," *New York Times*, June 16, 2021, https://www.nytimes.com/2021/06/16 /us/declining-birthrate-motherhood.html.

51. Fred Backus, "Most Americans Have Experienced True Love in Their Lives—CBS News Poll," *CBS News*, February 13, 2022, https://www .cbsnews.com/news/americans-experience-true-love-opinion-poll-02 -2022.

52. Miller, "Americans Are Having Fewer Babies."

53. Ann Berrington, "Childlessness in the U.K.," in *Childlessness in Europe: Contexts, Causes, and Consequences* (January 13, 2017), https://doi.org /10.1007/978-3-319-44667-7_3.

54. Zeynep Gurtin, "More Women Over 40 Are Getting Pregnant. But Is That Really About Their Choices?" *The Guardian*, April 17, 2019, https:// www.theguardian.com/commentisfree/2019/apr/17/more-women -over-40-pregnant-choices-motherhood.

55. Vegard Skirbekk, *Decline and Prosper!* (London: Palgrave Macmillan, 2022), 110.

56. Martha Gill, "Why a Shortage of Mr Rights Means Single Mothers Hold the Key to the Falling Birthrate," *The Guardian*, February 11, 2022, https: //www.theguardian.com/commentisfree/2023/feb/11/why-a-shortage -of-mr-rights-means-single-mothers-hold-the-key-to-the-falling -birthrate.

57. Jane Austen, *The Annotated Persuasion*, ed. David M. Shapard (New York: Anchor Books, 2010), 48.

58. Helen Fisher, *Anatomy of Love* (New York: W. W. Norton, 2016), 295.

59. *Singles in America* is an annual survey funded by Match.com that is conducted in collaboration with Dr. Fisher and the evolutionary biologist Dr. Justin Garcia of the Kinsey Institute. They take a demographically representative sample of five thousand singles between the ages of eighteen and ninety-eight about their attitudes toward dating, sex, and romance. See https://www.singlesinamerica.com.

60. Sarah Konrath, "What the Pandemic Has Done for Dating," *The Atlantic*, December 31, 2020, https://www.theatlantic.com/ideas/archive/2020/12/what-pandemic-has-done-dating/617502.

61. Interview with Helen Fisher, January 7, 2022.

62. Anna Miller, "Can This Marriage Be Saved?" American Psychological Association, *Monitor on Psychology* 44, no. 4 (April 2013): https://www.apa.org/monitor/2013/04/marriage.

63. Kasey J. Eickmeyer, "Generation X and Millennials Attitudes Toward Marriage & Divorce," National Center for Family & Marriage Research (2015), https://www.bgsu.edu/content/dam/BGSU/college-of-arts-and-sciences/NCFMR/documents/FP/eickmeyer-gen-x-millennials-fp-15-12.pdf.

64. Fisher, *Anatomy of Love*, 306.

65. Eliza Brown and Mary Patrick, "Time, Anticipation, and the Life Course: Egg Freezing as Temporarily Disentangling Romance and Reproduction," *American Sociological Review* 83, no. 5 (2018): 959, https://doi.org/10.1177/0003122418796807.

66. Ibid., 959.

67. Interview with Eliza Brown, November 21, 2021.

68. Brown and Patrick, "Time, Anticipation, and the Life Course," 960.

69. Ibid., 970.

70. Ramazan Amanvermez and Migraci Tosun, "An Update on Ovarian Aging and Ovarian Reserve Tests," *International Journal of Fertility and Sterility* 9, no. 4 (January–March 2016), 411.

71. Brown and Patrick, "Time, Anticipation, and the Life Course," 959.

72. Ibid., 968.

73. Ibid., 968–69.

74. Ibid.

75. Ibid., 971, 972, 970.

76. Ibid., 969, 973.

77. Ibid., 974.

78. Gina Kolata, "'Sobering' Study Shows Challenges of Egg Freezing," *New York Times,* September 23, 2022, https://www.nytimes.com/2022/09/23/health/egg-freezing-age-pregnancy.html.

79. Recommendations vary by provider, but most discourage sex for two weeks after each egg retrieval procedure. During ovarian stimulation, sex using barrier-method contraception is considered acceptable by some clinicians, though many couples undergoing IVF prefer to abstain during the course of treatment to avoid the chance of a multiple pregnancy.

80. Sarah Druckenmiller Cascante, Jennifer K. Blakemore, Shannon DeVore, et al., "Fifteen Years of Autologous Oocyte Thaw Outcomes from a Large University-Based Fertility Center," *Fertility and Sterility* 118, no. 1 (July 2022): 162, 160. https://doi.org/10.1016/j.fertnstert.2022.04.013.

81. Eva Illouz, *Consuming the Romantic Utopia* (Berkeley: University of California Press, 1997), 7.

82. For a classic study of the history of Western romantic ideals and the tension between matrimony and passion, see Denis de Rougemont's *Love in the Western World,* trans. Montgomery Belgion (Princeton, NJ: Princeton University Press, 1940).

83. The pregnancy plot is at the center of the fourth novel in Stephenie Meyer's Twilight saga, *Breaking Dawn* (2008). The book was adapted into a two-part movie, released in 2011 and 2012.

84. Sally Rooney, *Beautiful World, Where Are You* (New York: Farrar, Straus & Giroux, 2021), 334, 335.

85. Some social scientists have termed this phenomenon "coincidental childlessness" or "social infertility." Vegard Skirbekk, *Decline and Prosper! Changing Global Birth Rates and the Advantages of Fewer Children* (London: Palgrave Macmillan, 2022), 6; Anna Sussman, "The Case for Redefining Infertility," *New Yorker,* June 18, 2019, https://www.newyorker.com/culture/annals-of-inquiry/the-case-for-social-infertility.

86. Interview with Helen Fisher, January 7, 2022.

87. In the 2022 *Singles in America* survey, 68.7 percent of singles said that when entering a serious relationship it "wasn't important" for their partner to want kids. Helen Fisher and Justin Garcia, Match.com *Singles in America* dataset, 2022. *Singles in America* website, accessed March 18, 2023, https://www.singlesinamerica.com.

88. According to a 2016 survey conducted by the American Academy of Matrimonial Lawyers, 51 percent of responding attorneys claimed they'd observed a rise in the number of millennial clients asking for

prenuptial agreements. See American Academy of Matrimonial Lawyers, "Prenuptial Agreements on the Rise Finds Survey," AAML press release, October 28, 2016, https://www.prnewswire.com/news-releases/prenuptial-agreements-on-the-rise-finds-survey-300353444.html. A 2020 Credit Karma survey found that 59 percent of married millennials keep at least one separate bank account from their spouses and a quarter keep their finances completely separate. Paris Ward, "Many Millennial Couples Keep Finances Separate, Credit Karma Survey Shows," Credit Karma, February 28, 2020, https://www.creditkarma.com/insights/i/married-millennials-separate-finances. This tracks with a study released by Bank of America two years earlier, in which 28 percent of millennial respondents reported keeping their accounts separate from their partner's, and nearly one in five claimed to not know how much money their spouse or partner earns. Bank of America, *2018 Better Money Habits Millennial Report* (Winter 2018), https://bettermoneyhabits.bankofamerica.com/content/dam/bmh/pdf/ar6vnln9-boa-bmh-millennial-report-winter-2018-final2.pdf.

89. Taylor Lorenz and Joe Pinsker, "The Slackification of the American Home," *The Atlantic,* July 11, 2019, https://www.theatlantic.com/family/archive/2019/07/families-slack-asana/593584.

90. Jennifer Miller, "Family Life Is Chaotic. Could Office Software Help?" *New York Times,* May 27, 2020, https://www.nytimes.com/2020/05/27/style/family-calendar.html.

91. Ibid.

92. Rebecca Fishbein, "Is Therapy-Speak Making Us Selfish?" *Bustle,* April 7, 2023, https://www.bustle.com/wellness/is-therapy-speak-making-us-selfish.

93. Elizabeth Bruenig, "I Became a Mother at 25, and I'm Not Sorry I Didn't Wait," *New York Times,* May 7, 2021, https://www.nytimes.com/2021/05/07/opinion/motherhood-baby-bust-early-parenthood.html.

## CHAPTER 2: THE DIALECTIC OF MOTHERHOOD

1. Adrienne Rich, "Motherhood in Bondage," *New York Times,* November 20, 1976, https://timesmachine.nytimes.com/timesmachine/1976/11/20/91198580.html?pageNumber=19.

2. Nancy Friday, *My Mother/My Self* (New York: Delta Books, 1977), 3.

3. Nancy Felipe Russo, "The Motherhood Mandate," *Journal of Social Issues* 32, no. 3 (1976): 145.

4. For one recent example, see Peggy O'Donnell Heffington's introduction to *Without Children: The Long History of Not Being a Mother.*

5. Ann Davidman, "I Help People Decide if They Want to Have Kids. Here's My Advice," *Vox,* April 26, 2021, https://www.vox.com/first -person/22370250/should-i-have-kids-a-baby-decide-start-family -parenthood-kids-childfree.

6. Ann Davidman, "Treating Women Ambivalent About Motherhood: Best Practices for Patient-Provider Communication" (November 2022).

7. Amy Blackstone, "Amy Blackstone on Childfree Adults," interview by Barbara Risman, "The Society Pages" (blog), Council on Contemporary Families, July 2, 2019, https://thesocietypages.org/ccf/2019/07/02 /amy-blackstone-on-childfree-adults.

8. Tim Kreider, "The End of the Line," in *Selfish, Shallow, and Self-Absorbed: Sixteen Writers on the Decision Not to Have Kids,* ed. Meghan Daum (New York: Picador, 2015), 268.

9. Ella Alexander, "Why We Need to Stop Making Women Over 30 Feel Pressured to Have Children," *Harper's Bazaar,* August 7, 2019, https:// www.harpersbazaar.com/uk/culture/a28635150/why-we-need-to-stop -pressuring-women-over-30-to-have-children.

10. YouGov, "Do Women in the United States Come Under Pressure from Society to Have Children?" (New York: YouGov, 2022), https://today .yougov.com/topics/politics/survey-results/daily/2022/02/07/cc697/2.

11. Arland Thornton and Linda Young-DeMarco, "Four Decades of Trends in Attitudes Toward Family Issues in the United States: The 1960s Through the 1990s," *Journal of Marriage and Family* 63, no. 4 (November 2001): 1031, 1028. See also, Preston and Hartnett, *Future of American Fertility.*

12. Mary Ziegler, *Abortion and the Law in America* (Cambridge: Cambridge University Press), 2020.

13. *New York Times,* "Tracking the States Where Abortion Is Now Banned," accessed August 21, 2023, https://www.nytimes.com/interactive/2022 /us/abortion-laws-roe-v-wade.html.

14. Benjamin Rader, Ushma D. Upadhyay, Neil K. R. Sehgal, Ben Y. Reis, et al., "Estimated Travel Time and Spatial Access to Abortion Facilities in the US Before and After the *Dobbs v Jackson* Women's Health Decision," *JAMA* 328, no. 20 (November 22, 2022), DOI: 10.1001/ jama.2022.20424; Allison McCann, "What It Costs to Get an Abortion Now," *New York Times,* September 28, 2022, https://www.nytimes.com /interactive/2022/09/28/us/abortion-costs-funds.html; Katrina Kimport,

"Abortion After Dobbs: Defendants, Denials, and Delays," *Science Advances* 8, no. 6 (2022), DOI: 10.1126/sciadv.ade5327.

15. Society of Family Planning, *#WeCount Report,* June 15, 2023, DOI: https://doi.org/10.46621/XBAZ6145.

16. Kerry Jacoby, *Souls, Bodies, Spirits: The Drive to Abolish Abortion Since 1973* (Westport, CT: Praeger, 1998), 21–22.

17. Lizzie Widdicombe, "The Baby-Box Lady of America," *New Yorker,* December 18, 2021, https://www.newyorker.com/news/news-desk/the-baby-box-lady-of-america.

18. Euripides, *Medea,* trans. David Kovacs, in *Cyclopes. Alcestis. Medea, Euripides* 1, Loeb Classical Library 12 (Cambridge, MA: Harvard University Press, 1994), 307.

19. Simone de Beauvoir, *The Second Sex,* trans. Constance Borde and Sheila Malovany-Chevallier (New York: Vintage Books, 2011), 3–7.

20. Ibid., 40.

21. Ibid., 538.

22. Ibid., 538, 541–42.

23. Ibid., 538.

24. Ibid., 568.

25. Betty Friedan, *The Feminine Mystique* (New York: Dell Publishing, 1974), 11.

26. Beauvoir, *Second Sex,* 753.

27. Ibid., 549, 554, 566, 567.

28. Shulamith Firestone, *The Dialectic of Sex* (New York: Farrar, Straus and Giroux, 2003), epigraph.

29. Ibid., 8–9.

30. Ibid., 9.

31. Ibid., 11.

32. Ibid., 36.

33. Ibid., 179, 162–63, 186.

34. Among them are Firestone's contemporary Kate Millett, who in her 1970 treatise *Sexual Politics* (Urbana: University of Illinois Press, 2000) declared that "so long as every female, simply by virtue of her anatomy, is obliged, even forced, to be the sole or primary caretaker of childhood, she is prevented from being a free human being" (126). Later feminist thinkers have sought to undermine the notion that motherhood is innate but have shared Firestone's pessimistic reading of the institution under the current system. Take, for instance, Andrea Dworkin, in *Right-Wing Women* (New York: Perigee, 1983), who saw the sex and pregnancy un-

der patriarchy as inimical to freedom for free-thinking women: "Intelligence is also ambitious: it always wants more: not more being fucked, not more pregnancy; but more of a bigger world. A woman cannot be ambitious in her own right without also being damned" (43).

35. "What particularly fascinates me about the subject" of pregnancy, Lewis writes on the first page of her introduction, is its "morbidity, the little-discussed ways that, biophysically speaking, gestating is an unconscionably destructive business" (1). She goes on to note that the same genes that promote embryonic development are involved in the growth of cancer, and refers to the growing fetus as a kind of parasite that "enlarges and paralyzes the wider arterial system" that supplies it with blood (2). She marvels that the default status for those with "'viable' wombs," given the violence of pregnancy, entails "walking around in a state of physical implantability—no Pill, no IUD" (3). Sophie Lewis, *Full Surrogacy Now* (New York: Verso, 2019).

36. Ibid., 26.

37. Ibid., 29, 1, 3, 17.

38. Ibid., 124.

39. Lewis admiringly quotes Donna Haraway, one of her intellectual heroes, who said, "The point for me is parenting, not reproducing. Parenting is about caring for generations, one's own or not; reproducing is about making more of oneself to populate the future, quite a different matter" (311). Following her lead, Lewis praises the "beautiful militants hell-bent on regeneration, not self-replication" (326).

40. Sophie Lewis, *Abolish the Family* (New York: Verso, 2022), 9.

41. Ibid., 84.

42. Lewis, *Full Surrogacy Now*, 165.

43. Firestone, *Dialectic of Sex*, 85.

44. Rich, *Of Woman Born*, 11.

45. "Ideally, of course," Rich writes, "women would choose not only whether, when, and where to bear children, and the circumstances of labor, but also between biological and artificial reproduction. Ideally, the process of creating another life would be freely and intelligently undertaken, much as a woman might prepare herself physically and mentally for a trip across country by jeep, or an archeological 'dig'; or might choose to do something else altogether. But I do not think we can project any such idea onto the future—and hope to realize it—without examining the shadow-images we carry out of the magical thinking of Eve's curse and the social victimization of women-as-mothers. To do so is to deny

aspects of ourselves which will rise up sooner or later to claim recognition." Ibid., 174–75.

46. Ibid., epigraph.
47. Ibid., 21, 13.
48. Ibid., 174.
49. Ibid., 218.
50. Ibid., 226.
51. Ibid., 225.
52. Ibid., 40.
53. Ibid., 246.
54. Ibid., 33.
55. Audre Lorde, "Eye to Eye: Black Women, Hatred, and Anger," in *Sister Outsider* (New York: Penguin, 2020), 147.
56. Ibid., 143, 151–52.
57. Ibid., 152.
58. Alice Walker, "In Search of Our Mothers' Gardens," in *Within the Circle: An Anthology of African American Literary Criticism from the Harlem Renaissance to the Present,* ed. Angelyn Mitchell (Durham, NC: Duke University Press, 1994), 409.
59. For more on the evolving and interlocking feminist discourses on motherhood, see Lauri Umansky's *Motherhood Reconceived: Feminism and the Legacies of the Sixties* (New York: New York University Press, 1996).
60. E. Franklin Frazier, *The Negro Family in the United States* (Chicago: University of Chicago Press, 1939), 125.
61. Daniel Patrick Moynihan, *The Negro Family: The Case for National Action, Office of Policy Planning and Research,* U.S. Department of Labor, March 1965, 29–31.
62. Eldridge Cleaver, "The Allegory of the Black Eunuchs," in *Soul on Ice* (New York: Delta, 1968), 162. See chapter 3 of Umansky's *Motherhood Reconceived* for an extended discussion of the pro-motherhood strands within Black feminism and their response to the male-centered Black Power movement, "Black Nationalist Pronatalism, Black Feminism, and the Quest for a Multiracial Women's Movement," 77–102.
63. Angela Davis, "The Black Woman's Role in the Community of Slaves," *The Black Scholar* (December 1971), 5.
64. Ibid., 6.
65. Ibid., 7–8.

66. Fran Sanders, "Dear Black Man," in *The Black Woman: An Anthology* (New York: Washington Square Press, 2005), 88.

67. Umansky, *Motherhood Reconceived*, 88.

68. Rich, *Of Woman Born*, 224.

69. Jennie Klein, "Feminist Art and Spirituality in the 1970s," *Feminist Studies* 35, no. 3 (Fall 2009): 575–602.

70. Rich, *Of Woman Born*, 72.

71. Ibid., 92.

72. Mary Daly, *Gyn/Ecology: The Metaethics of Radical Feminism* (Boston: Beacon Press, 1990), 60.

73. Ibid., 355, 226, 3.

74. Clare Monagle, "Mary Daly's *Gyn/Ecology*: Mysticism, Difference, and Feminist History," *Signs* 44, no. 2 (2019): 333–53, DOI: 10.1086/699341.

75. Audre Lorde, "An Open Letter to Mary Daly," in *Sister Outsider* (New York: Penguin, 2020), 60.

76. Michelle Goldberg, "What Is a Woman?" *New Yorker*, July 28, 2014, https://www.newyorker.com/magazine/2014/08/04/woman-2.

77. Sara Ruddick, *Maternal Thinking: Toward a Politics of Peace* (Boston: Beacon Press, 1995), 7.

78. "Reason was failing me," Ruddick wrote, "as a lover, mother, and citizen." Yet "as destructive as Western ideals of Reason may be, the capacity to reason is a human good. . . . If I could not reject Reason, could I honor Reason differently? If I could no longer serve the Reason I had known, was it possible to reconceive a reason that strengthened passion rather than opposing it, that refused to separate love from knowledge?" Ibid., 8–9.

79. Ibid, 10.

80. Ibid., 6, 9 (Ruddick titles these values "Protection, Nurturance, and Training," respectively), 8.

81. Ibid., 148.

82. In 1993, in the pages of the feminist journal *Hypatia*, Patrice DiQuinzio charged that "Ruddick's analysis of mothering as a practice with characteristic goals, modes of thought, and virtues can be criticized for [its] universalizing and normative tendencies," based on her argument that "at least some needs of children are universal throughout the human species and require certain responses from mothers cross-culturally, thus implying that human needs, at least those experienced in infancy and childhood, are unmediated by culture or language." Patrice

DiQuinzio, "Exclusion and Essentialism in Feminist Theory: The Problem of Mothering," *Hypatia* 8, no. 3 (Summer 1993): 10.

83. In 1984, bell hooks wrote a critique of Ruddick's 1980 essay on "maternal thinking" where she laid out her preliminary ideas (which would be developed in greater detail in the 1989 book). hooks charged Ruddick with "romanticiz[ing] the idea of the 'maternal,'" and noted that the forms of intensive mothering Ruddick held up as ideals were often unattainable for working-class mothers. bell hooks, "Revolutionary Parenting," in *Feminist Theory: From Margin to Center* (Boston: South End Press, 1984), 138–40.

84. Ruddick, "Preface: Maternal Thinking, Revisited," *Maternal Thinking*, ix.

85. Élisabeth Badinter, *The Conflict,* trans. Adriana Hunter (New York: Metropolitan Books, 2006), 33, 100.

86. Edelman questions "reproductive futurism" (2) as a force in American politics and an "unquestioned good" (7). This normative attitude is characterized by appeals to think of the children or "fight" on their behalf. Rhetoric like this, Edelman says, "impose[s] an ideological limit on political discourse as such, preserving in the process the absolute privilege of heteronormativity by rendering unthinkable, by casting outside the political domain, the possibility of a queer resistance to this organizing principle of communal relations." Lee Edelman, *No Future: Queer Theory and the Death Drive* (Durham, NC: Duke University Press, 2004), 2.

87. Slaughter, "Why Women Still Can't Have It All."

88. Anne-Marie Slaughter, "'Having It All' Was Always a Poor Measure of Success," *FT,* January 27, 2023, https://www.ft.com/content/1580ed07-35ec-49ca-a314-1cea419493b6.

89. Elizabeth Kolbert, "Mother Courage," *New Yorker,* February 29, 2004, https://www.newyorker.com/magazine/2004/03/08/mother-courage.

90. Ibid.

91. Daphne de Marneffe, *Maternal Desire* (New York: Scribner, 2019), 223.

92. Angela Garbes, *Essential Labor: Mothering as Social Change* (New York: Harper Wave, 2022); Jessica Grose, *Screaming on the Inside: The Unsustainability of American Motherhood* (New York: Mariner Books, 2022); Nancy Reddy, *The Good Mother Myth* (New York: St. Martin's Press, 2025).

93. De Marneffe, *Maternal Desire,* 21.

94. Kolbert, "Mother Courage."

95. Ibid.

96. Rich, *Of Woman Born*, 215.

97. Ibid., xxxv.

98. Jacqueline Rose, *Mothers: An Essay on Love and Cruelty* (New York: Farrar, Straus and Giroux, 2018), 7.

99. hooks asserted that much of "feminism in the United States has so far been a bourgeois ideology," defined by "'competitive, atomistic liberal individualism' . . . to such an extent that it undermines the potential radicalism of feminist struggle." hooks, *Feminist Theory*, 8.

100. "Contemporary feminist analyses of family often implied that successful feminist movement would either begin with or lead to the abolition of family. This suggestion was terribly threatening to many women, especially non-white women. While there are white women activists who may experience family primarily as an oppressive institution, . . . many black women find the family the least oppressive institution." Ibid., 37.

101. Ibid., 98, 133, 134.

102. Ibid., 135–36.

103. Ibid., 138, 137.

104. Ibid., 137, 139.

105. Rich, *Of Woman Born*, 216, 209–10.

106. Schouten, *Liberalism, Neutrality, and the Gendered Division of Labor*, 3.

107. *Economist*, "Parents Now Spend Twice as Much Time with Their Children as 50 Years Ago," November 27, 2017, https://www.economist .com/graphic-detail/2017/11/27/parents-now-spend-twice-as-much -time-with-their-children-as-50-years-ago. A 2015 Pew Research study found that when surveying working parents, most report dividing household chores equitably (59 percent), child discipline (61 percent), and playing with the children (64 percent), as well as being equally focused on their work (62 percent). There were significant disparities in how men and women describe their domestic labor, however. The researchers found that when it came to individual tasks (like managing the children's schedules), men were more inclined than their spouses to say that the distribution of labor was equal. In the case of managing the family schedules, 64 percent of women said they did more, while 41 percent of the men said they contributed equally. Pew Research Center, "Raising Kids and Running a Household," 3.

108. During the pandemic, several news stories came out raising the alarm that the lockdown threatened to undo years of progress by forcing women to take on more work at home. See Claire Cain Miller, "Nearly Half of Men Say They Do Most of the Home Schooling. 3 Percent of

Women Agree," *New York Times*, May 6, 2020, https://www.nytimes
.com/2020/05/06/upshot/pandemic-chores-homeschooling-gender
.html, and Dalvin Brown, "Women Take on Greater Share of Parenting
Responsibilities Under Stay-at-Home Orders," *USA Today*, May 8, 2020,
https://www.usatoday.com/story/money/2020/05/08/women-take-on
-more-their-kids-remote-learning-responsibilities/5178659002. Yet
there are also indications that in some two-parent homes, especially
those that tended to be more egalitarian, the division of labor became
more evenly divided. A report for the Council on Contemporary Families found that, "according to both men and women, men are doing
more housework and childcare during the pandemic than before it began, leading to more equal sharing of domestic labor. Moreover, given
the conditions under which men are doing more, there is potential that
these changes may persist after the pandemic ends." See Daniel L. Carlson, Richard J. Petts, and Joanna R. Pepin, "Men and Women Agree:
During the COVID-19 Pandemic Men Are Doing More at Home,"
Council on Contemporary Families, May 20, 2020, https://sites.utexas
.edu/contemporaryfamilies/2020/05/20/covid-couples-division-of
-labor.

109. Sheila Heti, *Motherhood* (New York: Farrar, Straus and Giroux, 2018), 21.

110. Ibid.

111. Women in the United States today outnumber men in college enroll-
ment and have far higher degree completion rates. See Kim Parker,
"What's Behind the Growing Gap Between Men and Women in College Completion?" Pew Research Center, November 8, 2021. They
comprise nearly half of the workforce (see Institute for Women's Policy
Research, "Women's Labor Force Participation," *Status of Women in
the United States* [2015]), and hold slightly more than half of the professional and managerial positions (see U.S. Bureau of Labor Statistics,
Household Data Annual Averages [2022]). Women are also catching up
to men in their representation at the highest levels of leadership, though
they still lag behind. See *Women CEOs in America*, a report published
by the Women Business Collaborative (2022).

## CHAPTER 3: ANALYSIS PARALYSIS

1. Kim Brooks, "A Portrait of the Artist as a Young Mom," *The Cut*
(April 2016), https://www.thecut.com/2016/04/portrait-motherhood
-creativity-c-v-r.html.

2. Heti, *Motherhood*, 124; Rivka Galchen, *Little Labors* (New York: New Directions, 2016), 9; Rachel Cusk, *A Life's Work* (New York: Picador, 2021), 98.

3. Courtney Zoffness, *Spilt Milk* (San Francisco: McSweeney's, 2021), 203.

4. Heti, *Motherhood*, 1.

5. Ibid., 21.

6. Ibid., 83.

7. In a reflection on the vulnerability of pregnancy, Nelson writes, "I've begun to give myself over to the idea that the sensation might be forever changed, that this sensitivity is now mine, ours, to work with. Can fragility feel as hot as bravado? I think so, but sometimes struggle to find the way. Whenever I think I can't find it, Harry assures me that we can. And so we go on, our bodies finding each other again and again, even as they—we—have also been right here, all along." Maggie Nelson, *The Argonauts* (Minneapolis: Graywolf, 2015), 86.

8. Heti, *Motherhood*, 197.

9. Elizabeth Hardwick, *Sleepless Nights* (New York: New York Review Classics, 2001), 19.

10. Heti, *Motherhood*, 10.

11. Cusk, *Life's Work*, 57.

12. Maggie Doherty, "On Not Becoming a Mother," *New Republic*, April 25, 2018, https://newrepublic.com/article/148110/not-becoming-mother.

13. Jennifer Szalai, "The 50 Best Memoirs of the Past 50 Years," *New York Times*, June 26, 2019, https://www.nytimes.com/interactive/2019/06/26/books/best-memoirs.html.

14. *Publishers Weekly*, "PW Picks: Books of the Week," May 1, 2015, https://www.publishersweekly.com/pw/by-topic/industry-news/tip-sheet/article/66424-pw-picks-books-of-the-week-may-1-2015.html.

15. Rachel Cusk, "I Was Only Being Honest," *The Guardian*, March 21, 2008, https://www.theguardian.com/books/2008/mar/21/biography.women.

16. Cusk, *Life's Work*, 130.

17. Meaghan O'Connell, *And Now We Have Everything* (New York: Little, Brown and Company, 2018), 61.

18. Cusk, *Life's Work*, 57.

19. Galchen, *Little Labors*, 8.

20. Cusk, *Life's Work*, 133.

21. Ibid., 7.

22. See Galchen's "Notes on Some Twentieth-Century Writers" section. Galchen, *Little Labors*, 51; Jenny Offill, *Dept. of Speculation* (New York:

Vintage Contemporaries, 2014), 8; O'Connell, *And Now We Have Everything,* 214; Heti, *Motherhood,* 35.

23. Galchen, *Little Labors,* 9.
24. O'Connell, *And Now We Have Everything,* 33.
25. Zoffness, *Spilt Milk,* 54.
26. Galchen, *Little Labors,* 9.
27. Torrey Peters, *Detransition, Baby* (New York: One World, 2021), 266.
28. Ibid., 174.
29. Melanie Klein, "A Contribution to the Psychogenesis of Manic-Depressive States," *Love, Guilt and Reparation and Other Works,* in *The Writings of Melanie Klein,* vol. 1. (New York: The Free Press, 1975), 262–89.
30. Heti, *Motherhood,* 23.
31. Cusk, *Life's Work,* 1.
32. Ibid., 38, 107, 125, 131, 131, 155, 165, 200.
33. Ibid., 2.
34. Ibid., 135.
35. Galchen, *Little Labors,* 7.
36. Ibid., 18.
37. Ibid., 30.
38. Ibid., 32.
39. Peters, *Detransition, Baby,* 176.
40. Ibid, 178.
41. Ibid.
42. Elena Ferrante, "Elena Ferrante: 'Nothing Is Comparable to the Joy of Bringing Another Living Creature into the World,'" *The Guardian,* March 10, 2018, https://www.theguardian.com/lifeandstyle/2018/mar/10/elena-ferrante-nothing-comparable-joy-bringing-another-creature-into-world.
43. Ibid.
44. Elena Ferrante, *Frantumaglia: A Writer's Journey* (New York: Europa Editions, 2016), 123.
45. Elena Ferrante, *The Lost Daughter,* trans. Ann Goldstein (New York: Europa Editions 2020), 139.
46. Ibid., 117.
47. Ibid., 117.
48. Ibid., 117–18.
49. Ibid., 83.

50. Ibid., 140.

51. Ibid., 69.

52. Ibid., 10.

53. Ibid., 118.

54. Jacqueline Rose, "Mothers," *London Review of Books* 36, no. 12 (June 19, 2014), https://www.lrb.co.uk/the-paper/v36/n12/jacqueline-rose /mothers.

55. Ferrante, *Lost Daughter,* 118.


**CHAPTER 4: TO BE OR . . . ?**

1. Virginia Woolf, *Mrs. Dalloway* (New York: Penguin Classics, 2000), 98.

2. Ibid.

3. David Wallace-Wells, "The Uninhabitable Earth," *New York,* July 9, 2017, https://nymag.com/intelligencer/2017/07/climate-change-earth-too-hot -for-humans.html.

4. For a review, see Kyle Paoletta's "The Incredible Disappearing Dooms-day," *Harper's* (April 2023), https://harpers.org/archive/2023/04/the -incredible-disappearing-doomsday-climate-catastrophists-new-york -times-climate-change-coverage.

5. IPCC, "Climate Change 2022: Impacts, Adaptation and Vulnerability," contribution of Working Group II to the Sixth Assessment Report of the Intergovernmental Panel on Climate Change, ed. Hans-Otto Pört-ner and Debra C. Roberts (Cambridge: Cambridge University Press, 2022), DOI: 10.1017/9781009325844, 9.

6. Paoletta, "Incredible Disappearing Doomsday."

7. Alec Tyson, Brian Kennedy, and Cary Funk, "Gen Z, Millennials Stand Out for Climate Change Activism, Social Media Engagement with Is-sue," Pew Research Center (May 26, 2021), https://www.pewresearch .org/science/2021/05/26/gen-z-millennials-stand-out-for-climate -change-activism-social-media-engagement-with-issue; Brad Plumer, Raymond Zhong, and Lisa Friedman, "Time Is Running Out to Avert a Harrowing Future, Climate Panel Warns," *New York Times,* Febru-ary 28, 2022, https://www.nytimes.com/2022/02/28/climate/climate -change-ipcc-un-report.html.

8. G. W. F. Hegel, *Elements of the Philosophy of Right*, ed. Allen W. Wood, trans. H. B. Nisbet (Cambridge: Cambridge University Press, 2014), §47, 78.

9. Daniel Sherrell, *Warmth: Coming of Age at the End of Our World* (New York: Penguin, 2021), 17.

10. Ibid., 104.

11. Ibid., 118, 187, 232.

12. Shanna Swan, *Count Down: How Our Modern World Is Threatening Sperm Counts, Altering Male and Female Reproductive Development, and Imperiling the Future of the Human Race* (New York: Scribner, 2020); Landon Schnabel, "Secularism and Fertility Worldwide," *Socius* 7 (January–December 2021), https://doi.org/10.1177 /23780231211031320; Matthias Doepke, Anne Hannusch, Fabian Kindermann, and Michèle Tertilt, *The Economics of Fertility: A New Era*, CEPR Discussion Paper 17212 (London: Centre for Economic Policy Research, 2022); Ronald R. Rindfuss, S. Philip Morgan, and Kate Offutt, "Education and the Changing Age Pattern of American Fertility: 1963–1989," *Demography* 33, no. 3 (August 1996), 277–90; Ushma D. Upadhyay, Jessica D. Gipson, Mellissa Withers, Shayna Lewis, Erica J. Ciaraldi, Ashley Fraser, Megan J. Huchko, and Ndola Prata, "Women's Empowerment and Fertility: A Review of the Literature," *Social Science and Medicine* 115 (August 2014), DOI: 10.1016/j. socscimed.2014.06.014.

13. Britt Wray, *The Climate Baby Dilemma*, CBC, November 24, 2022, https://gem.cbc.ca/media/the-climate-baby-dilemma/s01e01; Umair Irfan, "We Need to Talk About the Ethics of Having Children in a Warming World," *Vox*, March 11, 2019, https://www.vox.com/2019/3 /11/18256166/climate-change-having-kids; Damian Carrington, "Want to Fight Climate Change? Have Fewer Children," *The Guardian*, July 12, 2017, https://www.theguardian.com/environment/2017/jul/12/want-to -fight-climate-change-have-fewer-children; Ezra Klein, "Your Kids Are Not Doomed," *New York Times*, June 5, 2020, https://www.nytimes.com /2022/06/05/opinion/climate-change-should-you-have-kids.html.

14. Miranda Green, "Ocasio-Cortez: It's 'Legitimate' to Ask if It's OK to Have Children in the Face of Climate Change," *The Hill*, February 25, 2019, https://thehill.com/policy/energy-environment/431440-ocasio-cortez-in -face-of-climate-change-its-legitimate-to-ask-if-ok.

15. Molly Lambert, "Miley Cyrus Has Finally Found Herself," *Elle*, July 11, 2019, https://www.elle.com/culture/music/a28280119/miley-cyrus-elle -interview.

16. Jane Goodall, "When the Duke of Sussex Interviewed Dr Jane Goodall About the Future of Sustainability," interview by Harry Charles Albert

David, *Vogue UK* (October 21, 2021), https://www.vogue.co.uk/article/prince-harry-jane-goodall-september-2019-issue.

17. Howard Stern, Interview with Seth Rogen, *Howard Stern Show,* podcast audio (May 11, 2021), https://www.youtube.com/watch?v=k5P6aPlSw3w.

18. Elizabeth Marks, Caroline Hickman, Panu Pihkala, Susan Clayton, et al., "Young People's Voices on Climate Anxiety, Government Betrayal and Moral Injury: A Global Phenomenon" *The Lancet Planetary Health* (September 7, 2021), http://dx.doi.org/10.2139/ssrn.3918955. After completing peer review, the paper was published three months later under the title "Climate Anxiety in Children and Young People and Their Beliefs About Government Responses to Climate Change: A Global Survey," *The Lancet Planetary Health* 5, no. 12 (December 2021), https://doi.org/10.1016/S2542-5196(21)00278-3.

19. Brown, "Growing Share of Childless Adults."

20. Ibid.

21. Katie O'Reilly, "To Have or Not to Have Children in the Age of Climate Change," *Sierra*, November 1, 2019, https://www.sierraclub.org/sierra/2019-6-november-december/feature/have-or-not-have-children-age-climate-change.

22. Stern, Interview with Seth Rogen.

23. Matthew Schneider-Mayerson, "The Environmental Politics of Reproductive Choices in the Age of Climate Change," *Environmental Politics* 31, no. 1 (2022), DOI: 10.1080/09644016.2021.1902700.

24. Ibid.

25. Ibid.

26. "Mission," Conceivable Future, accessed June 3, 2023, https://conceivablefuture.org/mission. In 2021, BirthStrike dissolved and ceased operations as an organized political campaign, citing the negative press coverage that cast them as neo-Malthusians, as well as the recognition that their message placed too much emphasis on individual choice rather than systemic change. Katharine Dow and Heather McMullen, "'Too Afraid to Have Kids'—How BirthStrike for Climate Lost Control of Its Political Message," *The Conversation*, September 15, 2022, https://theconversation.com/too-afraid-to-have-kids-how-birthstrike-for-climate-lost-control-of-its-political-message-181198.

27. Liza Featherstone, "If Politicians Want to Raise Birth Rates, They Should Pass Climate Policy," *New Republic,* October 1, 2021, https://newrepublic.com/article/163832/politicians-want-raise-birth-rates-pass-climate

-policy; Danielle McNally, "Women Are Deciding to Have Fewer Children, and Global Warming Is to Blame," *Marie Claire,* February 7, 2022, https://www.marieclaire.com/politics/climate-change-fertility-modern-fertility-survey.

28. Timothy Morton, "Introducing the Idea of 'Hyperobjects,'" *High Country News,* January 19, 2015, https://www.hcn.org/issues/47.1/introducing-the-idea-of-hyperobjects.

29. Amitav Ghosh, *The Great Derangement* (Chicago: University of Chicago Press, 2016), 32.

30. For a thorough overview of the theological and philosophical treatment of the question of the goodness of human life, see Rémi Brague's *The Legitimacy of the Human,* trans. Paul Seaton (South Bend, IN: St. Augustine's Press, 2017).

31. Theognis, "The Elegiac Poems of Theognis," in *Elegy and Iambus,* vol. 1, trans. J. M. Edmonds (Cambridge, MA: Harvard University Press; London: Heinemann Ltd., 1931; Perseus Digital Library), accessed August 14, 2023, 425–28. https://www.perseus.tufts.edu/hopper/text?doc=Perseus%3Atext%3A2008.01.0479%3Avolume%3D1%3Atext%3D11%3Asection%3D2#.

32. Ibid., 429–38. Not long after, Sophocles's chorus in *Oedipus at Colonus,* composed at the turn of the fifth century BCE, pronounces a remarkably similar verdict. The chorus's judgment is made on different grounds than Theognis's—deriving not from man's incorrigible folly but from the inevitability of suffering:

    > For while youth is with one, carrying with it light-headed thoughtlessness, what painful blow is far away? What hardship is not near? Murders, civil strife, quarrels, battles, and resentment! And the next place, at the end, belongs to much-dispraised old age, powerless, unsociable, friendless, where all evils of evils are our neighbors.

    But the conclusion is nearly identical:

    > Not to be born comes first by every reckoning; and once one has appeared, to go back to where one came from as soon as possible is the next best thing.

    Sophocles, *Oedipus at Colonus,* in *Sophocles: Antigone. The Women of Trachis. Philoctetes. Oedipus at Colonus,* vol. 2, trans. Hugh Lloyd-Jones, Loeb Classical Library 21 (Cambridge, MA: Harvard University Press, 1994), DOI: 10.4159/DLCL.sophocles-oedipus_colonus.1994, 546–47.

33. Plutarch, "Consolatio ad Apollonium," *Moralia,* trans. Frank Cole Babbitt (Cambridge, MA: Harvard University Press, 1928), §27, http://data
.perseus.org/citations/urn:cts:greekLit:tlg0007.tlg076.perseus-eng1:27.

34. No less interesting than the rare but pointed attention that the ancient
Greek and Roman authors paid to this question is what their disciples
tried to make of it. Many anonymous writers, active between the second
century BCE and first century CE, sought to extend the conversation
their illustrious predecessors had started. They were not content to have
the Silenic dictum merely passed down from generation to generation;
its practical implications had to be queried: If the anti-natalist dogma
is true, should humans change the way they live with a view to it? And
what would happen if they did? The author of a first-century-BCE letter,
purporting to be written three centuries earlier by the cynic Diogenes
of Sinope, writes that "one should not wed nor raise children, since
our race is weak and marriage and children burden human weakness
with troubles." See Pseudo-Diogenes, Letter 47, in *The Cynic Epistles:
A Study Edition,* ed. Abraham J. Malherbe (Atlanta: Society of Biblical
Literature, 1977), 179. But he does not stop there. Pseudo-Diogenes expresses skepticism that many (outside the circle of educated elites, that
is) would take up his proposal but assures the reader that even if this
were the case, it would be no reason for alarm:

> For now, perhaps only the one persuaded by me will go childless,
> while the world, unconvinced, will beget children. But even if the
> human race should fail, would it not be fitting to lament this as
> much as one would if the procreation of flies and wasps should fail?

To name another example: At around the same time, in an apocryphal Platonic dialogue likely written between 100 BCE and 50 CE,
Socrates tries to help a dying man named Axiochus overcome his fear
of death. Life is so full of torment and suffering, Socrates explains,
that death can only be understood as a "release"—"a transition from
something bad to something good." This claim echoes familiar themes
from Platonic dialogues (the *Phaedo,* in particular), but here another
question is raised, absent from the earlier texts. Axiochus asks Socrates
about the practical implications of this idea: "If you think that living is
bad, why do you remain alive?" This question goes unanswered. By the
end of the dialogue, Axiochus declares he is now so far from fearing
death that he "passionately desire[s] it." See *Axiochus,* trans. Jackson P.
Hershbell, in *Plato: Complete Works,* ed. John M. Cooper (Indianapolis:
Hackett Publishing Company, 1997).

The theme continued to be developed in Hellenistic and early Roman thought. Around 40 CE, the Roman Stoic philosopher Seneca wrote in his *Consolations*, addressing a mother mourning the death of her son: "Nothing is so deceptive as human life, nothing is so treacherous. Heaven knows! not one of us would have accepted it as a gift, were it not given to us without our knowledge. If, therefore, the happiest lot is not to be born, the next best, I think, is to have a brief life and by death to be restored quickly to the original state." See Seneca, "To Marcia on Consolation," *Moral Essays*, trans. John W. Basore, Loeb Classical Library 254 (Cambridge, MA: Harvard University Press, 1932), 78–79.

35. Friedrich Nietzsche, *The Birth of Tragedy*, in *Basic Writings of Nietzsche*, trans. Walter Kaufmann (New York: Modern Library, 2000), §3, 41–44.

36. David Benatar, *Better Never to Have Been: The Harm of Coming into Existence* (Oxford: Oxford University Press, 2006).

37. Genesis 1:28 (NKJV).

38. Ecclesiastes 1:2 (NKJV).

39. Ecclesiastes 4:2–3 (NKJV).

40. Eruvin 13b:14, William Davidson Talmud, digital edition of the Koren Noé Talmud, ed. Rabbi Adin Even-Israel Steinsaltz, "Sefaria," accessed August 11, 2023, https://www.sefaria.org/Eruvin.13b.14.

41. Another exception within the Jewish tradition to the more official party line is found in a Talmudic midrash on the book of Exodus from Sotah 12a. According to the sages, after Pharaoh commanded the midwives to put to death all newborn Jewish males, Moses's father, Amram, despaired. He decided to have no more children, as he would be "laboring for nothing by bringing children into the world [only] to be killed." He sends his wife away, and others follow his lead. Amram's daughter Miriam pleads with him to reconsider. His decree, says Miriam, is in the end harsher than Pharaoh's, for three reasons. First, Pharaoh endangered only the males, but Amram's proposal would condemn the females, too. Second, while Pharaoh had decreed to kill them only in this world, Amram decreed death in this world and in the world to come, as those not born will not enter the world to come. And, last, Miriam says of Pharaoh, "It is uncertain whether his decree will be fulfilled, and it is uncertain if his decree will not be fulfilled. You are a righteous person, and as such, your decrees will certainly be fulfilled." Amram is finally convinced and takes his wife back. The other men follow suit. (We thank Jacob Nadler for bringing this to our attention.) See Sotah 12a, William Davidson

Talmud, digital edition, ed. Rabbi Adin Even-Israel Steinsaltz, accessed August 11, 2023, https://www.sefaria.org/Sotah.12a.10.

42. Saint Augustine, *Treatises on Marriage and Other Subjects,* trans. Charles T. Wilcox et al., ed. Roy J. Deferrari, from *The Fathers of the Church: A New Translation* 27 (Washington, DC: Catholic University of America Press, 1999).

43. This fact was relayed to Berg by Moshe Halbertal, who himself first had it pointed out to him by Jacob Taubes.

44. Examples include the second-century ascetic Christian sect the Encratites, the early third-century New Testament apocryphal text the Acts of Thomas, and the third-century Gnostic religion Manichaeism.

45. Saint Gregory of Nyssa, "On Virginity," *Ascetical Works,* The Fathers of the Church: A New Translation 58, trans. Virginia Woods Callahan (Washington, DC: Catholic University of America Press, 1967), 48.

46. Lothario dei Segni (Pope Innocent III), *On the Misery of the Human Condition,* ed. Donald R. Howard, trans. Margaret Mary Dietz (Indianapolis and New York: Library of Liberal Arts 1969), 6.

47. While mainstream Islam, like Judaism, tended to favor procreation, even the Qur'an records the angels exasperated by the prospect of God placing the human being upon the earth: "What! wilt Thou place in it such as shall make mischief in it and shed blood, and we celebrate Thy praise and extol Thy holiness?" (2.30). Whether God's reply—"Surely I know what you do not know" (2.30)—appeased the irritated angels is left unsaid. And the early eleventh-century Arab poet al-Ma'arri, recognized as much for his withering pessimism and rejection of religious authority as for his verse, often railed against the unpardonable offense of siring children: "Better for Adam and all who issued forth from his loins / That he and they, yet unborn, created never had been!" Al-Ma'arri purportedly requested to have the following epitaph etched into a plaque on his tomb: "This is my father's crime against me, which I myself committed against none." See Reynold Alleyne Nicholson, *Studies in Islamic Poetry* (Cambridge: Cambridge University Press, 1921), 74.

48. E.g., Giannozzo Manetti's *On the Dignity and Excellence of Man,* his response to Pope Innocent III's *On the Misery of the Human Condition*; Giovanni Picco della Mirandola's *Oration on the Dignity of Man.*

49. William Shakespeare, *Hamlet,* Folger Library Shakespeare edition, ed. Barbara A. Mowat and Paul Werstine (New York: Simon & Schuster, 1992), 2.2.332. References are to act, scene, and line.

50. Ibid., 3.1.121–22.

51. Ibid., 3.1.163–64.

52. Nietzsche, *Birth of Tragedy*, §7, 60.

53. Though it is also worth mentioning that in *Paradise Lost* (1667), John Milton imagines Adam, reeling from his calamitous fall, railing against God: "Did I request Thee, Maker, from my clay / To mold me Man?" (10.743–44). The first man gradually comes to understand the true nature of his fate—a wretched life for which his children will blame him just as he now blames his own creator: "All that I eat or drink or shall beget, / Is propagated curse" (10.728–29). Horrified, Adam pleads, "Why do I overlive?" He demands death (10.773–79). See John Milton, *Paradise Lost,* ed. Gordon Teskey (New York: Norton, 2020), 254–56.

54. Arthur Schopenhauer, *The World as Will and Representation,* trans. E. F. J. Payne (New York: Dover Publications, 1969), 380.

55. Arthur Schopenhauer, "On the Sufferings of the World," in *The Essays of Arthur Schopenhauer: Studies in Pessimism,* trans. T. Bailey Saunders (London: George Allen & Company, 1913), 15.

56. In Thomas Mann's words, "Never probably in the history of the mind has there been so wonderful an example of the artist, the dark and driven human being, finding spiritual support, self-justification, and enlightenment in another's thought, as in this case of Wagner and Schopenhauer." Thomas Mann, *Essays of Three Decades,* trans. H. T. Lowe-Porter (London: Secker and Warburg, 1938), 345.

57. Both strains of the argument against procreation—i.e., both the argument from suffering and the argument from evil—appear in Lord Byron's poem "Cain," when Cain implores Satan: "Here let me die: for to give birth to those / Who can but suffer many years, and die, / Methinks is merely propagating death, / And multiplying murder." See Lord Byron, "Cain," *Poetry of Byron* (London: Macmillan, 1881). And both are threaded through the thought of the Italian philosopher Giacomo Leopardi, who was read approvingly by his contemporary Schopenhauer. Leopardi at once described the "burden of existence" foisted on every child from their first breath on and the corrupting nature of human society. Leopardi implicitly invoked the argument that producing more humans is to inflict evil on the world in stating that "unless he intends to carry off his children to live in the wild, [a decent man] should unquestioningly assume from the very first moment that his marriage will not bring into the world anything but a few more rogues"

(187), and the argument that reproducing is wrong because it inevitably causes suffering with the claim "in truth it is only fitting that the good father and the good mother, in trying to console their children, correct as best they can, and ease, the damage they have done by procreating them" (1087). Once they are born, the harm has already been done. See Giacomo Leopardi, *Zibaldone*, trans. Kathleen Baldwin, Richard Dixon, David Gibbons, Ann Goldstein, Gerard Slowey, Martin Thom, and Pamela Williams, ed. Michael Caesar and Franco D'Intino (New York: Farrar, Straus and Giroux, 2015).

58. Gustave Flaubert, *Memoirs of a Madman*, trans. Timothy Unwin (Liverpool: Liverpool Online Series Critical Editions of French Texts, 2001), 23.

59. Gustave Flaubert to Louise Colet, December 11, 1852, in *The Letters of Gustave Flaubert*, trans. Francis Steegmuller (New York: New York Review Books, 2023), 238.

60. D. H. Lawrence, *Women in Love* (New York: Penguin, 1920, 2006), 127.

61. For an example of one such atomic doomsday scenario, see Nevil Shute's 1957 apocalyptic novel *On the Beach* (New York: Vintage, 2010). Most famously, in 1968, Paul R. Ehrlich and Anne H. Ehrlich published *The Population Bomb,* which offered predictions of worldwide catastrophes, chief among them mass famines, due to population explosion. The book popularized the neo-Malthusian argument. Paul R. Ehrlich *The Population Bomb* (New York: Ballantine Books, 1968), 17. Though the predictions did not come to pass, as recently as 2009, the Ehrlichs claimed that "perhaps the most serious flaw in *The Bomb* was that it was much too optimistic about the future." Paul R. Ehrlich and Anne H. Ehrlich, "The Population Bomb Revisited," *Electronic Journal of Sustainable Development* 1, no. 3 (2009).

62. Philip Larkin, "This Be the Verse," in *Collected Poems,* ed. Anthony Thwaite (New York: Farrar, Straus and Giroux, 2003), 142.

63. Benatar, *Better Never to Have Been,* 1.

64. Sherrell, *Warmth,* 239.

65. Roy Scranton, "Learning to Die in the Anthropocene," *New York Times,* November 10, 2013, https://archive.nytimes.com/opinionator.blogs.nytimes.com/2013/11/10/learning-how-to-die-in-the-anthropocene.

66. Sherrell, *Warmth,* 241.

67. Ibid.

68. Ibid.

69. Ibid., 240.

70. Ibid., 242–43.

71. Meehan Crist, "Is It OK to Have a Child?" *London Review of Books* 42, no. 5 (March 5, 2020), https://www.lrb.co.uk/the-paper/v42/n05/meehan-crist/is-it-ok-to-have-a-child.

72. Ibid.

73. Tom Whyman, *Infinitely Full of Hope: Fatherhood and the Future in an Age of Crisis and Disaster* (London: Repeater Books, 2021).

74. Hannah Arendt, *The Human Condition* (Chicago: University of Chicago Press, 2018), 247, 246.

75. For a recent exploration of the significance of Arendt's concept of natality and how the concept of birth has figured into the thinking of Arendt, Friedrich Nietzsche, Mary Wollstonecraft, Mary Shelley, Sojourner Truth, Adrienne Rich, and Toni Morrison, see Jennifer Banks, *Natality* (New York: W.W. Norton, 2023).

76. Whyman, *Infinitely Full of Hope*, 22, 111.

77. Ibid., 157, 111. Crist is sharper on this point, writing, "If it is human nature to burn through this planet's resources as we have for the past 150 years, then we're done; if it is human systems that do this, then we've got a chance" (Crist, "Is It OK to Have a Child?").

78. Samuel Scheffler, "A World Without Children," *The Point* 20 (Fall 2019): 95.

79. Samuel Scheffler, *Why Worry About Future Generations?* (Oxford: Oxford University Press, 2018), 43.

80. Ibid., 44, 47.

81. Ibid., 48–49.

82. P. D. James, *Children of Men* (New York: Vintage Books, 1993), 11.

83. In *Why Worry About Future Generations?* Scheffler calls the reasons to value future generations that stem from our investment in long-term projects "reasons of interest," but there are also, in his account, reasons of "valuation" and "reciprocity" as well as "love" to concern ourselves with the future of humankind. The latter are the most interesting from the standpoint of the investigation undertaken here, insofar as they have to do with a direct positive affective attitude toward humanity itself. But we are not concerned with whether we, as a matter of fact, happen to have positive affective dispositions toward humanity but whether such attitudes, however prevalent they may or may not actually be, can be justified. Scheffler expounds on the idea of our love for humanity significantly in his to-date unpublished

manuscript, *One Life to Lead: The Mysteries of Time and the Goods of Attachment.*

84. After all, a paradigmatic example of a Schefflerian activity, as far as its formal features are concerned, would be eugenics: it would probably not make sense to put efforts into manipulating human procreation in order to improve the quality of the species or a subgroup within it were humanity to go extinct in the near future, but this fact hardly provides anyone with an objectively good reason for why they should work to ensure the future of humanity.

85. A freelance writer and novelist by the name of Dan Bloom has claimed credit for inventing the term "cli-fi" after writing a short novella in 2012 called *Polar City Red,* about a family forced to migrate to Alaska due to climate change. Bloom's novella itself remains obscure, but the term he coined has taken off. See Rodge Glass, "Global Warming: The Rise of 'Cli-Fi,'" *The Guardian,* May 31, 2013, https://www.theguardian.com /books/2013/may/31/global-warning-rise-cli-fi. The past decade saw the publication of so many new cli-fi novels that the critic Jo Livingstone said in 2020 that "the challenge facing the environmental writer now is standing out from the crowd (not to mention the headlines)." Jo Livingstone, "How to Write About Climate Change," *New Republic,* August 7, 2020, https://newrepublic.com/article/158838/write-climate -change.

86. Alexandra Alter, "The World Is Ending, and Readers Couldn't Be Happier," *New York Times,* September 5, 2014, https://www.nytimes.com /2014/09/06/books/station-eleven-joins-falls-crop-of-dystopian-novels .html.

87. Ghosh, *Great Derangement,* 9.

88. Alexandra Kleeman, *Something New Under the Sun* (London and New York: Hogarth, 2021), 105.

89. Joy Williams, *Harrow* (New York: Knopf, 2021), 69, 162, 98.

90. Edan Lepucki, *California: A Novel* (New York: Little, Brown, and Company, 2014), 4.

91. Claire Vaye Watkins, *Gold Fame Citrus* (New York: Riverhead, 2015), 4.

92. Lepucki, *California,* 58.

93. Richard Powers, *The Overstory* (New York: Norton 2018), 452.

94. Lydia Millet, *A Children's Bible* (New York: Norton 2020), 28, 17, 59.

95. Williams, *Harrow,* 100, 99, 182.

96. Millet, *Children's Bible,* 23.

97. Ibid., 5, 13, 5.

98. Powers, *Overstory*, 383.

99. Lydia Millet, "There Will Be Flood," interview by Christian Lorentzen, *Bookforum* (Summer 2020), https://www.bookforum.com/print/2702 /lydia-millet-discusses-her-new-novel-of-teens-biblical-allusions-and -plausible-environmental-disaster-24048.

100. Kleeman, *Something New Under the Sun*, 144.

101. Williams, *Harrow*, 92.

102. Richard Powers, *Bewilderment* (New York: Norton, 2021), 36.

103. Millet, *Children's Bible*, 22.

104. In *Mothers: An Essay on Love and Cruelty*, Jacqueline Rose analyzes the ways in which mothers have been consistently vilified for their alleged excess sexuality and blamed, in these terms, "for the ills of the world, the breakdown in the social fabric, the threat to welfare, to the health of the nation" (11). The "most recent version" of this campaign is "the charge that excessively reproducing mothers are responsible for climate change" (47).

105. Missouri Williams, *The Doloriad: A Novel* (New York: Farrar, Straus and Giroux 2022), 219.

106. Missouri Williams, "Aggressive Mirroring: An Interview with Missouri Williams," Interview by Nathan Stormer, *TriQuarterly* (March 4, 2022), https://www.triquarterly.org/interviews/aggressive-mirroring-interview -missouri-williams.

107. Millet is currently employed as the deputy creative director at the Center for Biological Diversity in Tucson. "Meet the Staff," Center for Biological Diversity, accessed June 3, 2023, https://www.biologicaldiversity. org/about/staff.

108. Millet, "There Will Be Flood."

109. Richard Powers, "Richard Powers: 'We're Completely Alienated from Everything Else Alive,'" interview by Emma John, *The Guardian*, June 16, 2018, https://www.theguardian.com/books/2018/jun/16/richard-powers -interview-overstory.

110. Joy Williams, "Save the Whales, Screw the Shrimp," in *Ill Nature: Rants and Reflections on Humanity and Other Animals* (New York: Vintage, 2001), 19.

111. Joy Williams, "The Case Against Babies," in *Ill Nature: Rants and Reflections on Humanity and Other Animals* (New York: Vintage, 2001) 88–89.

112. Joy Williams, "The Art of Fiction, No. 223," interview with Paul Winner, *The Paris Review* 209 (Summer 2014), https://www.theparisreview.org /interviews/6303/the-art-of-fiction-no-223-joy-williams.

113. Alter, "World Is Ending."

114. Ibid.

115. Ibid.

116. Jonathan Lear, *Imagining the End: Mourning and Ethical Life* (Cambridge, MA: Harvard University Press, 2022), 2.

117. In a short *New York Times* op-ed in 2014, George Marshall, the climate activist and founder of the Climate Outreach Information Network, anticipated this outcome. "I predict that 'cli-fi' will reinforce existing views rather than shift them," he wrote. "The unconvinced will see these stories as proof that this issue is a fiction, exaggerated for dramatic effect. The already convinced will be engaged, but overblown apocalyptic story lines may distance them from the issue of climate change or even objectify the problem." George Marshall, "Climate Fiction Will Reinforce Existing Views," *New York Times,* July 29, 2014, https://www.nytimes .com/roomfordebate/2014/07/29/will-fiction-influence-how-we-react -to-climate-change/climate-fiction-will-reinforce-existing-views.

118. Lear, *Imagining the End*, 7.

119. Ibid., 3, 8.

120. Ghosh, *Great Derangement,* 7.

121. Kieran Setiya, "The Midlife Crisis," *Philosophers' Imprint* 14, no. 31 (November 2014), 12.

122. Mary Shelley, *The Last Man* (Ware: Wordsworth Editions), 355.

123. Kyle Paoletta, "The Incredible Disappearing Doomsday," *Harper's* (April 2023); Hein de Haas, "Climate Refugees: The Fabrication of a Migration Threat," International Migration Institute (blog), June 8, 2020, https:// www.migrationinstitute.org/blog/climate-refugees-the-fabrication-of -a-migration-threat.

124. The asymmetry claim was introduced by Jan Narveson, who famously argued that we have a duty to make people happy, not to make happy people. See Jan Narveson, "Utilitarianism and New Generations," *Mind* 76, no. 301 (1967): 62–72. The label itself was coined by Jeff McMahan in "Problems of Population Theory," *Ethics* 92, no. 1 (October 1981), 96–127.

125. See, for example: Megan Howe, "Hurricane Matthew: How Are Haiti and Florida Coping?" *BBC News,* October 7, 2016, https://www.bbc.co .uk/news/world-us-canada-37584632.

126. To those familiar with contemporary philosophical debates in population ethics, the structure of the argument may remind them of the arguments of so-called longtermist effective altruists. Longtermists argue

that our highest moral priority is to prevent possible total extinction events—planetary collisions, murderous AI, etc. While these are incredibly unlikely, the magnitude of the possible disasters—the extinction of humanity from that point onward, i.e., the death of all those alive and the nonexistence of all those who would have otherwise lived—is so grave as to offset the very low likelihood of their occurrence and, in a utility calculation, trump any other potential cause for concern. Climate change, incidentally, does not feature high on the longtermist list of existential threats, since even under very pessimistic projections actual human extinction is not likely to take place.

127. Plato, *The Symposium*, 209cb-d6e, ed. M. C. Howatson and Frisbee C. C. Sheffield, trans. M. C. Howatson (Cambridge: Cambridge University Press, 2008), 44.

128. Heti, *Motherhood*, 120.

129. Sheila Heti, "A Common Seagull: On Making Art and Mourning," *Yale Review* (Winter 2019), https://yalereview.org/article/common-seagull.

## CONCLUSION

1. Agnes Callard, "Half a Person," *The Point* 20 (Fall 2019), 66.

2. Darja Filippova, "Annihilation," *The Point* 23 (Fall 2020), 159.

3. Ibid., 155.

4. Put one freezer bag inside another and fill the space with ice.

5. Shonda Rhimes, "Dartmouth Commencement Speech," Dartmouth University, filmed June 8, 2014, video of lecture, 24:01, https://www.youtube.com/watch?v=EuHQ6TH60_I.

6. Doris Lessing, "I Realise Now That Deserting My Children Was a Terrible Thing to Do," interview with Lucy Cavendish, *Evening Standard* 32, February 5, 2007.

7. Elizabeth Hardwick, "On Sylvia Plath," *New York Review of Books,* August 12, 1971, https://www.nybooks.com/articles/1971/08/12/on-sylvia-plath/.

8. Aurélie M. Athan, "Reproductive Identity: An Emerging Concept," *American Psychologist* 75, no. 4 (May–June 2020), 445–56. DOI: 10.1037/amp0000623. PMID: 32378941.

9. Nikki McCahon, "Matrescence," accessed September 14, 2023, https://www.nikkimccahon.com/discover-matrescence.

10. Rachel Bertsche, "When Your Name Becomes 'Mom,' Do Your Other Identities Matter?" *New York Times,* April 16, 2020, https://www.nytimes.com/2020/04/16/parenting/motherhood-identity-crisis.html.

11. Ibid.

12. Heti, *Motherhood*, 164.

13. Iris Murdoch, *The Sovereignty of Good* (New York: Schocken Books, 1971), 84.

14. Ibid., 53.

15. Wallace-Wells, "Uninhabitable Earth."

16. Elizabeth Bruenig, "I Became a Mother at 25, and I'm Not Sorry I Didn't Wait," *New York Times*, May 7, 2021, https://www.nytimes.com/2021/05/07/opinion/motherhood-baby-bust-early-parenthood.html.

# SOURCES

Alexander, Ella. "Why We Need to Stop Making Women Over 30 Feel Pressured to Have Children." *Harper's Bazaar,* August 7, 2019. https://www
.harpersbazaar.com/uk/culture/a28635150/why-we-need-to-stop
-pressuring-women-over-30-to-have-children.

Alter, Alexandra. "The World Is Ending, and Readers Couldn't Be Happier." *New York Times,* September 5, 2014. https://www.nytimes.com/2014/09
/06/books/station-eleven-joins-falls-crop-of-dystopian-novels.html.

Amanvermez, Ramazan, and Migraci Tosun. "An Update on Ovarian Aging and Ovarian Reserve Tests." *International Journal of Fertility and Sterility* 9, no. 4 (January–March 2016), 411–15. DOI: 10.22074/ijfs.2015.459.

American Academy of Matrimonial Lawyers. "Prenuptial Agreements on the Rise Finds Survey." AAML press release, October 28, 2016. On the PR Newswire website. https://www.prnewswire.com/news-releases/prenuptial
-agreements-on-the-rise-finds-survey-300353444.html.

Arendt, Hannah. *The Human Condition.* Chicago: University of Chicago Press, 2018.

Athan, Aurélie M. "Reproductive Identity: An Emerging Concept." *American Psychologist* 75, no. 4 (May–June 2020), 445–56. DOI: 10.1037/
amp0000623. PMID: 32378941.

Atwood, Meredith. "Mother's Day Is Nonsense." *Psychology Today,* May 9, 2020. https://www.psychologytoday.com/us/blog/the-doctor-nonsense
/202005/mothers-day-is-nonsense.

Augustine. *Treatises on Marriage and Other Subjects.* Translated by Charles T. Wilcox, Charles T. Huegelmeyer, John McQuade, Sister Marie Liguori,

Robert P. Russell, John A. Lacy, and Ruth Wentworth Brown. Edited by Roy J. Deferrari. From *The Fathers of the Church: A New Translation* 27. Washington, DC: Catholic University of America Press, 1999.

Austen, Jane. *The Annotated Persuasion*. Edited by David M. Shapard. New York: Anchor Books, 2010.

*Axiochus*. Translated by Jackson P. Hershbell. In *Plato: Complete Works*. Edited by John M. Cooper. Indianapolis: Hackett Publishing Company, 1997.

Backus, Fred. "Most Americans Have Experienced True Love in Their Lives-CBS News Poll." *CBS News*, February 13, 2022. https://www.cbsnews.com/news/americans-experience-true-love-opinion-poll-02-2022.

Badinter, Élisabeth. *The Conflict*. Translated by Adriana Hunter. New York: Metropolitan Books, 2012.

Bank of America. *2018 Better Money Habits Millennial Report* (Winter 2018). https://bettermoneyhabits.bankofamerica.com/content/dam/bmh/pdf/ar6vnln9-boa-bmh-millennial-report-winter-2018-final2.pdf.

Barrett, Jennifer. "Here's What Working Parents Should Envy About Norway (and It's Not Just the Electric Cars)." *Forbes*, February 12, 2021. https://www.forbes.com/sites/jenniferbarrett/2021/02/12/heres-what-working-parents-should-envy-about-norway-and-its-not-just-the-electric-cars/?sh=4452c5ea4ea8.

Barroso, Amanda, Kim Parker, and Jesse Bennett. "As Millennials Near 40, They're Approaching Family Life Differently Than Previous Generations." Pew Research Center, May 27, 2020. https://www.pewresearch.org/social-trends/2020/05/27/as-millennials-near-40-theyre-approaching-family-life-differently-than-previous-generations.

Beauvoir, Simone de. *The Second Sex*. Translated by Constance Borde and Sheila Malovany-Chevallier. New York: Vintage Books, 2011.

Benatar, David. *Better Never to Have Been: The Harm of Coming into Existence*. Oxford: Oxford University Press, 2006.

Berrington, Ann. "Childlessness in the U.K." In *Childlessness in Europe: Contexts, Causes, and Consequences* (January 13, 2017). https://doi.org/10.1007/978-3-319-44667-7_3.

Berry, Zoë. "The Rich Kids Who Want to Tear Down Capitalism." *New York Times*, November 27, 2020. https://www.nytimes.com/2020/11/27/style/trust-fund-activism-resouce-generation.html.

Bertsche, Rachel. "When Your Name Becomes 'Mom,' Do Your Other Identities Matter?" *New York Times*, April 16, 2020. https://www.nytimes.com/2020/04/16/parenting/motherhood-identity-crisis.html.

Blackstone, Amy. "Amy Blackstone on Childfree Adults." Interview by Barbara Risman. "The Society Pages" (blog), Council on Contemporary Families, July 2, 2019. https://thesocietypages.org/ccf/2019/07/02/amy-blackstone-on-childfree-adults.

Brague, Rémi. *The Legitimacy of the Human.* Translated by Paul Seaton. South Bend, IN: St. Augustine's Press, 2017.

Brooks, Kim. "A Portrait of the Artist as a Young Mom." *The Cut,* April 2016. https://www.thecut.com/2016/04/portrait-motherhood-creativity-c-v-r.html.

Brown, Anna. "Growing Share of Childless Adults in U.S. Don't Expect to Ever Have Children." Pew Research Center, November 19, 2021. https://www.pewresearch.org/fact-tank/2021/11/19/growing-share-of-childless-adults-in-u-s-dont-expect-to-ever-have-children.

Brown, Dalvin. "Women Take on Greater Share of Parenting Responsibilities Under Stay-at-Home Orders." *USA Today,* May 8, 2020. https://www.usatoday.com/story/money/2020/05/08/women-take-on-more-their-kids-remote-learning-responsibilities/5178659002

Brown, Eliza, and Mary Patrick. "Time, Anticipation, and the Life Course: Egg Freezing as Temporarily Disentangling Romance and Reproduction." *American Sociological Review* 83, no. 5 (2018): 959–82. https://doi.org/10.1177/0003122418796807.

Brown, Meta, and Andrew Haughwout, Donghoon Lee, Joelle Scally, and Wilbert van der Klaauw. "Measuring Student Debt and Its Performance." Federal Reserve Bank of New York Staff Reports 668 (April 2014). https://www.newyorkfed.org/medialibrary/media/research/staff_reports/sr668.pdf.

Bruenig, Elizabeth. "I Became a Mother at 25, and I'm Not Sorry I Didn't Wait." *New York Times,* May 7, 2021. https://www.nytimes.com/2021/05/07/opinion/motherhood-baby-bust-early-parenthood.html.

Lord Byron. "Cain." *Poetry of Byron.* London: Macmillan, 1881.

Callard, Agnes. "Acceptance Parenting." *The Point,* October 2, 2022. https://thepointmag.com/examined-life/acceptance-parenting.

Callard, Agnes. "Half a Person." *The Point* 20 (Fall 2019): 59–66.

Carlini, Denise L., and Ann Davidman. *Motherhood—Is It for Me?: Your Step-by-Step Guide to Clarity.* York, PA: Transformation Books, 2016.

Carlson, Daniel L., Richard J. Petts, and Joanna R. Pepin. "Men and Women Agree: During the COVID-19 Pandemic Men Are Doing More at Home." Council on Contemporary Families, May 20, 2020. https://sites.utexas.edu/contemporaryfamilies/2020/05/20/covid-couples-division-of-labor.

Carrington, Damian. "Want to Fight Climate Change? Have Fewer Children." *The Guardian,* July 12, 2017. https://www.theguardian.com/environment /2017/jul/12/want-to-fight-climate-change-have-fewer-children.

Cascante, Sarah Druckenmiller, Jennifer K. Blakemore, Shannon DeVore, Brooke Hodes-Wertz, M. Elizabeth Fino, Alan S. Berkeley, Carlos M. Parra, Caroline McCaffrey, James A. Grifo. "Fifteen Years of Autologous Oocyte Thaw Outcomes from a Large University-Based Fertility Center." *Fertility and Sterility* 118, no. 1 (July 2022): 158–66. DOI: 10.1016/j.fertnstert.2022.04.013. PMID: 35597614.

Center for American Progress. "When I Was Your Age: Millennials and the Wage Gap," report, March 3, 2016. https://www.americanprogress.org /article/when-i-was-your-age.

Center for Biological Diversity. "Meet the Staff." Accessed June 3, 2023. https:// www.biologicaldiversity.org/about/staff.

Center for Reproductive Rights. "After Roe Fell: Abortion Laws by State." Accessed June 4, 2023. https://reproductiverights.org/maps/abortion-laws -by-state.

Cerulli Associates. "A Look at Wealth 2019," October 16, 2019. https://blog .coldwellbankerluxury.com/a-look-at-wealth-millennial-millionaires.

Cerulli Associates. "Cerulli Anticipates $84 Trillion in Wealth Transfers Through 2045," January 20, 2022. https://www.cerulli.com/press-releases /cerulli-anticipates-84-trillion-in-wealth-transfers-through-2045.

Charles Schwab. *Retirement Reimagined.* Westlake, TX: Charles Schwab, 2022. https://content.schwab.com/web/retail/public/about-schwab /Retirement_Reimagined_Study_deck_0422-2S73.pdf.

Charles Schwab. *Modern Wealth Survey 2023.* Westlake, TX: Charles Schwab, 2023. "http://www.aboutschwab.com/schwab-modern-wealth" www .aboutschwab.com/schwab-modern-wealth-survey-2023.

Cleaver, Eldridge. "The Allegory of the Black Eunuchs," in *Soul on Ice.* New York: Delta, 1968.

Comolli, Chiara L., Gerda Neyer, Gunnar Andersson, Lars Dommermuth, Peter Fallesen, Marika Jalovaara, Ari Klængur Jónsson, Martin Kolk, and Trude Lappegard. "Beyond the Economic Gaze: Childbearing During and After Recessions in the Nordic Countries." *SocArXiv,* no. 37 (November 19, 2020): 473–520. DOI: 10.1007/s10680-020-09570-0.

Conceivable Future. "Mission." Accessed June 3, 2023. https://conceivablefuture .org/mission.

Cook, Alex. "Millennials' Net Worth Has Doubled Since Start of Pandemic."

*Magnify Money,* July 25, 2022. https://www.magnifymoney.com/news /net-worth-of-millennials.

Crist, Meehan. "Is It OK to Have a Child?" *London Review of Books* 42, no. 5 (March 5, 2020). https://www.lrb.co.uk/the-paper/v42/n05/meehan -crist/is-it-ok-to-have-a-child.

Cusk, Rachel. *A Life's Work.* New York: Picador, 2021.

Cusk, Rachel. "I Was Only Being Honest." *The Guardian,* March 21, 2008. https://www.theguardian.com/books/2008/mar/21/biography.women.

Daly, Mary. *Gyn/Ecology.* Boston: Beacon Press, 1978.

Davidman, Ann. "I Help People Decide if They Want to Have Kids. Here's My Advice." *Vox,* April 26, 2021. https://www.vox.com/first-person /22370250/should-i-have-kids-a-baby-decide-start-family-parenthood -kids-childfree.

Davidman, Ann. "Treating Women Ambivalent About Motherhood: Best Practices for Patient-Provider Communication" (unpublished memo, November 2022), PDF file. https://s3.amazonaws.com/kajabi-storefronts -production/sites/2147567692/themes/2150170949/downloads /HSwei49wRa2IhBdMqNnU_Best_Practice_Patient_Provider_Nov2022 .pdf.

Davis, Angela. "The Black Woman's Role in the Community of Slaves." *The Black Scholar* (December 1971).

Deloitte. *The Deloitte Global Millennial Survey,* 2019. https://www2.deloitte .com/content/dam/Deloitte/global/Documents/About-Deloitte/deloitte -2019-millennial-survey.pdf.

De Marneffe, Daphne. *Maternal Desire.* New York: Scribner, 2004; 2019.

DiQuinzio, Patrice. "Exclusion and Essentialism in Feminist Theory: The Problem of Mothering." *Hypatia* 8, no. 3 (Summer 1993).

Doepke, Matthias, Anne Hannusch, Fabian Kindermann, and Michèle Tertilt. *The Economics of Fertility: A New Era.* CEPR Discussion Paper 17212. London: Centre for Economic Policy Research, 2022.

Doherty, Maggie. "On Not Becoming a Mother." *New Republic,* April 25, 2018. https://newrepublic.com/article/148110/not-becoming-mother.

Donegan, Moira. "The Decline in the US Birth Rate Is Not About Moral Failure, It's About Economics." *The Guardian,* February 9, 2021. https://www .theguardian.com/commentisfree/2021/feb/09/us-birth-rate-decline -one-economics-coronavirus.

Dow, Katharine, and Heather McMullen. "'Too Afraid to Have Kids'— How BirthStrike for Climate Lost Control of Its Political Message."

*The Conversation*, September 15, 2022. https://theconversation.com/too-afraid-to-have-kids-how-birthstrike-for-climate-lost-control-of-its-political-message-181198.

Dworkin, Andrea. *Right-Wing Women.* New York: Perigee, 1983.

Echelon Insights. *Opening the Door to Opportunity: Millennials and Gen Z Speak,* October 2020.

*Economist.* "Parents Now Spend Twice as Much Time with Their Children as 50 Years Ago," November 27, 2017. https://www.economist.com/graphic-detail/2017/11/27/parents-now-spend-twice-as-much-time-with-their-children-as-50-years-ago.

Edelman, Lee. *No Future: Queer Theory and the Death Drive.* Durham, NC: Duke University Press, 2004.

Ehrlich, Paul R. *The Population Bomb.* New York: Ballantine Books, 1968.

Ehrlich, Paul R., and Anne H. Ehrlich. "The Population Bomb Revisited." *Electronic Journal of Sustainable Development* 1, no. 3 (2009).

Eickmeyer, Kasey J. "Generation X and Millennials Attitudes Toward Marriage & Divorce." National Center for Family & Marriage Research (2015). https://www.bgsu.edu/content/dam/BGSU/college-of-arts-and-sciences/NCFMR/documents/FP/eickmeyer-gen-x-millennials-fp-15-12.pdf.

Emmons, William R., Ana Hernández Kent, and Lowell R. Ricketts. "The Demographics of Wealth: How Education, Race and Birth Year Shape Financial Outcomes." Center for Household Financial Stability, Federal Reserve Bank of St. Louis, 2018.

Eruvin 13b:14. William Davidson Talmud. Digital edition. Edited by Rabbi Adin Even-Israel Steinsaltz. "Sefaria." Accessed August 11, 2023. https://www.sefaria.org/Eruvin.13b.14.

Euripides. *Medea.* Translated by David Kovacs, in *Cyclopes. Alcestis. Medea, Euripides* 1. Loeb Classical Library 12. Cambridge, MA: Harvard University Press, 1994.

Featherstone, Liza. "If Politicians Want to Raise Birth Rates, They Should Pass Climate Policy." *New Republic.* October 1, 2021. https://newrepublic.com/article/163832/politicians-want-raise-birth-rates-pass-climate-policy.

Federal Reserve. "Distribution of Household Wealth in the U.S. Since 1989." Accessed August 31, 2023. https://www.federalreserve.gov/releases/z1/dataviz/dfa/distribute/chart.

Ferrante, Elena. "Elena Ferrante: 'Nothing Is Comparable to the Joy of Bringing Another Living Creature into the World.'" *The Guardian,* March 10, 2018.

https://www.theguardian.com/lifeandstyle/2018/mar/10/elena-ferrante -nothing-comparable-joy-bringing-another-creature-into-world.

Ferrante, Elena. *Frantumaglia: A Writer's Journey.* New York: Europa Editions, 2016.

Ferrante, Elena. *The Lost Daughter.* Translated by Ann Goldstein. New York: Europa Editions, 2020.

Filippova, Darja. "Annihilation." *The Point* 23 (Fall 2020): 153–59.

Firestone, Shulamith. *The Dialectic of Sex.* New York: Farrar, Straus and Giroux, 2003.

Fishbein, Rebecca. "Is Therapy-Speak Making Us Selfish?" *Bustle,* April 7, 2023. https://www.bustle.com/wellness/is-therapy-speak-making-us-selfish.

Fisher, Helen. *Anatomy of Love.* New York: W. W. Norton, 2016.

Fisher, Helen, and Justin Garcia. *Singles in America.* Match.com, 2022. https://www.singlesinamerica.com.

Flaubert, Gustave. Gustave Flaubert to Louise Colet, December 11, 1852. In *The Letters of Gustave Flaubert.* Translated by Francis Steegmuller. New York: New York Review Books, 2023.

Flaubert, Gustave. *Memoirs of a Madman.* Translated by Timothy Unwin. Liverpool: Liverpool Online Series Critical Editions of French Texts, 2001.

Frazier, E. Franklin. *The Negro Family in the United States.* Chicago: University of Chicago Press, 1939.

Frejka, Tomáš. "Childlessness in the United States." In *Childlessness in Europe: Contexts, Causes, and Consequences,* edited by Michaela Kreyenfeld and Dirk Konitezka, 159–79. Demographic Research Monographs. Cham: Springer, 2017.

Friedan, Betty. *The Feminine Mystique.* New York: Dell Publishing, 1963; 1974.

Friday, Nancy. *My Mother/Myself.* New York: Delta Books, 1977.

Fry, Richard. "Young Adult Households Are Earning More than Most Older Americans Did at the Same Age." Pew Research Center, December 18, 2018. https://www.pewresearch.org/fact-tank/2018/12/11/young-adult -households-are-earning-more-than-most-older-americans-did-at-the -same-age.

Galchen, Rivka. *Little Labors.* New York: New Directions, 2016.

Garbes, Angela. *Essential Labor: Mothering as Social Change.* New York: Harper Wave, 2022.

Ghosh, Amitav. *The Great Derangement.* Chicago: University of Chicago Press, 2016.

Gietel-Basten, Stuart, Anna Rotkirch, and Tomáš Sobotka. "Changing the Perspective on Low Birth Rates: Why Simplistic Solutions Won't Work."

*BMJ* 379 (2022), November 15, 2022. http://dx.doi.org/10.1136/bmj -2022-072670.

Gill, Martha. "Why a Shortage of Mr Rights Means Single Mothers Hold the Key to the Falling Birthrate." *The Guardian,* February 11, 2022. https:// www.theguardian.com/commentisfree/2023/feb/11/why-a-shortage-of -mr-rights-means-single-mothers-hold-the-key-to-the-falling-birthrate.

Glass, Rodge. "Global Warming: The Rise of 'Cli-Fi.'" *The Guardian,* May 31, 2013. https://www.theguardian.com/books/2013/may/31/global-warning -rise-cli-fi.

Goldberg, Michelle. "What Is a Woman?" *New Yorker,* July 28, 2014. https:// www.newyorker.com/magazine/2014/08/04/woman-2.

González-Ramírez, Andrea. "Closing the Door on Motherhood." *The Cut,* July 3, 2023. https://www.thecut.com/2023/07/closing-the-door-on -motherhood-after-dobbs.html.

Goodall, Jane. "When the Duke of Sussex Interviewed Dr Jane Goodall About the Future of Sustainability." Interview by Harry Charles Albert David. *Vogue UK,* October 21, 2021. https://www.vogue.co.uk/article /prince-harry-jane-goodall-september-2019-issue.

Green, Miranda. "Ocasio-Cortez: It's 'Legitimate' to Ask if It's OK to Have Children in the Face of Climate Change." *The Hill,* February 25, 2019. https://thehill.com/policy/energy-environment/431440-ocasio-cortez -in-face-of-climate-change-its-legitimate-to-ask-if-ok.

Greene, David. "Millennials to Bear the Burden of Boomers' Social Safety Net." NPR, *Morning Edition,* March 4, 2014. https://www.npr.org/2014 /03/04/285581006/millennials-to-bear-burden-of-boomer-s-social -safety-net.

Gregory of Nyssa. "On Virginity." *Ascetical Works,* The Fathers of the Church: A New Translation 58. Translated by Virginia Woods Callahan. Washington, DC: Catholic University of America Press, 1967.

Grose, Jessica. *Screaming on the Inside.* New York: Mariner Books, 2022.

*Guardian.* "The Guardian View on a Demographic Paradox: The Rebirth of Pronatalism," November 17, 2022. https://www.theguardian.com /commentisfree/2022/nov/17/the-guardian-view-on-a-demographic -paradox-the-rebirth-of-pronatalism.

Gurtin, Zeynep. "More Women Over 40 Are Getting Pregnant. But Is That Really About Their Choices?" *The Guardian,* April 17, 2019. https://www .theguardian.com/commentisfree/2019/apr/17/more-women-over-40 -pregnant-choices-motherhood.

Haas, Hein de. "Climate Refugees: The Fabrication of a Migration Threat."

International Migration Institute (blog), June 8, 2020. https://www
    .migrationinstitute.org/blog/climate-refugees-the-fabrication-of-a
    -migration-threat.

Hamilton, Brady E., Joyce A. Martin, and Michelle J. K. Osterman. "Births:
    Provisional Data for 2020," *Vital Statistics Rapid Release*, no. 12. Hyatts-
    ville, MD: National Center for Health Statistics (May 2021). DOI: https://
    doi.org/10.15620/cdc:104993.

Hardwick, Elizabeth. "On Sylvia Plath." *New York Review of Books,* August 12,
    1971. https://www.nybooks.com/articles/1971/08/12/on-sylvia-plath/.

Hardwick, Elizabeth. *Sleepless Nights.* New York: New York Review Classics,
    2001.

Hartnett, Caroline Sten. "US Fertility Keeps Dropping—But That's Not a
    Reason to Panic." AP News, May 15, 2019. https://apnews.com/article/9
    ee9c55af1633f47cc1cc880d091c8cc.

Heffington, Peggy O'Donnell. *Without Children.* New York: Seal Press, 2023.

Hegel, G. W. F. *Elements of the Philosophy of Right.* Edited by Allen W. Wood.
    Translated by H. B. Nisbet. Cambridge: Cambridge University Press,
    2014.

Heti, Sheila. *Motherhood.* New York: Farrar, Straus and Giroux, 2018.

Heti, Sheila. "A Common Seagull: On Making Art and Mourning." *Yale Re-
    view* (Winter 2019). https://yalereview.org/article/common-seagull.

Holcombe, Madeline. "Mother's Day Isn't a Celebration for Everyone." CNN,
    May 9, 2022. https://www.cnn.com/2022/05/07/health/mothers-day
    -parental-grief-wellness/index.html.

hooks, bell. *Feminist Theory: From Margin to Center.* Boston: South End
    Press, 1984.

Horpedahl, Jeremy. "The Wealth of Generations: Latest Update." *Economist
    Writing Everyday,* December 21, 2022. https://economistwritingeveryday
    .com/2022/12/21/the-wealth-of-generations-latest-update/.

Hout, Michael. *State of the Union 2019: Social Mobility Report* (2019). https://
    inequality.stanford.edu/sites/default/files/Pathways_SOTU_2019
    _SocialMobility.pdf.

"How Do Countries Fight Falling Birth Rates?" BBC News, January 15, 2020.
    https://www.bbc.com/news/world-europe-51118616.

Howe, Megan. "Hurricane Matthew: How Are Haiti and Florida Coping?"
    *BBC News*, October 7, 2016. https://www.bbc.co.uk/news/world-us
    -canada-37584632.

Illouz, Eva. *Consuming the Romantic Utopia.* Berkeley: University of Califor-
    nia Press, 1997.

Insler, Sharon. "Do Millennials Have It Worse Than Generations Past?" Lending Tree, May 30, 2018. https://www.lendingtree.com/student/millennials-have-it-worse-study.

Institute for Women's Policy Research. "Women's Labor Force Participation." *Status of Women in the United States,* 2015. https://statusofwomendata.org/earnings-and-the-gender-wage-gap/womens-labor-force-participation.

IPCC. *Climate Change 2022: Impacts, Adaptation and Vulnerability.* Contribution of Working Group II to the Sixth Assessment Report of the Intergovernmental Panel on Climate Change, edited by Hans-Otto Pörtner, Debra C. Roberts, Melinda M. B. Tignor, Elvira Poloczanska, Katja Mintenbeck, Andrés Alegría, Marlies Craig, Stefanie Langsdorf, Sina Löschke, Vincent Möller, et al. Cambridge and New York: Cambridge University Press, 2022. DOI: 10.1017/9781009325844.

Irfan, Umair. "We Need to Talk About the Ethics of Having Children in a Warming World." *Vox,* March 11, 2019. https://www.vox.com/2019/3/11/18256166/climate-change-having-kids.

Jacoby, Kerry N. *Souls, Bodies, Spirits: The Drive to Abolish Abortion Since 1973.* Westport, CT: Praeger, 1998.

James, P. D. *Children of Men.* New York: Vintage Books, 1993.

Josephson, Amelia. "The Average Salary of a Millennial." SmartAsset, December 1, 2022. https://smartasset.com/retirement/the-average-salary-of-a-millennial.

Kearney, Melissa S., and Phillip B. Levine. "U.S. Births Are Down Again, After the COVID Baby Bust and Rebound." Brookings Institution (blog), May 31, 2023. https://www.brookings.edu/2023/05/31/us-births-are-down-again-after-the-covid-baby-bust-and-rebound.

Kearney, Melissa S., and Phillip B. Levine. "The U.S. Covid-19 Baby Bust and Rebound." *NBER Working Papers,* no. 30000, April 2022.

Kent, Ana Hernández, and Lowell R. Ricketts. "Millennials Are Catching Up in Terms of Generational Wealth." Federal Reserve Bank of St. Louis. *On the Economy* (blog), March 29, 2021. https://www.stlouisfed.org/on-the-economy/2021/march/millennials-catching-up-earlier-generational-wealth.

Kimport, Katrina. "Abortion After Dobbs: Defendants, Denials, and Delays." *Science Advances* 8, no. 6 (2022). DOI: 10.1126/sciadv.ade5327.

Kleeman, Alexandra. *Something New Under the Sun.* London and New York: Hogarth, 2021.

Klein, Ezra. "Your Kids Are Not Doomed." *New York Times,* June 5, 2020.

https://www.nytimes.com/2022/06/05/opinion/climate-change-should -you-have-kids.html.

Klein, Jennie. "Goddess: Feminist Art and Spirituality in the 1970s." *Feminist Studies* 35, no. 3 (Fall 2009): 575–602.

Klein, Melanie. "A Contribution to the Psychogenesis of Manic-Depressive States." *Love, Guilt and Reparation and Other Works,* in The Writings of Melanie Klein. Vol. 1. New York: The Free Press, 1975.

Kolata, Gina. "'Sobering' Study Shows Challenges of Egg Freezing." *New York Times,* September 23, 2022. https://www.nytimes.com/2022/09/23 /health/egg-freezing-age-pregnancy.html.

Kolbert, Elizabeth. "Mother Courage." *New Yorker,* February 29, 2004. https: //www.newyorker.com/magazine/2004/03/08/mother-courage.

Konrath, Sarah. "What the Pandemic Has Done for Dating." *The Atlantic,* December 31, 2020. https://www.theatlantic.com/ideas/archive/2020/12 /what-pandemic-has-done-dating/617502.

Kreider, Tim. "The End of the Line," in *Selfish, Shallow, and Self-Absorbed: Sixteen Writers on the Decision Not to Have Kids,* edited by Meghan Daum. New York: Picador, 2015.

Krivak, Andrew. *The Bear.* New York: Bellevue Literary Press, 2020.

Lambert, Molly. "Miley Cyrus Has Finally Found Herself. " *Elle,* July 11, 2019.        https://www.elle.com/culture/music/a28280119/miley-cyrus-elle -interview.

Larkin, Philip. "This Be the Verse," in *Collected Poems,* edited by Anthony Thwaite. New York: Farrar, Straus and Giroux, 2003.

Lear, Jonathan. *Imagining the End: Mourning and Ethical Life.* Cambridge, MA: Harvard University Press, 2022.

Lepucki, Edan. *California: A Novel.* New York: Little, Brown, and Company, 2014.

Lessing, Doris. "I Realise Now That Deserting My Children Was a Terrible Thing to Do." Interview with Lucy Cavendish. *Evening Standard* 32, February 5, 2007.

Lewis, Sophie. *Full Surrogacy Now.* New York: Verso, 2019.

Lewis, Sophie. *Abolish the Family.* New York: Verso, 2022.

Leopardi, Giacomo. *Zibaldone.* Translated by Kathleen Baldwin, Richard Dixon, David Gibbons, Ann Goldstein, Gerard Slowey, Martin Thom, and Pamela Williams, edited by Michael Caesar and Franco D'Intino. New York: Farrar, Straus and Giroux, 2015.

Livingston, Gretchen. "Childlessness." Pew Research Reports, May 7, 2015. https://www.pewresearch.org/social-trends/2015/05/07/childlessness/.

Livingstone, Jo. "How to Write About Climate Change." *New Republic,* August 7, 2020. https://newrepublic.com/article/158838/write-climate-change.

Lorde, Audre. "An Open Letter to Mary Daly," in *Sister Outsider,* 55–60. New York: Penguin, 2020.

Lorde, Audre. "Eye to Eye: Black Women, Hatred, and Anger." In *Sister Outsider,* 138–69. New York: Penguin, 2020.

Lorenz, Taylor, and Joe Pinsker. "The Slackification of the American Home." *The Atlantic,* July 11, 2019. https://www.theatlantic.com/family/archive/2019/07/families-slack-asana/593584.

Mann, Thomas. *Essays of Three Decades.* Translated by H. T. Lowe-Porter. London: Secker and Warburg, 1938.

Marks, Elizabeth, Caroline Hickman, Panu Pihkala, Susan Clayton, Eric R. Lewandowski, Elouise E. Mayall, Britt Wray, Catriona Mellor, and Lise van Susteren. "Young People's Voices on Climate Anxiety, Government Betrayal and Moral Injury: A Global Phenomenon." *The Lancet Planetary Health,* September 7, 2021. http://dx.doi.org/10.2139/ssrn.3918955.

Marks, Elizabeth, Caroline Hickman, Panu Pihkala, et al. "Climate Anxiety in Children and Young People and Their Beliefs About Government Responses to Climate Change: A Global Survey." *The Lancet Planetary Health* 5, no. 12 (December 2021). https://doi.org/10.1016/S2542-5196(21)00278-3.

Marshall, George. "Climate Fiction Will Reinforce Existing Views." *New York Times,* July 29, 2014. https://www.nytimes.com/roomfordebate/2014/07/29/will-fiction-influence-how-we-react-to-climate-change/climate-fiction-will-reinforce-existing-views.

Martinchek, Kassandra. "Young Millennials and Gen Zers Face Employment Insecurity and Hardship During the Pandemic." Urban Institute, December 18, 2020. https://www.urban.org/urban-wire/young-millennials-and-gen-zers-face-employment-insecurity-and-hardship-during-pandemic.

Martinez, Gladys M., and Kimberly Daniels. "Fertility of Men and Women Aged 15–49 in the United States: National Survey of Family Growth, 2015–2019." *National Health Statistics Reports* 179 (January 10, 2023).

Mathews, T. J., and Brady E. Hamilton. "Mean Age of Mother, 1970–2000." *National Vital Statistics Reports* 51, no. 1 (December 11, 2002).

McCahon, Nikki. "Matrescence." Accessed September 14, 2023. https://www.nikkimccahon.com/discover-matrescence.

McCann, Allison. "What It Costs to Get an Abortion Now." *New York Times,* September 28, 2022. https://www.nytimes.com/interactive/2022/09/28 /us/abortion-costs-funds.html.

McCoy, Terrence. "'Do It for Denmark!' Campaign Wants Danes to Have More Sex. A Lot More Sex." *Washington Post,* March 27, 2014. https:// www.washingtonpost.com/news/morning-mix/wp/2014/03/27/do-it -for-denmark-campaign-wants-danes-to-have-more-sex-a-lot-more -sex/.

McNally, Danielle. "Women Are Deciding to Have Fewer Children, and Global Warming Is to Blame." *Marie Claire,* February 7, 2022. https:// www.marieclaire.com/politics/climate-change-fertility-modern-fertility -survey.

Miller, Anna. "Can This Marriage Be Saved?" American Psychological Association, *Monitor on Psychology* 44, no. 4 (April 2013). https://www.apa .org/monitor/2013/04/marriage.

Miller, Claire Cain. "Americans Are Having Fewer Babies. They Told Us Why." *New York Times,* July 5, 2018. https://www.nytimes.com/2018/07 /05/upshot/americans-are-having-fewer-babies-they-told-us-why.html.

Miller, Claire Cain. "Nearly Half of Men Say They Do Most of the Home Schooling. 3 Percent of Women Agree." *New York Times,* May 6, 2020. https://www.nytimes.com/2020/05/06/upshot/pandemic-chores -homeschooling-gender.html.

Miller, Claire Cain, Sarah Kliff, and Larry Buchanan. "Childbirth Is Deadlier for Black Families, Even When They're Rich, Expansive Study Finds." *New York Times,* February 12, 2023.

Miller, Jennifer. "Family Life Is Chaotic. Could Office Software Help?" *New York Times,* May 27, 2020. https://www.nytimes.com/2020/05/27/style /family-calendar.html.

Millet, Lydia. *A Children's Bible.* New York: Norton, 2020.

Millet, Lydia. "There Will Be Flood." Interview by Christian Lorentzen. *Bookforum* (Summer 2020). https://www.bookforum.com/print/2702 /lydia-millet-discusses-her-new-novel-of-teens-biblical-allusions-and -plausible-environmental-disaster-24048.

Millett, Kate. *Sexual Politics.* Urbana: University of Illinois Press, 2000.

Milton, John. *Paradise Lost.* Edited by Gordon Teskey. New York: Norton, 2020.

Monagle, Clare. "Mary Daly's *Gyn/Ecology*: Mysticism, Difference, and Feminist History." *Signs: Journal of Women in Culture and Society* 44, no. 2 (2019): 333–53. DOI: 10.1086/699341.

Monte, Lindsay. "More Women in Early 30s Are Childless." U.S. Census Bureau, November 30, 2017. https://www.census.gov/library/stories/2017 /11/women-early-thirties.html.

Morton, Timothy. "Introducing the Idea of 'Hyperobjects.'" *High Country News*, January 19, 2015. https://www.hcn.org/issues/47.1/introducing -the-idea-of-hyperobjects.

Moynihan, Daniel Patrick. *The Negro Family: The Case for National Action, Office of Policy Planning and Research.* U.S. Department of Labor, March 1965.

Murdoch, Iris. *The Sovereignty of Good.* New York: Schocken Books, 1971.

Narveson, Jan. "Utilitarianism and New Generations." *Mind* 76, no. 301 (1967): 62–72.

Nelson, Maggie. *The Argonauts.* Minneapolis: Graywolf, 2015.

*New York Times.* "Tracking the States Where Abortion Is Now Banned." Accessed September 12, 2023. https://www.nytimes.com/interactive/2022 /us/abortion-laws-roe-v-wade.html.

Nicholson, Reynold Alleyne. *Studies in Islamic Poetry.* Cambridge: Cambridge University Press, 1921.

Nietzsche, Friedrich. *The Birth of Tragedy,* in *Basic Writings of Nietzsche.* Translated by Walter Kaufmann. New York: Modern Library, 2000.

Ocasio-Cortez, Alexandria. Twitter post. March 3, 2021, 2:42 P.M. https:// twitter.com/AOC/status/1367213849963859968.

O'Connell, Meaghan. *And Now We Have Everything.* New York: Little, Brown and Company, 2018.

OECD. *Under Pressure: The Squeezed Middle Class.* Paris: OECD Publishing, 2019. https://doi.org/10.1787/689afed1-en.

Offill, Jenny. *Dept. of Speculation.* New York: Vintage Contemporaries, 2014.

O'Reilly, Katie. "To Have or Not Have Children in the Age of Climate Change." *Sierra,* November 1, 2019. https://www.sierraclub.org/sierra /2019–6-november-december/feature/have-or-not-have-children-age -climate-change.

Osterman, Michelle J. K., Brady E. Hamilton, Joyce A. Martin, Anne K. Driscoll, and Claudia P. Valenzuela. "Births: Final Data for 2021." *National Vital Statistics Reports* 72, no. 1 (January 31, 2023).

Paoletta, Kyle. "The Incredible Disappearing Doomsday." *Harper's,* August 2023. https://harpers.org/archive/2023/04/the-incredible-disappearing -doomsday-climate-catastrophists-new-york-times-climate-change -coverage.

Parker, Kim. "What's Behind the Growing Gap Between Men and Women in College Completion?" Pew Research Center, November 8, 2021. https://www.pewresearch.org/fact-tank/2021/11/08/whats-behind-the -growing-gap-between-men-and-women-in-college-completion.

Parker, Kim, and Rachel Minkin. "Public Has Mixed Views on the Modern American Family." Pew Research Center, September 2023.

Peters, Torrey. *Detransition, Baby.* New York: One World, 2021.

Pew Research Center. "Raising Kids and Running a Household: How Working Parents Share the Load." November 2015.

Pew Research Center. "Millennial Life: How Young Adulthood Today Compares with Prior Generations." February 14, 2019.

Plath, Sylvia. *The Bell Jar.* New York: Harper Perennial Classics, 1999.

Plato. *The Symposium.* Edited by M. C. Howatson and Frisbee C. C. Sheffield. Translated by M. C. Howatson. Cambridge: Cambridge University Press, 2008.

Plumer, Brad, Raymond Zhong, and Lisa Friedman. "Time Is Running Out to Avert a Harrowing Future, Climate Panel Warns." *New York Times,* February 28, 2022. https://www.nytimes.com/2022/02/28/climate/climate -change-ipcc-un-report.html.

Plutarch. *Moralia.* Translated by Frank Cole Babbitt. Cambridge, MA: Harvard University Press; London: William Heinemann Ltd., 1928.

Powers, Richard. "Richard Powers: 'We're Completely Alienated from Everything Else Alive.'" Interview by Emma John. *The Guardian,* June 16, 2018. https://www.theguardian.com/books/2018/jun/16/richard-powers -interview-overstory.

Powers, Richard. *The Overstory.* New York: Norton, 2018.

Powers, Richard. *Bewilderment.* New York: Norton, 2021.

Preston, Samuel H., and Caroline Sten Hartnett. *The Future of American Fertility.* NBER Working Paper Series, 2008.

Pseudo-Diogenes. Letter 47. In *The Cynic Epistles: A Study Edition,* edited by Abraham J. Malherbe. Atlanta: Society of Biblical Literature, 1977.

*Publishers Weekly.* "PW Picks: Books of the Week: May 4, 2015," May 1, 2015. https://www.publishersweekly.com/pw/by-topic/industry-news /tip-sheet/article/66424-pw-picks-books-of-the-week-may-1-2015 .html.

Rabin, Roni Caryn. "Pregnancy's Most Dangerous Time: After New Mothers Come Home." *New York Times,* May 28, 2023. https://www.nytimes.com /2023/05/28/health/pregnancy-childbirth-deaths.html.

Rader, Benjamin, Ushma D. Upadhyay, Neil K. R. Sehgal, Ben Y. Reis, John S. Brownstein, and Yulin Hswen. "Estimated Travel Time and Spatial

Access to Abortion Facilities in the US Before and After the *Dobbs v Jackson Women's Health Decision.*" *JAMA* 328, no. 20 (November 22, 2022). DOI: 10.1001/jama.2022.20424.

Rhimes, Shonda. "Dartmouth Commencement Speech." Dartmouth University, filmed June 8, 2014. Video of lecture, 24:01. https://www.youtube.com/watch?v=EuHQ6TH60_I.

Rich, Adrienne. "Motherhood in Bondage." *New York Times,* November 20, 1976. https://timesmachine.nytimes.com/timesmachine/1976/11/20/91198580.html?pageNumber=19.

Rich, Adrienne. "Dreams Before Waking." In *Your Native Land, Your Life.* New York: W. W. Norton, 1986.

Rich, Adrienne. *Of Woman Born.* New York: Norton, 1996.

Rindfuss, Ronald R., S. Philip Morgan, and Kate Offutt. "Education and the Changing Age Pattern of American Fertility: 1963–1989." *Demography* 33, no. 3 (August 1996), 277–90.

Rooney, Sally. *Beautiful World, Where Are You.* New York: Farrar, Straus & Giroux, 2021.

Rose, Jacqueline. "Mothers." *London Review of Books* 36, no. 12 (June 12, 2014). https://www.lrb.co.uk/the-paper/v36/n12/jacqueline-rose/mothers.

Rose, Jacqueline. *Mothers: An Essay on Love and Cruelty.* New York: Farrar, Straus and Giroux, 2018.

Rougemont, Denis de. *Love in the Western World.* Translated by Montgomery Belgion. Princeton, NJ: Princeton University Press, 1940.

Ruddick, Sara. *Maternal Thinking: Toward a Politics of Peace.* Boston: Beacon Press, 1995.

Russo, Nancy Felipe. "The Motherhood Mandate." *Journal of Social Issues* 32, no. 3 (1976).

Sanders, Fran. "Dear Black Man." In *The Black Woman: An Anthology.* New York: Washington Square Press, 2005.

Scheffler, Samuel. *Why Worry About Future Generations?* Oxford: Oxford University Press, 2018.

Scheffler, Samuel. "A World Without Children." *The Point* 20 (Fall 2019): 89–95.

Schnabel, Landon. "Secularism and Fertility Worldwide." *Socius* 7 (January–December 2021). https://doi.org/10.1177/23780231211031320.

Schneider-Mayerson, Matthew. "The Environmental Politics of Reproductive Choices in the Age of Climate Change." *Environmental Politics* 31, no. 1 (2022). DOI: 10.1080/09644016.2021.1902700.

Schopenhauer, Arthur. "On the Sufferings of the World." In *The Essays of*

*Arthur Schopenhauer: Studies in Pessimism.* Translated by T. Bailey Saunders, 1913.

Schopenhauer, Arthur. *The World as Will and Representation.* Translated by E. F. J. Payne. New York: Dover Publications, 1969.

Schouten, Gina. *Liberalism, Neutrality, and the Gendered Division of Labor.* Oxford: Oxford University Press, 2019.

Scranton, Roy. "Learning to Die in the Anthropocene. *New York Times,* November 10, 2013. https://archive.nytimes.com/opinionator.blogs.nytimes.co/2013/11/10/learning-how-to-die-in-the-anthropocene.

Segni, Lothario (Pope Innocent III). *On the Misery of the Human Condition.* Edited by R. Donald Howard. Translated by Margaret Mary Dietz. Indianapolis and New York: Library of Liberal Arts, 1969.

Seneca. "To Marcia on Consolation." *Moral Essays.* Translated by John W. Basore. Loeb Classical Library 254. Cambridge, MA: Harvard University Press, 1932.

Setiya, Kieran. "The Midlife Crisis." *Philosophers' Imprint* 14, no. 31 (November 2014).

Shakespeare, William. *Hamlet.* Folger Library Shakespeare edition, edited by Barbara A. Mowat and Paul Werstine. New York: Simon & Schuster, 1992.

Shelley, Mary. *The Last Man.* Ware: Wordsworth Editions, 2004.

Sherrell, Daniel. *Warmth: Coming of Age at the End of Our World.* New York: Penguin, 2021.

Shierholz, Heidi, and Lawrence Mishel. "The Worst Downturn Since the Great Depression." Economic Policy Institute. January 2, 2009. https://www.epi.org/publication/jobspict_200906_preview.

Shute, Nevil. *On the Beach.* New York: Vintage, 2010.

Silva, Jennifer M. *Coming Up Short.* Oxford: Oxford University Press, 2013.

Skirbekk, Vegard. *Decline and Prosper.* London: Palgrave Macmillan, 2022.

Slaughter, Anne-Marie. "Why Women Still Can't Have It All." *The Atlantic* (July/August 2012). https://www.theatlantic.com/magazine/archive/2012/07/why-women-still-cant-have-it-all/309020.

Slaughter, Anne-Marie. "'Having It All' Was Always a Poor Measure of Success." *FT,* January 27, 2023. https://www.ft.com/content/1580ed07-35ec-49ca-a314-1cea419493b6.

Sobotka, Tomáš, Anna Matysiak, and Zuzanna Brzozowska. *Policy Responses to Low Fertility: How Effective Are They? Working Paper No. 1.* United Nations Population Fund, May 2019.

Society of Family Planning. *#WeCount Report.* June 15, 2023. DOI: https://doi.org/10.46621/XBAZ6145.

Sophocles. *Oedipus at Colonus.* In *Sophocles: Antigone. The Women of Trachis. Philoctetes. Oedipus at Colonus.* Vol. 2. Translated by Hugh Lloyd-Jones, Loeb Classical Library 21. Cambridge, MA: Harvard University Press, 1994. DOI: 10.4159/DLCL.sophocles-oedipus_colonus.1994.

Sotah 12a. William Davidson Talmud. Digital edition, ed. Rabbi Adin Even-Israel Steinsaltz. Accessed August 11, 2023. https://www.sefaria.org/Sotah.12a.10.

Statistics Denmark. "Total Fertility Rate (Ages 15–49) by Ancestry." Accessed September 1, 2023. https://www.statbank.dk/FERT1.

Statistics Finland. "Total Fertility Rate, 1776–2022." Accessed September 1, 2023. https://statfin.stat.fi/PxWeb/pxweb/en/StatFin/StatFin__synt/statfin_synt_pxt_12dt.px.

Statistics Iceland. "Fertility and Reproduction Rates 1853–2022." Accessed September 1, 2023. https://px.hagstofa.is/pxen/pxweb/en/Ibuar/Ibuar__Faeddirdanir__faeddir__faedingar/MAN05202.px.

Statistics Norway. "Household Payments for Kindergarten, January 2023," April 25, 2023. https://www.ssb.no/en/utdanning/barnehager/artikler/houshold-payments-for-kindergarten-january-2023.

Statistics Norway. "Total Fertility Rate, Women (C) 1968–2002." Accessed September 1, 2023. https://www.ssb.no/en/statbank/table/04232.

Statistics Sweden. "Summary of Population Statistics 1960–2022." Accessed September 1, 2023. https://www.scb.se/en/finding-statistics/statistics-by-subject-area/population/population-composition/population-statistics/pong/tables-and-graphs/population-statistics—summary/summary-of-population-statistics.

Stern, Howard. Interview with Seth Rogen. *Howard Stern Show,* May 11, 2021. Podcast audio. https://www.youtube.com/watch?v=k5P6aPlSw3w.

Sussman, Anna. "The Case for Redefining Infertility." *New Yorker,* June 18, 2019. https://www.newyorker.com/culture/annals-of-inquiry/the-case-for-social-infertility.

Sussman, Anna. "The End of Babies." *New York Times,* November 16, 2019. https://www.nytimes.com/interactive/2019/11/16/opinion/sunday/capitalism-children.html.

Swan, Shanna. *Count Down.* New York: Scribner, 2020.

Szalai, Jennifer. "The 50 Best Memoirs of the Past 50 Years." *New York Times,* June 26, 2019. https://www.nytimes.com/interactive/2019/06/26/books/best-memoirs.html.

T. Rowe Price. "How Do You Compare?" *T. Rowe Price Investor* (Spring 2019).

Tavernise, Sabrina, Claire Cain Miller, Quoctrung Bui, and Robert Gebel-off. "Why American Women Everywhere Are Delaying Motherhood." *New York Times,* June 16, 2021. https://www.nytimes.com/2021/06/16/us/declining-birthrate-motherhood.html.

Theognis. "The Elegiac Poems of Theognis." In *Elegy and Iambus.* Vol. 1. Translated by J. M. Edmonds. Cambridge, MA: Harvard University Press; London: Heinemann Ltd., 1931; Perseus Digital Library. Accessed August 14, 2023. https://www.perseus.tufts.edu/hopper/text?doc=Perseus%3Atext%3A2008.01.0479%3Avolume%3D1%3Atext%3D11%3Asection%3D2#.

Thornton, Arland, and Linda Young-DeMarco. "Four Decades of Trends in Attitudes Toward Family Issues in the United States: The 1960s Through the 1990s." *Journal of Marriage and Family* 63, no. 4 (November 2001).

Tikkanen, Roosa, Robin Osborn, Elias Mossialos, Ana Djordjevic, and George A. Wharton. International Health Care System Profiles: Norway (June 5, 2020). https://www.commonwealthfund.org/international-health-policy-center/countries/norway.

Twenge, Jean M. "The Myth of the Broke Millennial." *The Atlantic,* April 17, 2023. https://www.theatlantic.com/magazine/archive/2023/05/millennial-generation-financial-issues-income-homeowners/673485.

Tyson, Alec, Brian Kennedy, and Cary Funk. "Gen Z, Millennials Stand Out for Climate Change Activism, Social Media Engagement with Issue." Pew Research Center, May 26, 2021. https://www.pewresearch.org/science/2021/05/26/gen-z-millennials-stand-out-for-climate-change-activism-social-media-engagement-with-issue.

Umansky, Lauri. *Motherhood Reconceived: Feminism and the Legacies of the Sixties.* New York: New York University Press, 1996.

United Nations Regional Information Centre for Western Europe. "Family Day: Nordic Fertility Rates in Steady Decline," May 15, 2023. https://unric.org/en/family-day-nordic-fertility-rates-in-steady-decline.

Upadhyay, Ushma D., Jessica D. Gipson, Mellissa Withers, Shayna Lewis, Erica J. Ciaraldi, Ashley Fraser, Megan J. Huchko, and Ndola Prata. "Women's Empowerment and Fertility: A Review of the Literature." *Social Science and Medicine* 115 (August 2014). DOI: 10.1016/j.socscimed.2014.06.014.

U.S. Bureau of Labor Statistics. Household Data Annual Averages (2022). https://www.bls.gov/cps/cpsaat11.htm.

U.S. Census Bureau. S1301 Fertility Data, in "American Community Survey,"

September 2022. Accessed September 12, 2023. https://data.census.gov /table?q=S1301&tid=ACSST1Y2019.S1301.

Valerio, Tayelor, Brian Knop, Rose M. Kreider, and Wan He. *Childless Older Americans: 2018.* U.S. Census Bureau, Current Population Reports (August 2021).

Van Dam, Andrew. "The Unluckiest Generation in U.S. History." *Washington Post,* June 5, 2020. https://www.washingtonpost.com/business/2020/05 /27/millennial-recession-covid.

Walker, Alice. "In Search of Our Mothers' Gardens." In *Within the Circle: An Anthology of African American Literary Criticism from the Harlem Renaissance to the Present,* edited by Angelyn Mitchell. Durham, NC: Duke University Press, 1994.

Wallace-Wells, David. "The Uninhabitable Earth." *New York,* July 9, 2017. https://nymag.com/intelligencer/2017/07/climate-change-earth-too -hot-for-humans.html.

Ward, Paris. "Many Millennial Couples Keep Finances Separate, Credit Karma Survey Shows." Credit Karma, February 28, 2020. https://www .creditkarma.com/insights/i/married-millennials-separate-finances.

Warner, Judith, Nora Ellmann, and Diana Boesch. "The Women's Leadership Gap: Women's Leadership by the Numbers." Center for American Progress, November 20, 2018.

Warnock, Rob. "Apartment List's 2023 Millennial Homeownership Report." Apartment List, April 18, 2023. https://www.apartmentlist.com/research /millennial-homeownership-2023.

Watkins, Claire Vaye. *Gold Fame Citrus.* New York: Riverhead, 2015.

Whyman, Tom. *Infinitely Full of Hope: Fatherhood and the Future in an Age of Crisis and Disaster.* London: Repeater Books, 2021.

Williams, Joy. *Ill Nature: Rants and Reflections on Humanity and Other Animals.* New York: Vintage, 2001.

Williams, Joy. "The Art of Fiction, No. 223." Interview with Paul Winner. *The Paris Review* 209 (Summer 2014). https://www.theparisreview.org /interviews/6303/the-art-of-fiction-no-223-joy-williams.

Williams, Joy. *Harrow.* New York: Knopf, 2021.

Williams, Missouri. "Aggressive Mirroring: An Interview with Missouri Williams." Interview by Nathan Stormer, *TriQuarterly*, March 4, 2022. https://www.triquarterly.org/interviews/aggressive-mirroring-interview -missouri-williams.

Williams, Missouri. *The Doloriad: A Novel.* New York: Farrar, Straus and Giroux, 2022.

Widdicombe, Lizzie. "The Baby-Box Lady of America." *New Yorker,* December 18, 2021. https://www.newyorker.com/news/news-desk/the-baby-box-lady-of-america.

Women Business Collaborative. *Women CEOs in America* (2022). https://www.wbcollaborative.org/women-ceo-report.

Wong, Venessa. "It's Not Just Millennials—Gen Z Is Dealing with a Lot of Debt Now Too." Buzzfeed, September 17, 2019. https://www.buzzfeednews.com/article/venessawong/millennials-average-debt-2019.

Woolf, Virginia. *Mrs. Dalloway.* New York: Penguin Classics, 2000.

World Bank. "Fertility Rate, Total (Births per Woman)" (2021). Accessed September 1, 2023. https://data.worldbank.org/indicator/SP.DYN.TFRT.IN.

Wray, Britt. *The Climate Baby Dilemma.* CBC, November 24, 2022. https://gem.cbc.ca/media/the-climate-baby-dilemma/s01e01.

YouGov. "Do Women in the United States Come Under Pressure from Society to Have Children?" New York: YouGov, 2022. https://today.yougov.com/topics/politics/survey-results/daily/2022/02/07/cc697/2.

YouGov. "The American Dream Survey." New York: YouGov, 2023. https://docs.cdn.yougov.com/wgu9xa8nwm/crosstabs_The%20American%20Dream.pdf.

Ziegler, Mary. *Abortion and the Law in America.* Cambridge: Cambridge University Press, 2020.

Zoffness, Courtney. *Spilt Milk.* San Francisco: McSweeney's, 2021.

# ABOUT THE AUTHORS

Rory O'Connell

ANASTASIA BERG is an assistant professor of philosophy at the Hebrew University of Jerusalem. Her writing has appeared in *The New York Times*, *The Atlantic*, *The Times Literary Supplement*, the *Los Angeles Review of Books*, *The Chronicle Review*, and *The Point*, where she is a senior editor.

RACHEL WISEMAN is a writer and the managing editor of *The Point*. Her writing has appeared in *The Atlantic*, *The Point*, *The New Republic*, and *The Chronicle of Higher Education*.